COLLECTION MANAGEMENT

9/09 8 — 1 5/09		
5-12	13-1	12-18-11

Ornamental Bamboos

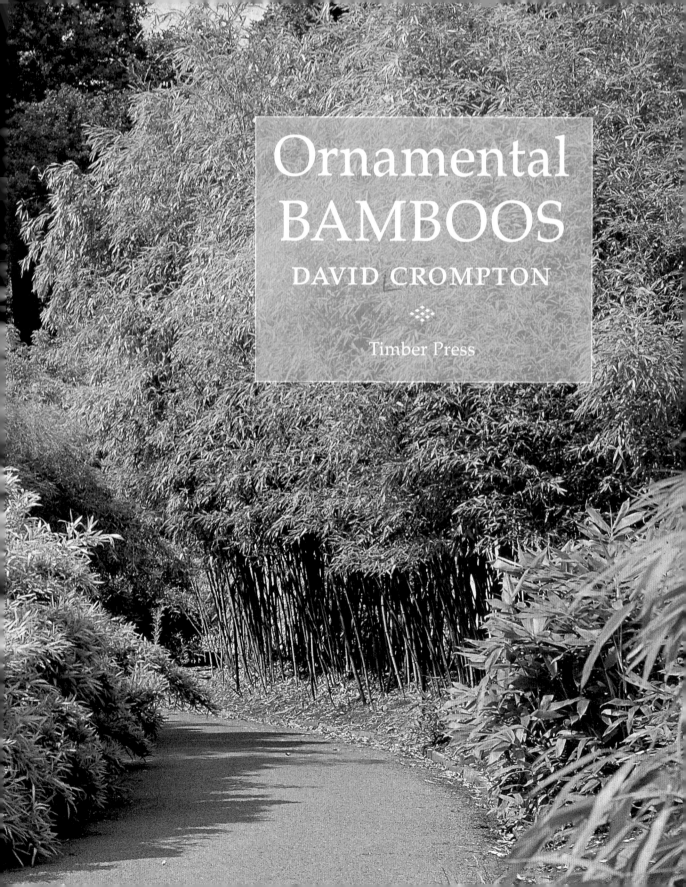

Ornamental BAMBOOS

DAVID CROMPTON

❖

Timber Press

Previous spread: Part of the Bamboo Garden at Royal
Botanic Gardens, Kew. The variegated bamboo
surrounding the rock is *Pleioblastus shibuyanus*
'Tsuboi', and to the right is *Phyllostachys viridiglaucescens*. This page: A young culm of *Borinda papyrifera*.

Photographs by author unless otherwise noted.
Drawings by Yasmin Ineson.

Published in 2006 by
Timber Press, Inc.
The Haseltine Building
133 S.W. Second Avenue, Suite 450
Portland, Oregon 97204-3527, U.S.A.
www.timberpress.com

For contact information regarding editorial, marketing,
sales, and distribution in the United Kingdom, see
www.timberpress.co.uk.

Designed by Susan Applegate
Printed in Hong Kong

Library of Congress Cataloging-in-Publication Data

Crompton, David.
    Ornamental bamboos/David Crompton.
        p. cm.
    Includes bibliographical references and index.
    ISBN-13: 978-0-88192-790-0
    ISBN-10: 0-88192-790-2
    1. Bamboo. 2. Bamboo—Varieties. 3. Bamboo—
Utilization. I. Title.
    SB413.B2C756 2006
    635.9′349—dc22   2006013497

A catalog record for this book is available from the
British Library.

635.9349

Contents

Foreword

I first met David Crompton in 1986, through an official visit on behalf of the National Council for the Conservation of Plants and Gardens (NCCPG). A colleague and I had been asked to visit David's small specialist nursery, which was then situated on London Clay and in a remote location on the borders of Essex and Hertfordshire. Our task was to assess David's suitability to hold a National Collection of bamboos.

David was very pleased to show us round his nursery, where he had been steadily amassing a collection of all the bamboos that were in cultivation at that time. Both I and my colleague were impressed with David's enthusiasm and knowledge when it came to talking about bamboos, in particular with regard to their growing requirements and propagation. We had no hesitation in recommending that he hold a National Collection.

Before leaving the nursery, I invited David to visit my garden at Stream Cottage, in Fittleworth, West Sussex. David visited me about a month later and found the garden something of a revelation. I don't think he had envisaged that so many different bamboos could be associated with other shrubs and plants in a way that demonstrated the bamboos to their best advantage.

Shortly after this, David moved to a larger nursery in Fordingbridge, Hampshire, where he has remained ever since. He has had no formal training in horticulture and is entirely self-taught—and all the better for it, in many ways. He is very honest and straightforward, and I am sure his customers get very direct responses to their sometimes difficult questions.

In the years since we first met, David and I have become firm friends, both of

Chusquea culeou towers over its
dwarf form, 'Tenuis', seen at right.

us concerned with the best ways of incorporating bamboos into the horticultural landscape. I concentrate on the artistic side, while David focuses more on the practicalities of growing bamboos, an indication of a good nurseryman. I hope the interest and affection that David has for bamboos will encourage his readers to see these plants as a welcome addition to any garden.

I have long felt a need for a book that properly covers the growing of bamboos and that is easy to read and suitable for the ordinary gardener wishing to acquire more knowledge. David has a natural writing ability and can explain complicated subjects in a way that is enjoyable and simple to understand. Having followed the creation of this book in all its stages, I can thoroughly recommend it to experts and amateurs alike.

PETER ADDINGTON
Past president
The Bamboo Society
(Great Britain)

Preface

I have written this book with the gardener in mind, rather than the scientist. Although chapter 7, the descriptive list of bamboo genera, species, and cultivars, could be considered scientific in nature, this is by coincidence and not by design. In recent years several excellent books have appeared that more than adequately cover the technical side of these intriguing plants. Although I have occasionally drawn upon their material and content, I do not seek to emulate or reproduce their style here. I have, however, followed the traditional format for a book such as this, with various chapters about growing bamboos preceding the descriptive list. My intention has always been to provide an easy-to-read reference that is free from excessive scientific jargon. Of course, some technical terms are necessary, but a full explanation of such terms can be found in the glossary. This approach is ideal for the gardener or enthusiast wanting a simple guide to growing bamboos in a garden setting. It serves as an easy reference, an aid to identification, and offers straightforward help in choosing appropriate species and cultivars for a given situation. One note: For the sake of brevity, in the descriptive list "differs from the species" is used when meaning "differs from the more common form of the species."

In this book I offer a personalized account of my experiences, both as a bamboo enthusiast and as a nurseryman who has specialized in bamboos for some 20 years. In this time, I have encountered the many joys, wonders, and successes of bamboo gardening, not to mention some of the pitfalls and disasters that can be avoided with a little foreknowledge. Moreover, having a nursery and demonstration garden full of bamboos to scrutinize and examine, just a short distance from my writing desk, has been of the utmost usefulness in helping me to ensure the accuracy of the various measurements and colors given throughout the book.

Although I have been interested in plants since I was a child, my preoccupation with bamboos started in my late teens, shortly after I left school and started work in central London. I already had ideas of perhaps one day starting a nursery, and possibly even having a public garden. But the dictates of social convention, along with parental concerns that I get a proper job, overrode my more entrepreneurial proclivities, at least for the time being. Starting work in London was not such a bad thing, really. London is such a great capital city. There are huge areas given over to parks and open spaces, and with the milder microclimate among all the buildings, various exotic-looking plants flourish in profusion. In the late 1970s, bamboos were obscure in cultivation in Britain and not grown to the extent that they are nowadays. Still, occasional rather dusty-looking specimens could be encountered in sheltered courtyards dwarfed by tall skyscrapers in the area known as the City of London, or found bursting out of narrow beds in private gardens in the West End. Many of these specimens had quite obviously been there for an eternity, possibly dating back to the late 19th or early 20th centuries, when these properties were first planted. I was intrigued. Were these plants hardy outside of central London? And why were they not more widely grown in horticulture?

I found the answer to these questions and others while visiting the Royal Botanic Gardens, Kew. Within Kew Gardens lies an area given over entirely to bamboos, known as the Bamboo Garden. In the late 1970s it was much overgrown and neglected (though now beautifully restored), with great thickets of aged canes arching and leaning or straining against the thick ropes tying them together. Under this jungle-like mass, narrow paths snaked and tunneled about in the stygian gloom. Here was a world apart. All outside noise was muted and distant, even the sounds of the aircraft overhead coming and going from nearby Heathrow. There was hardly a label to be found in a decipherable state, but regardless, I was utterly spellbound. This was fantastic! So exotic and tropical-looking. If only I could identify some of the species and forms and grow them in my own garden. At that time the guide to the gardens offered little help, barely giving this feature a mention, and only to state that the Bamboo Garden was a relic of the Victorian period when such things were in vogue. So started my journey into the wonderful world of bamboos.

By the age of 24, I could stand city life no more and left my secure, well-paying office job to start my first nursery just a few miles north of London. At first I grew unusual and Mediterranean shrubs, but my interest in bamboos was close to the surface, and soon I began collecting different types with a view to offering some for sale in the nursery when I had built up enough stock. There lay the problem. Apart from a few very common varieties, in the early 1980s virtually all the choice or better types were difficult or nigh impossible to obtain in Britain. They could only be read about in books from abroad and could only occasionally be found in the larger botanic gardens. Bear in mind that Alexander High Lawson in *Bamboos: A Gardener's Guide to Their Cultivation in Temperate Climates* (1968) listed only about 50 bamboos that were at least to some extent available in Britain. And this of course did not include more than a small fraction of the beautiful colored-culm forms available today.

Nonetheless I persevered and by 1986 had built up a collection of some 40 species, forms, and cultivars. At about this time two things happened that were to have a great influence on my life and on my career with bamboos.

In the summer of 1986 my bamboos were given National Collection status. The National Collections Scheme is administered by an organization called the National Council for the Conservation of Plants and Gardens. The NCCPG is dedicated to conserving the rich heritage of garden plants in Britain, which might otherwise be lost to cultivation through obscurity, supercession by modern varieties, or even extinction. National Collections are living reference libraries of plants and are open to visits by the gardening public.

I soon discovered that holding a National Collection was not exactly a sinecure. There were all sorts of conditions to be met, and furthermore, within a few years the collection was being visited by considerable numbers of people. However, the great benefit to me was that this brought me into contact with many other bamboo enthusiasts and collectors, and we were able to exchange not just plants but also knowledge and experience.

My first nursery was always something of a struggle. The location 10 miles from where I lived was an imposition, and its situation on heavy soil on top of a hill was far from ideal. In 1989 I moved to my nursery in Hampshire, where I now grow bamboos on a fine river valley soil composed of a dark brown sandy loam. A decade and a half later, so much has changed in the world of bamboos.

Many people helped me in the completion of this book. I wish to acknowledge as many as I can, knowing that it is impossible to name all the individuals who provided assistance, either directly or indirectly, with their kindness and knowledge.

Most of all, I would like to thank the late Peter Addington, my gardening friend and mentor, to whom this book is dedicated. His influence is everywhere within these pages, as a subtle infusion. It was his intimate knowledge of ornamental horticulture that I always found so infinitely compelling, and his unique style of combining bamboos with other garden plants that I found to be the best way to grow bamboos.

I met Peter just prior to my bamboos becoming a National Collection. He had accompanied David McClintock on a formal visit in the spring of 1986, for the purpose of accessing my bamboo collection for its worthiness to become a National Collection. At first I could hardly see Peter, for he was obscured by the foliage of a huge pot of *Himalayacalamus falconeri* 'Damarapa', which he knew I wished to obtain and so had brought as a gift. We immediately became firm friends, even discovering that we shared the same birthday, 9 October, and there started a rewarding association that was to lead to visits to each other's gardens, trips abroad to acquire new bamboos, and endless happy hours of sharing our interest in bamboo gardening. Peter had a huge influence on both my life and my career with bamboos, largely through my incessant visits to his famous garden, Stream Cottage, in West Sussex.

On my very first visit to Stream Cottage, I remarked to Peter upon alighting from my car, "This is like arriving in paradise!" An apt description, for this wonderful garden, which is the setting for many of the photographs in this book, was to become through the 1980s and 1990s the mecca for bamboo enthusiasts in Britain. Its unique combination of various bamboos and other types of plants, set in a lush fold of the Sussex countryside, somehow showed bamboo gardening at its most excellent. Regretfully Peter eventually had to give up the garden due to his advancing age, but it survives in the care of new owners, albeit with modifications. It is my treasured experience that for all the hundred times or so that I visited Peter at Stream Cottage over a 14-year period, the sun shone on every occasion, with not a drop of rain. To anyone familiar with British weather, this is some record!

I am also deeply indebted to the late David McClintock, who so patiently gave much valuable help and insight into matters of taxonomy, an important element even in a book such as this, if we are to make any sense of the confusing naming of bamboos and the ridiculous number of synonyms attached to the bamboos in cultivation.

I would like to express my gratitude to all at Timber Press, for their almost endless patience and tolerance regarding the time it has taken me to complete the manuscript. Without their interest, support, and encouragement, this book would not exist.

Thanks to Alan Edwards for being such a wizard with a computer and helping me with all the technical difficulties of writing a book in the modern way.

Further thanks are due to Steve Renvoize, Ray Townsend, and Chris Stapleton of the Royal Botanic Gardens, Kew, for the many illuminating conversations we have had about bamboos. Last but not least I would like to acknowledge all my friends and fellow enthusiasts in The Bamboo Society (Great Britain), notably Mike Bell, the current president, and Les Cathery, for their seemingly tireless efforts to organize and lead the various meetings, trips, and expeditions to bamboo gardens and places of interest. Special thanks to Anthony and Jane Rogers at Carwinion, for making their wonderful garden available for me to photograph. Thanks, too, to David Helliwell and John Vlitos for all the lively visits we have shared over the years of growing bamboos in our respective gardens. And thanks to all the many people whom I have met through my work at the nursery and from whom I have learned so much.

Introduction

For centuries past, travelers to the Far East have been impressed by the remarkable beauty of bamboo in the natural landscape and by its well-nigh incredible usefulness to humankind. Bamboo has a tremendous importance in Eastern cultures, particularly in China and Japan, where it has acquired a symbolic status in religion, philosophy, and art. The cultivation of bamboo in these countries is an ancient practice; there are references to it in Chinese records dating back to at least 100 BC.

Until the middle of the 19th century, it was mistakenly supposed that all bamboos were of tropical origin and therefore too tender to be grown outdoors in the gardens of Europe and North America. When the pioneer plant hunters of the Victorian era began to penetrate deeper into the Asian subcontinent, away from the warm coastal regions and into the foothills of the Himalaya, they discovered bamboos growing in conditions that were far from tropical. In fact, many of the species they brought back to Western gardens were found to be completely hardy.

Gardens of all sizes can accommodate bamboos. Even in the smallest urban gardens, which can be little more than a terrace or balcony, certain varieties can be utilized for ornament and delight. Bamboos are not out of place when incorporated in a cottage garden or within mixed borders, so long as suitable varieties are chosen. In larger gardens, the almost limitless scope of these plants can be explored; the dedicated enthusiast can even construct a garden devoted exclusively to bamboos.

This book is all about growing bamboos as ornamental plants. My aim is to inspire and enthuse, and to engender a deeper appreciation of how different types of bamboo can be used in the garden. Even now, with bamboos more widely grown, there remains much misunderstanding and misconception. It is amazing

A clump of *Fargesia murielae* provides a backdrop
to azaleas, hostas, and ferns at Stream Cottage.

how many people still think there is only one type of bamboo, or believe bamboos only grow in swamps in a tropical jungle. Moreover, there is still a hardened core of skeptics, both amateur and professional, who openly revile bamboos and consider them to be invasive weeds at best! Perhaps with the help of the descriptions and photographs in these pages, I can bring about a change of view. For those of us already enlightened, we now have at our disposal a veritable painter's palette of color, shape, and form, diversely useful throughout our gardens and estates.

Bamboos can be endlessly fascinating. There is an air of mystery surrounding them; they are quite unlike other woody plants, definitely exotic and yet able to harmonize superbly in Western gardens. It is often astounding how quickly a newcomer to the subject will develop a profound interest, whether through exploring all the horticultural possibilities or by delving into the utilization of bamboo as a raw material. (The latter is itself an entire subject about which much has been written, and is the subject of ongoing research.) The cultivation of bamboos seems to have an appeal for people from all walks of life, not just the established horticultural community. When I first became interested in bamboos as ornamental plants, I mistakenly thought my enthusiasm was something unique, something not shared by others, even those who were already keen gardeners. Imagine my surprise when I discovered that there are no boundaries when it comes to who will be susceptible to the all-consuming, magnificent obsession that can develop so quickly from the most fleeting exposure to these enchanting and bewitching plants. This curious phenomenon may be explained by the undoubted fact that bamboos are so completely different from other plants. Their unusual growth cycle, their vigor and tremendous power of growth, and their diverse range of size and form all add to their attraction. And just about anybody can enjoy growing them, from the keen gardener to the novice or even the nongardener.

Western gardeners now have access to a wealth of bamboo species and varieties from the temperate regions of the world, including some of the finest and most handsome of garden ornamentals. Bamboos are so very useful in the garden. Some are tall and stately, an established stand capable of producing culms more than 8 m (26 feet) tall even in cool-temperate conditions, while others have culms that arch gracefully under the weight of their elegant foliage. Many of these taller varieties can be used as imposing specimen plants, yet others are more suitable as dense hedges or screens. Some of the dwarfer species are appropriate for groundcover, effectively dominating even the toughest weeds. There is hardly a need to be fulfilled or a problem to be mastered where some sort of bamboo cannot provide the answer. Indeed, few groups of plants can claim to be so versatile and adaptable. Bamboos are not at all difficult to grow, so long as one has at least a rudimentary understanding of their characteristics, and there are bamboos suitable for almost every site and situation.

Bamboos are enjoying a considerable return to popularity. They are being planted more widely than ever before in Western horticulture, not only in gardens but also in municipal developments, parks, and other public places. This is, I think, largely due to the coincidental rekindling of interest in exotic-looking plants in general. I myself am an enthusiastic proponent of this style of gardening and have coined the term New Exoticism to describe the movement. The New Exoticists have joyously abandoned the more traditional forms of gardening to embrace a more adventurous approach. We try to create gardens that evoke the atmosphere of a warmer climate, perhaps even a jungle-like paradise. This effect can be produced with evergreen plants that have large or spiky-looking leaves, or with plants that have a strong structural element to their growth habit, such as bamboos. Indeed, the architectural quality of bamboos has come firmly to the attention of the modern landscape gardener, who now employs these plants to produce an exotic effect, making particular use of varieties with very thick culms or large, tropical-looking leaves.

Although the popularity of bamboos as ornamental plants has waxed and waned since their first introduction to Western gardens, the revival of interest has coincided with the introduction of many new species and cultivars, many of which have exciting colored culms or strikingly variegated leaves. Approximately 200 different bamboos now available are hardy enough for use in most cool-temperate gardens. With the ever-increasing number of nurseries stocking bamboos, or indeed specializing in bamboos, it is now easier to acquire even the rarest or most recently introduced types and forms.

The growing of bamboos is no longer an eccentricity. Since the 1990s a proliferation of books have appeared, providing the budding enthusiast with a rich storehouse of information and knowledge. Various societies and clubs devoted to bamboos now exist in most Western countries, where amateurs and professionals alike can share experiences and skills. More than ever before, bamboos can be seen flourishing in gardens everywhere. These beautiful plants, imbued with an age-old essence of Far Eastern horticulture, are at last gaining the appreciation they deserve in the gardens of the West.

CHAPTER 1

Discovering Bamboo

Bamboos are very different from other plants we can grow in our gardens. Most of us, whether familiar with garden plants or not, have at least some sense of what bamboo looks like, at least in its harvested or cured state. In this form it has a certain color, usually beige-brown. The outer surface feels smooth. It is very light to hold and somewhat flexible. And most of all, it has a distinctive jointed structure. Since childhood, most of us will likely have encountered the ubiquitous cut bamboo canes used as plant supports or perhaps manufactured into furniture or other household objects. But if we are to grow bamboos in our gardens, it is helpful to know exactly what distinguishes them from other garden plants. So, without delving too deeply into the finer points of botanical science, how can we recognize bamboo as a living plant?

General Appearance

When viewing living bamboos from a short distance, we can see that they usually have a number of vertical stems, called culms, and that these culms have swollen joints, called nodes, that are visible at regular intervals. There are branches, which are like smaller versions of the culms, and leaves, most of which seem to occur in the middle and upper parts of the plant, with a portion of culm visible at the base, which is bereft of branching.

Upon slightly closer inspection, we can see that the leaves are usually more or less long and narrow and end in a sharp point. Some plants appear as a tightly circumscribed dense clump of slender culms, others have a more thicket-like habit with ragged edges, and yet others exist as a more open grove of tree-like, thicker culms, with enough space to walk between them. All these characteristics are typical of bamboos. The only other plants that have any resemblance to them are grasses.

Bamboos as Members of the Grass Family

The popular conception of bamboos as large, woody, grass-like plants, grown in China and eaten by pandas, is to some extent correct. In fact, bamboos are members of the grass family, Poaceae (Gramineae), and are far more closely related to the grass in our lawns than to the shrubs and trees in our ornamental borders. The grass family is a very large group of plants that, according to botanists, comprises approximately 650 genera divided into more than 10,000 species. Among the many members

An extensive grove of *Hibanobambusa tranquillans* 'Shiroshima'.

of the grass family are cereals such as wheat, corn, and barley and other commercially important plants such as rice and sugar cane. Bamboos are classified as Bambusoideae, a subfamily of the Poaceae.

There is considerable contention among taxonomists as to the exact number of bamboo genera and species to be found in the wild, but between 90 and 115 genera and 1200 species are recognized. The taxonomy of bamboos has always been very provisional, with frequent changes and reclassifications. At one time all bamboos were defined as being lignified (woody), and herbaceous bamboos were not thought to exist. More recent research, in particular molecular data, has confirmed that there are herbaceous bamboos, although they are mainly tropical in origin. The herbaceous bamboos are not widely cultivated in Western gardens and are not covered in this book.

Before we look at bamboos more closely, I would like to stress just how essential it is to have a fundamental understanding of how members of the grass family differ from other plants, and how bamboos differ from other grasses. This is a necessary prerequisite to gaining a proper perception of the remarkable growth characteristics of bamboos, which will be explained in greater depth in chapter 2.

Distinguishing Grasses from Other Plants

The more sophisticated flowering plants (angiosperms) found in nature are divided by botanists into two distinct groups, depending on the number of initial leaves produced when germinating from a seed. The monocotyledons, such as grasses and bamboos, produce just one initial seed leaf, whereas the dicotyledons, such as broad-leaved shrubs and trees, produce two initial seed leaves. These simple differences at the seedling stage set the scene for much more important differences in growth characteristics as the respective types develop into proper plants.

Grasses are distinct from other plants by having jointed aerial stems, or culms, although tussock-forming grasses may appear more or less stemless because the stem is present in diminished form. From these culms, leaves are present at the joints, arranged alternately in two ranks along the culm and in one plane. The leaves are attached by means of a sheath that surrounds or wraps around the culm. Usually the culms are hollow, although they may be solid, and they are interrupted at regular intervals by nodes, which contain an internal dividing wall. The underground parts of the plant consist of further jointed stems, called rhizomes, from which the true roots emerge at the joints. These underground stems are connected together so that the plant is a colony rather than having a central main stem. The leaves are usually long and narrow and normally consist of an unbranched midrib with parallel veins on each side.

In grasses, all growth or development starts from buds at the joints of each stem, and once a bud has developed at a joint, any further growth from that bud normally takes place in one phase or growth spurt. As a bud begins to grow, the diameter of the stem that elongates from it is fixed and does not expand. Once that initial growth spurt has been completed, there is no further increase in the length of the culm. The plant expands by developing its system of underground stems and can thus produce larger aerial stems, which feed the production of more underground stems, and so on.

Broad-leaved plants such as shrubs and trees do not have a regular jointed structure of growth. There is usually a central main stem or trunk, which branches randomly. Belowground the roots emerge from the lower parts of the main trunk and also branch randomly. This main stem consists of an outer layer, called a cambium, where all new growth takes place. Outside the cambium is a protective layer, the phloem, which becomes the bark and is shed periodically or continually expanded. Under the cambium are progressively older layers or rings of wood that are no longer living but contribute to the strength and wind resistance of the plant. The plant expands through growth of the cambium, through the growing tips of the twigs and branches, and by the tips of the roots. The leaves emerge from leaf axils on the twigs and minor branches, and have veins that are usually at an angle to the central midrib, which itself may be branched.

Though greatly oversimplified, these descriptions of monocotyledons and dicotyledons serve the purpose of illustrating the principal differences between these two plant types. Interestingly, I have found over the years that most of the visitors to my bamboo collection are unaware of these distinctions and simply expect bamboos to grow in the same way as shrubs and trees. I would urge further reading of a more scientific nature for anyone wishing to gain a better understanding of how plants grow.

Distinguishing Bamboos from Other Grasses

In the past, botanists have tended to regard bamboos as forest grasses with broader leaves, specialized leaf anatomy, and relatively simple flowers, and the woody bamboos have always formed the core of this classification. Contemporary molecular techniques have considerably helped to clarify exactly what is and what is not a bamboo. From our perspective as gardeners, we only need to make simple distinctions between true woody bamboos and other grasses. The greatest difficulties arise in trying to differentiate between herbaceous grasses

and herbaceous bamboos, since many grasses mimic bamboos to some extent in their growth habit. Many of these bamboo-like grasses appear within the houseplant trade and are offered for sale purporting to be bamboos. The true herbaceous bamboos are mostly tropical and are too tender to be grown outside in cool-temperate gardens. They have softer, not properly lignified culms that cannot grow to great heights nor support a complex branch structure.

Woody bamboos can be differentiated from other grasses and from herbaceous bamboos by two simple characteristics. Firstly, each culm, when fully developed after the passage of one complete growing season, should have a properly lignified branch structure. Secondly, the true foliage leaf blades (as opposed to the blades of the culm sheaths, which are discussed in later chapters) are attached to the sheaths that bear them by means of a short stalk, or pseudopetiole, which can be clearly seen. In true grasses, as opposed to woody bamboos, the base of the leaf is connected directly to the sheath in such a way that the base of the leaf itself seems to be wrapped around the culm. There is one further distinction between woody bamboos and other grasses and herbaceous bamboos that is valid but of less use to gardeners. The woody bamboos have two separate phases of shoot development: a shoot elongation phase and a vegetative branching phase. Unfortunately, certain important groups of woody bamboos that are cultivated as garden ornamentals tend to overlap these two phases, or begin the branching phase before the elongation phase is completed. However, the two prior distinguishing characteristics are reliable guides and apply without exception to all the woody bamboos in cultivation, including all the bamboos featured in this book.

Bamboos in the Wild

True grasses are vegetation of more open environments and often coexist with grazing animals, whereas bamboos have evolved superbly as vegetation of the forest or forest fringes. Their structural characteristics, such as a tall lignified culm with its complex branch structure, and the comparatively large pseudopetiolate leaves (explained in chapter 2), enable bamboos to make efficient use of lower light levels and compete with other vegetation. With their rapid growth and ability to colonize large areas in a relatively short time, bamboos can quickly take advantage of any changes or disturbances to forest dynamics. For example, bamboos often invade the small clearings created by fallen trees, or colonize and stabilize areas denuded by landslides or the activities of humans.

Although said to be primitive in terms of their structure, bamboos have specialized leaf anatomy compared with other grasses, and relatively simple flowering characteristics. Bamboos show a high degree of adaptation to different environments. This can be demonstrated by examining the various growth habits found among bamboos. Some are tropical, while others are hardy enough to withstand the severest winters. Some are robust, perennial groundcovers of the forest floor; others are delicate-looking, airy, and arching, adapted to light woodland or the forest fringes; and still others are strong-growing, upright, and tree-like, forming the dominant vegetation. Some bamboos are even adapted to climb into surrounding larger plants and can suppress seed germination and overwhelm all lesser vegetation.

A mature grove of *Semiarundinaria fastuosa* brightly lit by spring sunshine in the upper garden at Penjerrick, Cornwall.

Evolution

Bamboos are among the most ancient of flowering plants. The earliest antecedents of the bamboos that we can grow in our gardens were probably the herbaceous grasses, which are thought to have originated in the tropical or subtropical forests of the southern hemisphere in the latter part of the Cretaceous period, or perhaps the early Tertiary period, some 65 to 135 million years ago. These ancestral grasses are believed to have coexisted with the dinosaurs. Yet these grasses or their descendents somehow survived whatever sudden and cataclysmic happening exterminated the dinosaurs and so many other organisms.

It is generally considered that all proper bamboos, in the form recognized today, originate from a common ancestor and probably evolved in the Miocene or Oligocene epochs between approximately 5 and 34 million years ago. Fossil records dating back this far are scant, because grasses, which are less substantial than animal remains, tend to leave traces or imprints rather than becoming fossilized. However, Miocene fossil bamboo remains have been discovered in France, dating back to approximately 6½ million years ago. It is thought that the earliest woody bamboos originated in tropical lowlands of the southern hemisphere and eventually radiated into the northern hemisphere and temperate regions.

Distribution

Bamboos are distributed over a wide area, although the distribution is very uneven. They occur in more or less all tropical and subtropical regions of the world and are also found in the temperate zones. Bamboos are in their greatest abundance along the southern and eastern parts of Asia, from India across China to Japan and Malaysia. The only two continents that have no native bamboos are Europe and

Antarctica. Although there are no native European bamboos, some of the more invasive temperate species have escaped European gardens and become naturalized. The United States has only two native bamboos (*Arundinaria gigantea* and *A. gigantea* subsp. *tecta*), which are restricted to areas known as canebrakes in the warmer southern states. Further south, bamboos occur from Mexico to Argentina. The greatest diversity of bamboos in the southern hemisphere occurs in South America. Interestingly, 40 percent of the bamboos of the New World are of the genus *Chusquea*, which is found over a large geographic area. The continent of Africa is remarkably depauperate (impoverished) in endemic bamboos, having only a few species, whereas the neighboring island of Madagascar has some 30 species. Three species are native to Australia, found only in the northern tropical extremities.

Bamboos originate over a considerable range of climate and altitude. They are known to tolerate extremes of rainfall from 75 to 650 cm (30 to 256 inches) per year and temperatures ranging from −20°C to 45°C (−4°F to 113°F). The geographical limits of bamboo extend from 46° north, where *Sasa kurilensis* may be found on the island of Sakhalin, to 47° south for *Chusquea culeou* in Argentina. Although bamboos are predominantly vegetation of the middle to lower altitudes, they do occur at great elevations, not far below the tree line in certain montane regions. *Thamnocalamus spathiflorus* has been recorded growing above 3300 m (11,000 feet) between eastern Nepal and Sikkim, and *Borinda yulongshanensis* grows at 4200 m (13,800 feet) in the Yunnan province of China. Some species of *Chusquea* occur at 3600 m (12,000 feet) in the Andes.

The overall distribution of bamboo today is largely determined by climatic factors, particularly moisture and humidity. Essentially

bamboos are vegetation of the forest floor and woodland fringes. Some species have adapted to more open conditions, but bamboos are seldom found in very dry localities. It is probable that bamboos were once much more extensive in their range of distribution and that worldwide climatic changes brought about during the Pleistocene Ice Age caused a contraction of their natural environments. This may be the cause of the curious dearth of bamboos in Africa.

Since bamboos are ancient in origin, it is also considered that continental drift has played an important part in determining their present distribution. Geomorphologists, who study the movement of rocks and the creation of landforms, believe that all the continents were once joined together in the form of a supercontinent. Over innumerable millions of years, this supercontinent broke into smaller landmasses, which drifted apart to form the arrangement of the continents as we now know them. This helps to explain why bamboos are so uneven in their natural distribution, and offers a plausible reason (in addition to climatic factors) for why Europe has no native bamboos.

The activities of humans have greatly modified the geographical range of bamboos throughout the world. Cultivation for timber and food in tropical areas, combined with use as an ornamental plant in Europe and the United States, has considerably extended the boundaries of distribution. Unfortunately, the equation is more than balanced by the wholesale elimination of many natural stands through land clearance for agricultural use, particularly in South America. The canebrakes of the United States have been significantly diminished in this way, and much bamboo continues to be lost in the destruction of tropical rain forests worldwide.

Some species of bamboo have become naturalized through human intervention. One of the most often naturalized species is *Bambusa vulgaris*, pantropic in origin, whose culms have long been used as plant supports in local agriculture and have consequently taken root, thus extending the parameters of the species. *Sino-bambusa tootsik*, a subtropical bamboo originally from China, has escaped from cultivation as an ornamental in Honolulu, Hawaii, to become a pernicious weed among the native vegetation. In Japan, where bamboos have been cultivated since ancient times, many species originally introduced from China have become naturalized to such an extent that they have modified the appearance of the landscape in many regions. This has given rise to disagreement among contemporary horticulturists as to whether certain species are indeed native or just naturalized.

Bamboos in Asiatic Culture

Bamboo has been an important component of Chinese and Japanese gardens for thousands of years. During the fourth century BC, the philosopher Meng-tzu wrote of gardens in ancient China that included bamboo. There are records of what is thought to be the world's earliest known botanic garden at Yun Ming Tai, created by the first emperor of the Qin Dynasty in the third century BC, where bamboos were used among designs to display a wide variety of plants. In the first century BC, as Buddhism became the national religion in many parts of China, bamboo shoots attained great significance in the vegetarian diet of Buddhist monks. The first known monograph on bamboos was written in AD 450, and by the end of the seventh century, many Chinese gardening manuals appeared that contained advice on the planting of bamboo.

Throughout Chinese art and literature, bamboo is depicted as one of the four noble plants,

the others being the orchid, chrysanthemum, and flowering plum. Chinese calligraphy, including the painting of bamboo with great delicacy, by brush and ink, has long been an important art form, but it assumed profound importance during the Mongol rule of China in the 13th and 14th centuries. Under Mongol domination, the Chinese saw bamboo as a symbol of the wise man who, when shaken violently by a storm, bends but never breaks.

In Japan the three most revered plants are bamboo, flowering plum, and pine. The ancient Japanese made considerable use of bamboo, employing it as a decorative plant perhaps more often than the Chinese. They also exploited its full potential in construction, furniture, and handicrafts. Certain species of bamboo were used to make the equipment that is of such importance in the Japanese tea ceremony, and many other Japanese ceremonies became closely related to bamboos. Calligraphy was taken from China to Japan in AD 400 when many Chinese artists and scholars facing persecution fled to Japan and settled there. Japanese artists embraced calligraphy and refined it almost to abstraction. By the seventh century, bamboo was a regular subject for poetry and literature, and great emphasis was placed on its longevity and stability, themes that have continued through the centuries.

Garden design in China and Japan is regarded as an art form similar to landscape painting. Although there are important differences between Chinese and Japanese gardens, both are constructed according to rules and conventions based on assumptions entirely different from those of Western gardens. Humankind and nature are considered to be inseparable in these countries, and therefore gardens aim to reflect nature, yet stimulate the imagination. Such gardens are strongly symbolic. Water is usually present, suggesting human life and profound thought. Instead of lawns, there are gravel beds and impressive rock formations that symbolize mountains. Plants are seen in isolation rather than in groups or patterns, thus aiding meditation. Japanese gardeners of the 16th century refined this art still further by using raked sand or gravel to symbolize a flowing river, and surrounding this with hardly any plants at all, perhaps just moss growing on rocks and a few living stems of bamboo used to represent an entire forest. Many examples of this type of garden can still be seen.

Bamboos in Western Horticulture

The cultivation of bamboos as ornamental plants is a comparatively recent phenomenon in Western horticulture, dating back only some 200 years. References to bamboos in early European literature are common, but the erroneous supposition that these plants were too delicate for even the mild English climate no doubt contributed at least in part to the lack of introductions prior to the early 19th century.

Derivation of the Word *Bamboo*

I have adapted this section, with some alterations as a result of further research of the original works, from *Bamboos: A Gardener's Guide to Their Cultivation in Temperate Climates* (Lawson 1968) and *The Bamboo Garden* (Freeman-Mitford 1896).

The exact derivation of the word *bamboo* will probably remain obscure, but it seems to be Asian in origin. In his monograph of 1839, Ruprecht stated that one of the earliest known references to bamboos by a European author occurred around 400 BC in the works of Ctesias, then private physician to King Artaxerxes Mnemon of Persia. Later, in a letter to Aristotle, Alexander the Great referred to canes big enough to be used as boats, although this was

doubtless something of an exaggeration. Pliny also referred to bamboos in his *Natural History.*

After this there appears to be a considerable blank until the writings of Marco Polo, who in 1298, upon his return from China, described at length the importance of bamboo as a raw material in the local economy. William Marsden inserted *bamboo* in his Malay dictionary, but it was Colonel Henry Yule, the translator of Polo's travels, who extensively researched the word for *Hobson-Jobson: Being a Glossary of Anglo-Indian Colloquial Words and Phrases* (1886). Yule used several passages from the old writers to illustrate the earliest uses of the word. Garcia de Orta, for example, made the following statement in *Colloquios dos simples e drogas e cousas medicinaes da India* (1563), referring to *tabashir*, an ancient elixir obtained from certain bamboos: "The people from whom it is got call it sacar-mambum . . . because the canes of that plant are called by the Indians Mambu." A passage in Jan Huygen van Linschoten's *Discours of Voyages into ye East & West Indies* (1598) referred to "a thick reede as big as a man's legge, which is called bambus." And Ralph Fitch, in Richard Hakluyt's *Principall Navigations, Voyages, and Discoveries of the English Nation* (1589), wrote: "All the houses are made of canes, which they call bambos, and bee covered with straw." Colonel Yule noted that the word *bamboo* in its present form was used by the Portuguese before the end of the 16th century and that English speakers probably adopted the word from them, as is true with many other words.

Early Introductions

Bamboos started to appear in Western gardens in the early part of the 19th century, with the first introductions made almost entirely in Europe. In North America, bamboos began to be cultivated more toward the middle part of the 19th century, although a few tropical species

Summer at Stream Cottage. The tall bamboo dominating the back of this scene is *Chusquea gigantea*.

may have been brought into cultivation a little earlier. Most of the now long-established hardy species were introduced by the famous plant collectors of the Victorian era, in the latter half of the 19th century, following the exploration of inland China and the Himalayan region. It was during this period that the popularity of bamboos reached a peak not equaled until the revival of enthusiasm that began in the 1990s. The Victorians were keenly interested in Asiatic arts and customs, and the exotic, subtropical appearance of bamboos was considered fashionable.

Phyllostachys nigra was the first hardy bamboo introduced to Europe. Some authorities assert that it arrived in 1827; whatever the date, it was almost certainly introduced long before any of the other hardy species. Next came *Pseudosasa japonica* (then called *Arundinaria japonica*), which was introduced to France by Philipp Franz von Siebold in 1850 and thence to England a year or two later, whereupon it became the most commonly cultivated bamboo in the British Isles until its flowering in the 1980s.

Many species of bamboo were introduced to the United States shortly after their arrival in

Europe. *Pseudosasa japonica* is believed to have been the first, arriving circa 1860. Three species of *Phyllostachys* (*P. aurea*, *P. bambusoides*, and *P. edulis*) were introduced to the United States by 1890, but there are no definite records of any other successful introductions prior to this date. In 1898 the U.S. Department of Agriculture (USDA) began the mass introduction of plants from around the world with potential significance as agricultural crops, and from the beginning there was a strong interest in bamboos. Many of the earliest attempts to introduce bamboos were unsuccessful, but nonetheless, a number of species were brought into cultivation this way.

Establishment in Cultivation

Through the early years of the 20th century, bamboos sustained their popularity in the large private gardens of Europe, but the outbreak of the First World War heralded the beginning of a virtual hibernation in the use of bamboo as a garden plant. Apart from a brief revival of interest in the 1960s, bamboos languished in obscurity across Europe, particularly so in Britain, until the 1990s, with very little new material having been introduced in this period.

In the United States, interest in bamboos was maintained in the first half of the 20th century largely through the efforts of the USDA, who, as mentioned, had undertaken a large-scale program of plant introductions, both directly from the Far East and from nurseries in Europe. The USDA extensively promoted bamboo as an economically viable crop for American agriculture, extolling its potential for a wide variety of uses. By 1961 the USDA had to acknowledge that bamboo had not proved suitable in this respect, due to insufficient market for bamboo products in the United States, and in 1965 all major research projects were terminated. Nonetheless, considerable knowledge and insight had been gained into all aspects of bamboo growth, and the cultivation of these plants had become firmly established across the United States.

Particular groups of plants seem to experience cycles of popularity, and bamboos are no exception. There is no doubt that Western gardeners, particularly those in Europe, have seriously neglected bamboos in the past, probably due to various misconceptions regarding hardiness and garden worthiness. Recent years, however, have seen a rekindling of interest in all things bamboo in almost every Western country. There has always been a dedicated core of enthusiasts maintaining private collections, but the number of gardeners attracted to bamboos has increased significantly, coupled with a growing awareness of bamboo worldwide.

CHAPTER 2

The Bamboo Plant

Although bamboos are members of the grass family (Poaceae), they possess various characteristics that make them a distinct group of plants. Chapter 1 briefly discussed the differences between grasses and broad-leaved plants such as shrubs and trees, and how to distinguish bamboos from other grasses. Let us now consider how the bamboo grows and look in more detail at its component parts.

Growth Habit

A developing bamboo plant has a system of rhizomes that can advance indefinitely at rates and distances determined by the species. From the rhizomes emerge culms (formerly referred to as canes, a term best used to describe culms in their cut or harvested state). The culms grow more or less vertically and produce lateral branches. The rhizomes and culms are the main structural parts of a bamboo, and they all have a jointed, segmented habit of growth, consisting of an alternating series of nodes and internodes. This segmented pattern of growth, combining the hollow internodes and solid nodes, gives the bamboo its light weight and considerable strength, allowing the culms to bend with the wind but not break.

A bamboo plant is really just a branching system of segmented stems. The only non-jointed or nonsegmented parts of a bamboo are its foliage and roots. There is no central trunk or root system common to other types of woody plant. For bamboos, the nodes are the centers of growth activity, and from the nodes all new branches of segmented growth originate, as does the foliage. From the nodes at the bases of the culms and from the nodes of the rhizomes, the true roots of a bamboo emerge.

Each culm bears leaves from the culm branches, allowing minerals obtained through the roots to be converted by photosynthesis into plant foods, which are then stored in the rhizomes. This enables the system of rhizomes to be extended and new culms to be produced, thus enlarging the bamboo grove. In a mature bamboo clump or grove, the rhizome linkages between the original culms may perish over the course of time, and therefore it makes sense to think of an established bamboo not as a single plant but as a colony.

Life Cycle

The life cycle of a bamboo can be divided into three distinct stages. The initial seedling stage is very brief, lasting only a few weeks from the point of germination until the full complement of vegetative structures has been attained: the first culm and its foliage, the first rhizome and its roots. A bamboo is most commonly encountered in its developmental stage, an intervening period of many years between the seedling stage and the ultimate flowering stage. Often, though not always, the flowering stage portends the death of the bamboo. However, seed is produced to continue the species and to allow the species to evolve.

Nodes and Internodes

The segmented parts of a bamboo plant are simply a succession of almost identical units. Each complete unit, comprising a node and an internode, is enclosed or wrapped in a protective sheath at the time of its initial development. The nodes, which are always solid, are usually larger in diameter than the usually hollow internodes that connect them together.

Nodes consist externally of the sheath scar, the supranodal ridge, and a dormant bud, although in some cases the bud is absent. The sheath scar appears as a thin, sometimes cork-like ring that surrounds the culm completely. It marks the point of attachment of the protective sheath, which may or may not have been discarded. The supranodal ridge defines the upper limit of the node and is extremely variable in size and prominence. Inside the node is a dividing wall that separates the usually hollow internodes on either side. Usually, each successive node along the culm has a dormant bud that faces the opposite direction to the one on the node before it, though all are in the same plane.

The internodes are the portions of the culm that exist between the nodes, and they can vary in length considerably, thus allowing the culms to reach great heights and the rhizomes to reach great distances. As previously mentioned, internodes are nearly always hollow, although there are exceptions, such as the bamboos of the genus *Chusquea*, which have solid internodes.

In common with other members of the grass family, the nodes and internodes of a bamboo stem form their basic dimensions in one growth spurt. Once this growth spurt is completed, the diameter and length of each node and internode is fixed and does not increase.

Buds and Necks

No growth of any sort can emerge from anywhere along the internodes of a bamboo plant. All new segmented stems of a bamboo plant have to emerge from a dormant bud present on the node of an existing segmented stem.

Culms of *Chusquea culeou* can be seen in various stages of development.

For example, the branches of a culm emerge from the culm nodes, and the smaller branches and twigs emerge from the nodes of the main branches. Underground, each section of rhizome will have begun its life from the node of an existing rhizome or a node at the base of an existing culm. The dormant bud at a node consists of a whole new section of segmented growth all tightly compressed and covered in overlapping scales or bracts. As the bud germinates, so the compressed nodes and internodes begin to enlarge and elongate, rather like extending a telescope of many sections. Dormant buds are usually present on most nodes of culms and rhizomes, apart from some lower nodes of thicker culms, and on the neck.

An important structural part of every segmented stem of a bamboo plant is the neck. Each developed bamboo stem, whether aboveground or underground, be it a culm, branch, or rhizome, has at its base a distinct constricted section of very tightly compressed segments that are nearly always narrower than the rest of the stem that ensues from it. This is the neck. The nodes and internodes of the neck are enclosed in their initial development by much reduced scale-like sheaths. Each node along the neck is bereft of buds. The main function of the neck is to allow the bamboo to create a new branch of segmented stem that may be of a different diameter to the section of stem from which it arose. It is also a device that, if need be, can help alter the orientation of the new stem so that it can grow in a certain direction. At the bases of the culms and rhizomes, the neck can be recognized clearly. However, the neck is less obvious at the bases of the culm branches of many bamboos, and often appears either much reduced or virtually absent.

Rhizomes

The term *rhizomes* is used to describe all the underground stems of a bamboo and technically includes the lowermost portions of the culms that are beneath the soil surface, although for our purposes it is easier to think of the culms as being separate entities to the rhizomes. Rhizomes are the structural foundations of a bamboo and serve to anchor and support the aerial culms that arise from them. They also store plant foods and are the primary means of the plant reproducing itself vegetatively.

Rhizomes are of the utmost importance because their nature and growth characteristics determine the rate of invasion for a particular bamboo and the spacing between the culms. All bamboos are invasive to some extent, but it is the rate of invasion that concerns us most as gardeners. We need to have at least a rudimentary understanding of how rhizomes behave, and an awareness of the two basic types found in bamboos, in order to ascertain the suitability of a particular bamboo for a given situation or area.

The rhizomes are the most seldom seen parts of a bamboo. They are typically subterranean and ivory-colored, only developing pigment when exposed to daylight. A developing rhizome will always try to grow in a straight line directly away from the parent plant. It will change direction only if it encounters some obstacle, and then only to loop around and regain its original direction. At the tip a rhizome is hard and pointed so that it may easily penetrate the surrounding soil. Additionally, a small amount of moisture is secreted from the tip as the rhizome moves forward, softening the soil slightly for easier penetration. The tip is formed of closely overlapping sheaths, enclosing newly forming nodes and internodes, compressed tightly together and elongating as the tip moves forward. Each section (one node and internode) is enclosed in its own simply constructed protective sheath that is fixed at its base to the node. The life of these sheaths is short, lasting only until the section of rhizome is properly developed, whereupon the sheath quickly rots away.

At each node along the rhizome is a dormant bud (always solitary), from which either new culms or new rhizomes develop. Every rhizome will have originated from a bud as a branch from an existing rhizome, or less usually as a lateral bud from the base of a culm. These buds can remain dormant for many months, even years, before they are stimulated into growth by warmer weather in spring or an increased supply of water after a dry period. As the rhizome grows, so it normally orientates itself so that each bud, dormant or developing, lies at a right angle to the force of gravity.

The characteristics and growth habit of a rhizome system vary considerably between different genera and species of bamboo. Since the early 20th century, various terms have been coined by botanists to classify the main types of rhizome system and the spatial distribution of the culms. None of these classifications are completely satisfactory, for bamboos, with all their fascinating oddities and exceptions, stubbornly resist our efforts to parcel them into neat categories.

The most straightforward and logical system, however, is the classification devised by the late American botanist Floyd Alonzo McClure in his books of 1925 and 1966. McClure recognized two principal types of rhizomes, pachymorph and leptomorph, each type determined by growth habit. This is the classification I use in this book. However, I also show similar terms in parentheses where appropriate, as it is worthwhile to understand the connection between terms which, though apparently different, actually describe the same phenomenon. In particular, the terms *sympodial* and *monopodial* have often been used as categories for rhizome behavior, but these terms really only describe the branching characteristics, not the basic morphology. They could equally be used for other parts of a bamboo plant, such as the flowers, and so are less satisfactory than McClure's straightforward *pachymorph* and *leptomorph*.

Pachymorph (Sympodial) Rhizomes
Pachymorph rhizomes are common in bamboos of tropical and subtropical origin, although they can also occur in bamboos from high-altitude temperate regions. They are usually short and thick, and nearly always curved, with the tip turning upward to form a culm. The diameter of the rhizome is normally slightly greater than the culm produced at its tip, and each internode is larger in diameter than in length due to retarded elongation. The nodes are not perceptibly larger in diameter than the internodes. Every internode is solid (very rarely hollow), has a single dormant bud, and is asymmetrical (longer on the bud-bearing side and, when growing horizontally, often slightly flattened). Roots are produced at or near the node, usually less so on the upper surface and more so on the lower surface.

After the terminal bud at the tip of a pachymorph rhizome has transformed into a culm, the lateral buds along the rhizome break from dormancy to develop into new rhizomes. A lateral bud on a true pachymorph rhizome can only produce another rhizome, culms being produced only from the terminal bud at the apex of such rhizomes.

The clumping habit of this type of rhizome system keeps the culms close together, typically forming a single, closely circumscribed, caespitose group, expanding outward very slowly. Examples can be found among members of *Bambusa* (tropical bamboos) and *Fargesia* (high-altitude temperate bamboos). The rate of spread for this rhizome type in cool-temperate climates is approximately 10 to 15 cm (4 to 6 inches) per year, though often less. Warmer conditions do not significantly increase the rate of spread.

Certain pachymorph bamboos can produce rhizomes with elongated rhizome necks, giving a more open, more invasive habit, with scattered groups of culms. This is true of *Yushania* bamboos, for example, and some species of *Chusquea*. The approximate annual rate

Pachymorph (sympodial) rhizome. Each rhizome turns upward and is short and thicker than the aerial culm that develops from the terminal bud at the tip. The lateral buds produce further rhizomes. New shoots are shown in various stages of development.

of spread for this rhizome type in cool-temperate climates is 15 to 50 cm (6 inches to 1⅝ feet). Again, warmer conditions do not significantly increase the rate of spread.

Leptomorph (Monopodial) Rhizomes

Most bamboos from temperate regions have this type of rhizome. A typical leptomorph rhizome is more or less cylindrical, slender, and elongated. Its diameter is nearly always less than that of the culms that develop from it. Internodes are symmetrical, hollow (very occasionally solid), and greater in length than diameter, the length of each internode being fairly uniform throughout.

In most genera, the nodes in this type of rhizome are noticeably larger in diameter than the internodes, although there are some exceptions not covered here. Each node normally bears a

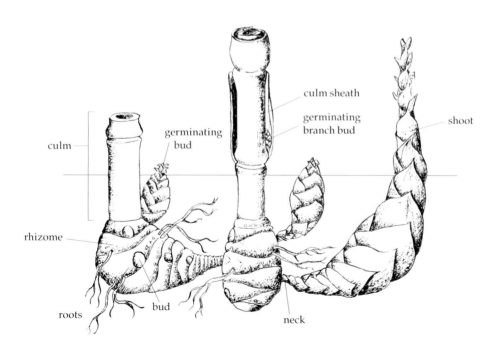

solitary dormant bud, although in certain bamboos (particularly some species of *Sasa*) there may be sections of rhizome comprising two or more adjacent nodes where buds may be absent and root development poor or even entirely absent.

Lateral buds of a leptomorph rhizome often remain dormant for a considerable period, though their ability to germinate is often reduced after three or more seasons. Most of the buds that germinate will grow into a culm directly, while a few will produce new rhizomes. A leptomorph rhizome can extend itself indefinitely from its terminal bud. Occasionally in some bamboos (more particularly *Phyllostachys*) the terminal bud will turn upward to produce a culm, often at the end of the growing season, although the culm will sometimes not emerge until the following season. This terminates the extension of the rhizome, with new rhizome growth continuing from the lateral buds.

The clump habit of this type of rhizome system is more open, producing a diffuse grove of individual freestanding culms. *Phyllostachys*, *Pleioblastus*, and *Sasa* bamboos are all good examples. It is difficult to estimate a rate of spread for this rhizome type, since it is so variable from bamboo to bamboo, and since it is much affected by growing conditions. An annual spread could be anywhere from 15 cm (6 inches) to as much as 5 m (16 feet) for a vigorous, strongly leptomorph bamboo, even in a cool-temperate climate. The running propensity of leptomorph rhizomes is increased by

Leptomorph (monopodial) rhizome. Each rhizome grows horizontally and is long and noticeably thinner than the aerial culms that develop from lateral buds. Some lateral buds on the rhizome produce further rhizomes. The culm at left was produced at the start of the main shooting season in early summer and is large in diameter; a section has been cut away above the dark area to show the internal structure. The culm at right was produced later in the shooting season and is slightly thinner.

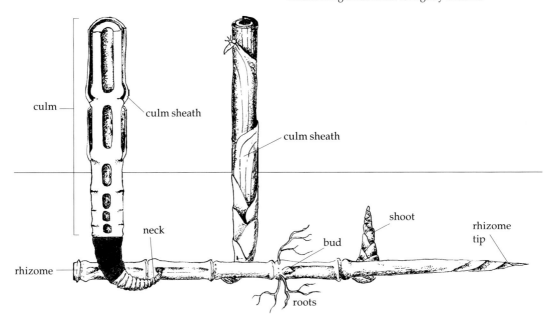

warmer conditions, often considerably, with a spread of 8 m (26 feet) in a single year not uncommon. However, in more cool-temperate places such as the British Isles, many leptomorph bamboos, particularly some species of *Phyllostachys*, are almost static and consequently more or less caespitose.

Metamorph Rhizomes

Most bamboos can be classified without difficulty as having either pachymorph or leptomorph rhizomes. However, certain bamboos show types of rhizome growth that do not fit exactly into these categories. Metamorph rhizomes can occur in the transitional parts of a bamboo plant, where a rhizome transforms into a culm. In a typical bamboo the underground parts of the plant can be clearly defined as a rhizome neck, the rhizome proper, a culm neck, or a culm base, with the transformation between these states taking place abruptly. Metamorph growth exists when the distinction between these states is not clear.

Metamorph 1 rhizomes are found between the rhizome neck and a culm proper, in the position normally occupied by the culm base. It is intermediate in form between a pachymorph rhizome and a normal culm base. This type of growth often appears in *Pleioblastus* and *Shibataea* bamboos, when culms originating from lateral buds on leptomorph rhizomes are said to tiller. This means that culms grow directly out from the base of a culm, without an intervening rhizome, to form groups of culms. In such cases, metamorph 1 growth is barely distinct from an elongated culm neck, although this should not be confused with an elongated rhizome neck between two pachymorph rhizomes.

Metamorph 2 rhizomes can occur at the apex of both pachymorph and leptomorph rhizomes, when the transformation of the rhizome into a culm takes place gradually instead of abruptly. Such a phenomenon is found where a leptomorph rhizome turns upward to produce a culm from its terminal bud, as commonly occurs with *Phyllostachys* bamboos. The type of metamorph 2 rhizome that occurs between a pachymorph rhizome and the culm it transforms into is much less common and does not apply typically to any of the bamboos featured in this book. It is known to exist in certain obscure species of *Chusquea*.

Roots

From the rhizome nodes emerge the true roots of a bamboo, which often burst through the remains of the sheath. The roots are also ivory-white when young but are not jointed and do not have a protective sheath. Bamboo roots are randomly and sparsely branched, fibrous, and usually more or less equal in thickness within any particular plant. They do not usually penetrate to any great depth; for most species the network of rhizomes and roots seldom delves deeper than the top 30 cm (1 foot) of soil. The primary purpose of the roots is to absorb water and nutrients from the soil, but they also help anchor the plant as the aerial parts are moved about by wind.

The roots of bamboos are said to be adventitious, meaning they emerge from unusual locations compared with other types of plant. In a tree or shrub there is usually one central root system from the base of the trunk, but the roots of bamboos are initiated adventitiously from the nodes of the rhizomes. It is also common for roots to be initiated from nodes at the bases of the culms, particularly from the thicker culms, since the thickened roots can act as a prop, helping to support the culm against the action of the wind. In some tropical and subtropical bamboos, root primordia may be visible on higher nodes up the culm and sometimes on the branches. This is much less common in the temperate bamboos, but there are a few notable examples. *Chimonobambusa quadrangularis*, the square-stemmed bamboo, has root primordia present on most lower culm nodes, which can be clearly seen and felt as sharp points or hooks.

Culms

Culms arise from the rhizome, either as extensions from the tip or as lateral branches, determined by whether the rhizome is pachymorph or leptomorph. Culms may also originate by tillering. In common with all the other main structural parts of a bamboo, the culm has segmented growth, consisting of an alternating series of nodes and internodes. The growth of a culm can be divided into two distinct phases: the shoot elongation phase, where the culm ex-

Section of a bamboo culm (*Phyllostachys*), showing the principal parts.

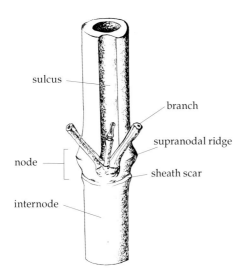

sulcus

branch

supranodal ridge

node

sheath scar

internode

tends itself upward, and the branching phase, where the lateral branches develop from the culm nodes. These two phases of growth can be separate or may overlap.

The culm grows from the rhizome as a series of tightly compressed nodes and internodes wrapped in scale-like, overlapping sheaths. In common with the tips of the rhizomes, a small amount of moisture is secreted at the tip of a new culm as it pushes its way upward through the soil, softening and easing its passage until it emerges from the ground. When the ground is very dry, a small moist patch appearing overnight heralds the new culm below, which is now near the surface and about to emerge. As the culm pushes its way through the soil surface it is then known as a new shoot.

New Shoots

One of the most fascinating and rewarding aspects of growing bamboos is the emergence of new shoots. In addition to the daily interest of checking for any new shoots that may have appeared overnight, and noting how far they are from the rest of the plant, there is the excitement of finding a big increase in culm diameter compared with the previous year's growth, particularly when it comes to varieties with larger culms. New shoots are often very colorful, with the overlapping sheaths at the tip sometimes blotched, flushed, or tinted pink, red, purple, beige, or brown, in all sorts of combinations. Additionally they may be fringed or covered with hairs of varying thickness and density. These characteristics are a useful aid to the identification of certain groups of bamboos. The genus *Phyllostachys*, for example, comprises many similar species, and sometimes the only effective way to be sure of an identification is by comparing the colors and structures of the culm sheaths.

The shooting season, as it is sometimes

called by bamboo enthusiasts, begins for most temperate bamboos in late spring or early summer, once the weather has started to warm up (as a general guide, this means daytime temperatures constantly above 5°C [41°F]). Some bamboos send up new shoots much earlier than others. The shoots of *Fargesia robusta*, for example, appear closely around the perimeter of the clump often as early as February in cool-temperate Europe and the United States. At the other extreme, the shoots of *Phyllostachys bambusoides* can appear as late as June or July in the same regions. Once shooting has begun, shoots continue to appear for a period of several weeks, onward into summer, with the thickest culms for that particular year usually produced in this period. Many bamboos produce further new shoots off and on until the weather begins to cool in autumn, but these later shoots often have a smaller diameter.

Not all bamboos conform to this pattern; indeed, some species of *Chimonobambusa*, as well as most tropical or subtropical bamboos, can send up shoots at almost any time of year if the weather is warm enough.

Upon emergence, the culm extends itself upward by elongating the internodes as they are formed, whereupon the sheaths, their purpose in protecting the new culm now complete, become desiccated and are discarded, revealing an ever-increasing length of culm surface. This surface is often covered with a waxy whitish powdery bloom that can be thick enough to scrape off with a thumbnail. With some bamboos, however, the dead sheaths may remain attached to the culm for a considerable period, especially on the culm branches.

New shoots of *Phyllostachys viridis*. Five days later these shoots were more than 2 m (6 feet) high.

Diagrammatic new shoot of a bamboo (cut away). The shoot emerges from the ground at its finished diameter. As the shoot grows, so the compressed internodes expand vertically and begin to harden, thus forming the aerial culm.

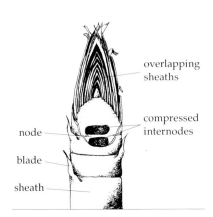

overlapping sheaths

compressed internodes

node

blade

sheath

As the new culm grows upward from the ground, so it starts to harden and begin the process of lignification. This process is very rapid, for the culm will need to support the complement of branches and leaves that are to soon to follow. Yet the hardening process continues even after the branches and leaves have developed, and a culm does not attain its maximum strength until the passing of at least two, more often three, complete growing seasons.

Dimensions and Profile

Generally a bamboo culm is thickest at the base, where the greatest strength is needed, and gradually tapers toward the tip, similar to a telegraph pole or the mast of a ship. Curiously, however, some thicker culms, particularly those of the genus *Phyllostachys*, can be seen to have a slight increase in diameter for several nodes and internodes from the base before beginning the usual long taper toward the tip; the thickest part of the culm may be some 60 cm (2 feet) or more from the ground in a cool-temperate climate.

In a developing bamboo plant, the oldest culms are usually the shortest and thinnest, and the youngest culms are usually the tallest and thickest. This is because the diameter of a bamboo culm does not increase from the time it emerges from the ground, and each new culm grows to its full height in one season, after which the height does not increase. Branches and leaves may be produced in subsequent seasons, but the basic dimensions of the culm (its diameter and height) remain the same throughout its life. There is no secondary thickening or extension, as with shrubs and trees. In fact, by the time the eighth or ninth sheath has emerged aboveground, the diameter of the shoot will indicate the basic diameter of the finished culm. Each successive year, the developing bamboo will produce culms that emerge with greater diameters and that reach correspondingly greater heights, until the typical mature dimensions of the species have been attained for a particular set of climatic and growing conditions. The only exception to this is when there is some change in the growing conditions, such as drought, or when the plant is disturbed, as when it is dug up and moved or divided for the purposes of propagation. In these instances the bamboo is able to adjust the diameter and height of the culms to take account of the changed growing circumstances.

The culms of *Phyllostachys edulis* often attain larger dimensions in the warm-temperate conditions of the Bambouseraie de Prafrance in southern France than they do in their native China. The culm in the foreground is 22 cm (8½ inches) in diameter at the base.

Sulcus

The culms of most bamboos are more or less cylindrical, although in cross section many thicker culms may be somewhat oval. In certain bamboos there may also be a shallow groove or flattened depression on one side of the internodes, always above and in line with the branch complement. This is called a sulcus. The action of the branch bud creates a sulcus in the internode above as the internode elongates in its development. In genera such as *Semiarundinaria* the sulcus is only partly developed, whereas in *Phyllostachys* the sulcus is well developed and highly visible, making it an almost infallible guide to identifying the genus. Many of the bamboos most prized for their colored culms have a panel or stripe of a different color in the sulcus. A sulcus may only be present in the branched part of a culm, and very thick culms of bamboos with a sulcus are usually completely cylindrical below the lowest node with a branch bud.

Growth Period

Culms from pachymorph bamboos normally complete their growth in two to four months. Culms from leptomorph bamboos usually achieve some 90 percent of their growth within just one month, with the remaining growth spread over the next one or two months. When a bamboo culm has reached approximately half its final height, the rate of growth is usually at it fastest. Indeed, I have measured *Phyllostachys vivax* growing in my garden in southern England, rocketing skyward at an astonishing 38 cm (1¼ feet) in a single 24-hour period during a spell of hot weather. In warm-temperate or subtropical conditions, a growth rate of 90 cm (3 feet) a day is not uncommon. The relatively sudden growth and abrupt halt to growth in a bamboo culm can be explained by the fact that a culm is not a complete plant in itself but merely a component of the overall clump or grove.

The life span of a bamboo culm can vary considerably between species. Some high-altitude bamboos of the Himalayan region die down annually under the winter snows, replacing their culms each spring, and only when cultivated in milder environments do these species retain their culms to build up a mature stand. However, the usual life of a bamboo culm, whether temperate or tropical, is between five and ten years, although some species may have culms that live 20 years or more.

Color

The basic color of living bamboo culms is green, but all sorts of other colors and color combinations are possible through mutation of the outer layers of the culm wall. The most frequently found exception to the basic green culm is a culm with yellow pigment, or a yellow culm with green striping, or even a green culm with yellow striping. In the woody bamboos, any such striping always appears as vertical or longitudinal sections or panels on the culms, never as horizontal bands. Other colors are also possible, as with the black culms of the well-known *Phyllostachys nigra*. Many bamboos develop red tones and tinges, such as *Himalayacalamus falconeri* 'Damarapa', caused by exposure to sunlight. Certain species have an unusually copious covering of waxy powder on the young culms that can appear whitish, grayish, or bluish. In the temperate bamboos the greatest variation in terms of color is to be found among the large genus *Phyllostachys*, which mutates quite readily and has provided some excellent colored-culm bamboos for Western gardens. Colored-culm forms and varieties do also exist in many other genera but are much less common.

Arching, Geniculations, and Distortions

Very few culms grow completely vertical and straight, except perhaps when very young. There is normally some degree of arching near the summit as the culm ages and as more and more foliage develops, particularly in later years. However, there are also bamboos with distortions to the normal shape or length of the culm nodes or internodes. One fairly common distortion is a slight noticeable zigzag from node to node on some culms, particularly in the phyllostachoid genera of *Phyllostachys* and *Semiarundinaria*, although it can occur elsewhere. In some species and cultivars, this tendency to zigzag may be extremely pronounced in the lower part of the culm. In *P. aureosulcata*, for example, there are often sinuous or sharply angled changes of direction from node to node near the base of the culm but seldom higher up. These more extreme zigzags are known as geniculations, a word derived from the Greek, meaning "knees" or "knee-like."

Phyllostachys aurea and its colored forms frequently produce a clustering of nodes and internodes at the base of the culm, giving a knobbly effect, and because of this the species is known in the United States as the fishpole

Many bamboos have colorful or distinctive culms: 1. *Chusquea gigantea*, 2. *Phyllostachys bambusoides* 'Marliacea', 3. *Phyllostachys aurea*, 4. *Phyllostachys bambusoides* 'Castillonis', 5. *Phyllostachys bambusoides* 'Holochrysa', 6. *Chimonobambusa quadrangularis*, 7. *Thamnocalamus crassinodus*, 8. *Himalayacalamus falconeri* 'Damarapa', 9. *Phyllostachys aureosulcata* 'Spectabilis', 10. *Phyllostachys nigra* 'Boryana', 11. *Phyllostachys viridiglaucescens*, 12. *Chimonobambusa tumidissinoda*, 13. *Phyllostachys nigra*, 14. *Phyllostachys bambusoides* 'Castillonis Inversa', 15. *Phyllostachys vivax* 'Aureocaulis', 16. *Drepanostachyum khasianum*. Photo by Derek St. Romaine

bamboo. Another interesting example is *Pseudosasa japonica* 'Tsutsumiana', which develops bottle-like swellings in the internodes of larger culms. If we were to dig up the rhizomes, the swellings would be revealed there too, rather like a series of bulbous tires laid next to each other.

Culm Branches

The culms of all species of woody bamboo produce branches at successive nodes, on alternate sides of the culm. Indeed, one of the most important ways of distinguishing bamboos from other grasses is by noting the presence of a woody branch structure. The sequence of branch development on a young culm can vary between different genera. In *Phyllostachys* bamboos, for example, the branch buds awaken into growth as soon as the internode immediately above them has completed its elongation, which produces a wave of branch emergence from base to summit. Bamboos of other genera, such as *Fargesia*, *Pleioblastus* (the taller species), *Thamnocalamus*, and *Yushania*, tend to produce their branches in the order of summit to base. In some bamboos, particularly certain species of *Chusquea*, the branch buds of a fully grown culm may remain dormant for a period and then break into growth more or less simultaneously.

Immature bamboo plants often bear branch buds at all of the culm nodes, but in a mature clump of bamboo the lower nodes of the culms (aboveground) are usually without branches. In fact, progressively larger culms tend to have a progressively greater portion of their length, from the ground upward, devoid of branches. It is quite common for the culms of a mature bamboo to lack branches for half or even three-quarters of their length. This is often considered a desirable characteristic in bamboos grown ornamentally and is also beneficial for handicraft applications that require a culm free of the marks or scars caused by the removal of branches.

All the bamboos described in this book, except those of the genus *Chusquea*, produce their branch complement from a primary bud that is always solitary at the culm nodes. Many bamboos may appear to have two or more main branches growing directly out of the culm node, but these will all have originated from the primary branch, which will have branched or divided at its base, in some cases precociously. Each main branch axis may produce smaller branches at each node all along its length, and these in turn will produce yet smaller branches, twigs, and twiglets.

In *Sasa* bamboos there is only one main branch axis at culm nodes, because the primary branch has no basal buds. *Phyllostachys* bamboos, however, have a binary branch complement; the primary bud divides into two usually unequal main branch axes, with an occasional much smaller third branch coming from the base of the smaller main branch axis. The ramification of the primary bud can vary in extent quite considerably between different bamboo genera. Where such ramification is very precocious, the original primary branch may be indistinguishable in size from all the other branches that have emerged in a sunburst from its base.

Certain bamboos, such as *Phyllostachys aureosulcata* 'Spectabilis', are prone to producing extreme geniculations.

Chusquea bamboos are exceptional in usually having one large, central, primary branch bud at each culm node (in the branched part of the culm) flanked at either side by additional, independent, smaller branch primordia, extending sometimes almost completely round the culm. The central branch is always dominant, when properly developed, often being nearly as thick and long as the culm from which it originated, particularly in the midculm region. This is characteristic of bamboos that in their natural habitat are loosely scandent. However, *C. culeou*, the species that most commonly represents *Chusquea* in Western gardens, has no primary branch but a series of small, independent branch primordia extending in a narrow band two-thirds of the way around the culm.

Some smaller bamboos, such as *Shibataea* species, have short, simple branches that seldom rebranch into smaller branches or twigs. However, many larger bamboos, such as *Phyllostachys* species, have long branches that rebranch into complex orders of smaller branches, with great numbers of small twigs. The branch complement of any species is usually at its most typical in the midculm region. Often the lowermost branches on a culm are not fully developed or are lacking entirely. Nearer the summit of the culm the branches tend to be progressively shorter, with correspondingly less development of smaller orders of branching.

Many tropical bamboos have further developed their branching characteristics by compressing, reducing, or extending the branch complement, or by adapting the smaller branches and twigs into weak thorns. These thorns, though weakly developed, are still quite sharp and offer some degree of protection from larger grazing animals.

Sheaths

Bamboo sheaths are actually the foliar organs of the plant, but a distinction should be made between a sheath proper and a leaf proper. Some modern botanists, such as the authors of *American Bamboos* (Judziewicz et al. 1999), regard all parts of a bamboo sheath as parts of a leaf, since a sheath may be green when exposed to light and has the ability to photosynthesize. Based on this reasoning, the term *culm leaves* has gained some credence to describe the culm sheaths. However, since this can be misleading for ordinary bamboo gardeners, and since it may not become widely accepted even among botanists, in this book I keep to the traditional terminology for describing sheaths.

At the time of their original development,

Examples of culm branching patterns found in bamboos.

Sasa *Phyllostachys* *Pleioblastus* *Semiarundinaria*

all segmented parts of a bamboo are enclosed by a protective sheath. Every node, whether aboveground or belowground, will have a sheath attached to it just below the supranodal ridge, enclosing the elongating internode immediately above. There are six principle types of sheath to be found on a bamboo plant: culm sheaths, branch sheaths, rhizome sheaths, neck sheaths, leaf sheaths, and prophylla, which are scale-like sheaths found in the earliest stages of development of a branch bud on any segmented part of a bamboo. With the exception of leaf sheaths, which have a separate and dis-

The attractively colored sheaths on a new culm of *Chusquea gigantea*.

tinct function, all types of bamboo sheath tend to be short-lived, with abscission taking place promptly once the enclosed internode is fully developed.

The only part of a bamboo sheath that resembles a leaf is the sheath blade, or limbus, an appendage to the top of the sheath. The true leaves of a bamboo are the blades of the leaf sheaths. All members of the grass family bear their leaves in this way, but the woody bamboos have their leaves separated from the leaf sheaths by a pseudopetiole, which is actually just an extension of the midrib of the leaf. True grasses and herbaceous bamboos have the bases of their leaves sessile to the leaf sheaths, without a stalk between them. A bamboo sheath comprises four distinct parts: the sheath proper and its three principle appendages, the limbus, the ligule, and the auricles.

Sheath Proper

The sheath proper envelopes and supports the elongating internode immediately above the node to which the sheath is attached. The outer surface may be textured with shallow striations or may be completely smooth, and is sometimes covered with short adpressed hairs. It may also be stained or blotched with colors other than green. All bamboo sheaths have a glazed, lustrous interior surface to facilitate the elongation of the young internode it contains.

Limbus

The limbus, or sheath blade, is an appendage to the top of the sheath. It can be broadly triangular to narrowly linear but is usually smaller overall than the sheath proper (except in the case of leaf sheaths). The limbus is often different in color from the rest of the sheath. It is usually carried at an angle to the sheath proper (although it may be nearly upright) and is often shorter lived, falling off while the rest of the sheath remains attached to the plant. At the uppermost ends of the culms and culm branches are the leaf sheaths, whose blades are the true leaves of a bamboo plant and are usually larger overall than the sheaths proper that bear them.

Ligule

The ligule is an upward projection of the sheath proper. It occurs along the inner surface behind the base of the sheath blade, or in the case of leaf sheaths, behind the base of the pseudopetiole. It can vary considerably in size, shape, and texture between different species of bamboo. The ligule is an effective waterproofing device, preventing moisture from penetrating downward to the young internode.

Examples of a culm sheath and leaf sheath. Each complete node and internode of a bamboo is enclosed in a protective sheath at the time of its original development. At the top of the culm sheath there is usually a blade-like appendage called the limbus or sheath blade. At the summit of the culms and at the ends of all orders of branches and twigs, these blades are longer and become the "leaves" of a bamboo plant. At this stage the sheaths are known as leaf sheaths.

Auricles

The auricles are ear-like projections appended to the sheath proper so as to flank the ligule. They may be borne in pairs, one on either side of the ligule, singly, or may be completely absent. They are often fringed with short, stiff hairs known as oral setae or fimbriae. Sometimes these hairs are present on the sheath, while the auricles themselves are absent, in which case they are properly known as shoulder bristles.

Variations in Color and Form

Many species of bamboo can be identified from the color and form of their culm sheaths. This is particularly useful where species are closely related and difficult to distinguish, as are many *Phyllostachys* species. It is not an infallible guide by any means, for there can be considerable variation within a clump of bamboo and even within a single culm. However, the sheaths found in the midculm region of a mature stand of bamboo can be expected to represent the most typical color and form for a given species. Those found near the base of a culm

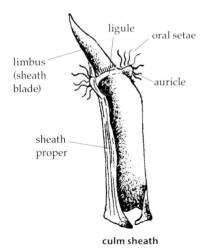

culm sheath

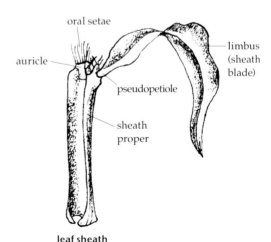

leaf sheath

A naturally occurring path through an extensive colony of *Sasa palmata* 'Nebulosa' reveals the zebra-like effect created by the desiccated culm sheaths still attached at each node.

New shoot of *Phyllostachys nigra* 'Henonis'.

tend to show a marked reduction in the size of the sheath blade and an absence of auricles, whereas those found on the uppermost nodes of a culm take the form of leaf sheaths, complete with pseudopetiole and leaf blade. The transition from culm sheaths to leaf sheaths at the top of a culm is often quite abrupt. Interestingly, the leaves borne at the tip of a culm and at the tips of the main culm branches are often considerably larger than those produced on the lower orders of branches and branchlets.

Branch Sheaths

Branch sheaths are usually scaled-down versions of the culm sheaths, alike in all their parts. Indeed, those produced on the large primary branches of many scandent species of *Chusquea* closely resemble in size and form those of the mother culm.

Rhizome Sheaths

Unlike culm sheaths, rhizome sheaths show a strong uniformity in size and form from node to node, particularly in leptomorph bamboos, where the diameter of any one rhizome axis tends to be constant throughout its length. The appendages on rhizome sheaths are usually very small or entirely lacking. There is also a pronounced overlapping, each sheath extending in length beyond the internode that it encloses to partially cover the next node and internode. Such sheaths are said to be imbricate and as a consequence are usually persistent.

Leaves

As previously mentioned, the true leaves of a bamboo are the blades of the leaf sheaths. Leaves are carried at the uppermost extremities of culms and at the ends of all orders of branches, from the main branch axes to the smallest twigs and twiglets. They develop acropetally, from base to tip, each one emerging tightly furled through the open top of the previous sheath, opening out on alternate sides but always on the same plane. When fully opened, the leaf is then orientated to favor the strongest incidence of light.

Bamboo leaves can vary in size quite significantly between species, from the tiny leaves of *Pleioblastus pygmaeus* to the enormous leaves of *Sasa palmata* 'Nebulosa'. However, the shape is more or less similar in every species: linear-lanceolate to broadly linear. The leaf base

is obtuse and the leaf tip is acute, although some bamboo leaf tips can be more acute than others. The leaf margins are entire and usually fringed with minute bristly hairs that all point sharply toward the leaf tip. Sometimes these hairs appear to be present on one margin only, but they are usually found, to a greater or lesser extent, on both margins. Their presence is barely visible to the naked eye, and often the only means of detecting them is to run a finger gently along the leaf margins, from tip to base, whereupon the friction of the forward-pointing bristles can be clearly felt.

The upper surface of the leaf is usually smooth and lustrous, having a strong reflective quality, particularly when wet. The lower surface is

Unfurling bamboo leaves (cut away). Each new leaf blade emerges tightly rolled up from inside the top of the preceding leaf sheath and then opens out and orientates itself to favor the highest incidence of light.

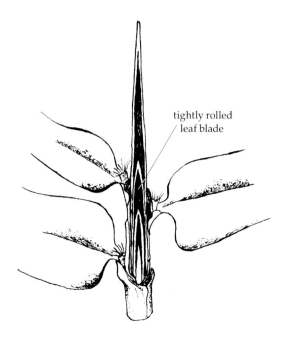

tightly rolled leaf blade

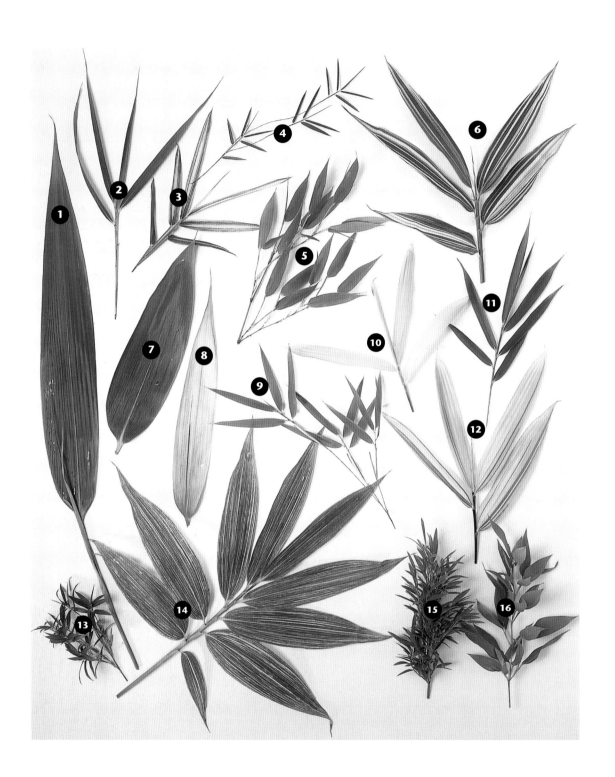

often covered with minute hairs and is invariably dull and matte. The matte effect is caused by small projections from the many stomata, and this effect is increased by the presence of any hairs. Close inspection of several different species will reveal that the dull matte coloration does not always extend uniformly across the leaf. Some species have a strip of a different color, usually less grayish matte, on one side of the leaf. The reason for this is not yet fully explained.

Veins

Each leaf is bisected by the midrib, of which the leaf stalk or pseudopetiole is merely an extension. It is the primary vein carrying nutrients to and from the leaf for photosynthesis, and it extends right along the leaf to its tip. In some species of bamboo the midrib can be clearly seen and felt, while in others (particularly those with small, thin leaves) it may be so fine as to be almost imperceptible. Parallel to the midrib, at a short distance on either side, are the secondary veins, which are smaller. Even smaller still, and normally visible only with the aid of a magnifying glass, are the intermediate or tertiary veins. Connecting all three orders of veins are transverse veinlets, which create a latticework pattern of roughly square or rectangular sections. This is known as tessellation or tessellated venation.

Tessellation is more conspicuous in some bamboos than others. Some people believe that hardiness can be determined by the degree of tessellation visible in the leaves, but this cannot be an absolute truth. While all the hardy bamboos seem to have well-tessellated leaves, there are also tropical species that have visible tessellation but that are unable to tolerate the slightest frost. Nonetheless, we can make the observation that all of the hardiest bamboos are clearly tessellated and that no species has proved hardy that does not have such tessellation.

Leaf Change

Nearly all woody bamboos are evergreen, and all the hardy bamboos cultivated in Western gardens are evergreen or nearly so. Some species, such as *Pleioblastus auricomus*, may lose a considerable portion of their foliage naturally by the end of winter but would still be classed as evergreen. The genus *Borinda* contains some species that lose most of their leaves through winter but otherwise retain them in very mild growing conditions.

Bamboos renew their leaves annually, just like deciduous plants, but do so gradually during the growing season. Foliage is often shed and replaced with greater activity during the main shooting period in spring and early summer. There is usually a complete change of leaves every year, the older leaves yellowing and falling away as new ones develop. The process goes largely unnoticed in the garden, becoming apparent only when there is a fresh carpet of beige and brown beneath the plant, as the growing season progresses.

Variegation

Many bamboos have variegated forms, in which white or yellow or a different shade of

Bamboo leaves vary in size and color: 1. *Indocalamus tessellatus*, 2. *Pleioblastus linearis*, 3. *Pleioblastus shibuyanus* 'Tsuboi', 4. *Thamnocalamus crassinodus* 'Kew Beauty', 5. *Phyllostachys nigra* 'Henonis', 6. *×Hibanobambusa tranquillans* 'Shiroshima', 7. *Sasa palmata* 'Nebulosa', 8. *Pseudosasa japonica* 'Akebono', 9. *Thamno-calamus spathiflorus*, 10. *Pleioblastus auricomus* 'Chrysophyllus', 11. *Fargesia robusta*, 12. *Pleio-blastus auricomus*, 13. *Pleioblastus pygmaeus*, 14. *Sasa kurilensis* 'Shimofuri', 15. *Chusquea culeou*, 16. *Shibataea kumasasa*. Photo by Derek St. Romaine

green is present in the leaf blades. One colorful example is ×*Hibanobambusa tranquillans* 'Shiroshima', whose leaves have conspicuous bands of creamy white mixed with the basic green. Variegation is common among the dwarfer bamboos but occurs sparingly in taller types. Some bamboos have conspicuously variegated young leaves in early summer, but the variegation tones down or loses its intensity as the season progresses, due to ripening of the leaf and exposure to sunlight, as in the case of *Sasaella masamuneana* 'Albostriata'. Some types of variegation are unstable, and the variegation may be variable from leaf to leaf, with some leaves almost completely white or yellow and others almost completely or completely green. In some

cases there may be entire culms without variegated leaves, as occurs among the notoriously beautiful but difficult variegated forms of *Shibataea kumasasa*.

Flowers

Bamboo flowers are very small and inconspicuous and rather resemble the flowers of cereals or herbaceous grasses. In evolutionary terms, bamboo flowers are fairly primitive in their structure. Each individual flower has one ovary and one ovule and therefore produces just one seed. The flowers are arranged in groups of three or four as spikelets, and these in turn are grouped together as spikes, racemes, or panicles. In common with other grasses, bamboo flowers are generally wind-

Young leaves of ×*Hibanobambusa tranquillans* 'Shiroshima'

pollinated. Because of this, petals are absent or much reduced, and nectaries are entirely lacking, but pollen is produced copiously.

The flowering of bamboos is a phenomenon still not fully understood by botanists. Ever since bamboos were first studied scientifically, many different theories have evolved to explain the act of flowering, to the extent that the subject has become confused and rife with fallacy and misconception.

In the past it was believed that when a clump of bamboo came into flower in one part of the world, all other clumps of that species, wherever else in the world they might be, came into flower at the same time. There have been many examples of simultaneous flowering. Indeed,

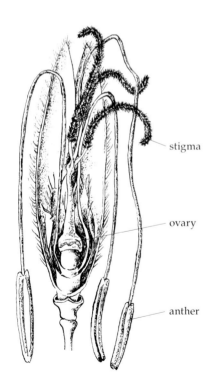

Flower of a bamboo (*Phyllostachys*), greatly enlarged.

stigma

ovary

anther

Thamnocalamus spathiflorus flowered in many locations throughout Europe in 1876, and also flowered in North Africa and Sikkim, prompting many authorities at the time to state that when a bamboo comes into flower in one location, it does so everywhere. This idea has since proved to be only a partial truth. Most of the established bamboo species in Western gardens originate from only one clonal source, which has been divided and redivided over the years. Every division, no matter how small, retains the botanical identity of its parent clump and may therefore be expected to come into flower at approximately the same time. But the seedlings that arise from the flowering of a bamboo are all unique in terms of their botanical identity, varying within narrow limits from the botanical characteristics of the parent, and are therefore likely to flower at different times.

Flowering Intervals

For the vast majority of bamboos, flowering is not an annual occurrence. Indeed, the intervals between flowerings may be 10, 50, or even more than 100 years. There are even some bamboos that have not been known to flower since proper records began. *Fargesia nitida* was once thought to be such a bamboo, but in 1993 a clump was found to be flowering in Cornwall, in southwestern England—the first known flowering of the species since it was brought into cultivation circa 1889. Since then, many older clones of *F. nitida* have come into flower across Europe and the United States. On the other hand, *Pleioblastus auricomus* is frequently in flower, with no apparent ill effect. It was once believed that the intervals between flowerings were always constant for a particular species, but this theory has long been disproved. Alexander High Lawson demonstrated this in *Bamboos: A Gardener's Guide to Their Cultivation in Temperate Climates* (1968) by quoting the flowering intervals of two well-known species as they occurred prior to the publication of his book: *Himalayacalamus falconeri* flowered in 1876, 1890, 1929, and 1936, with intervals of 14, 39, and 7 years. *Phyllostachys aurea* flowered in 1876, 1904, 1922, and 1936, with intervals of 28, 18, and 14 years. We can conclude that flowering does not form a regular pattern and that it is not possible to accurately predict future flowerings based on the intervals of the past.

There have always been two major difficulties in keeping authentic records of flowerings. The first problem is in correctly identifying the species in flower. This is absolutely essential if the record is to have any value. The second problem is in defining exactly what is meant by flowering. A bamboo can produce just a single floret, buried in a mass of foliage, occurring on a single culm of just one clump, and appearing in only one year. Sometimes a more obvious flowering can be seen, whereby some culms in a clump have flowers and other culms do not. Quite often it may be observed that one clump of a given species is in flower, while an adjacent clump of the same species and of the same clonal origin is not in flower. At the furthest extreme is full gregarious flowering, the rarest condition, in which every plant of a given clone flowers profusely, at the same time, the world over. The uncertainty of flowering is further complicated by the fact that a bamboo may flower on and off for several years, sometimes decades. Many clumps of *Semiarundinaria fastuosa*, for example, began flowering in Western gardens in 1957 and continued to do so on and off until the early 1980s.

Floyd Alonzo McClure (1966) observed that, in terms of their flowering cycle, most bamboos

Pseudosasa japonica in flower.

known to science can be said to exist some-where between two extremes: continuous or annual flowering and constant sterility, if such a state really exists. Relatively few bamboos are designated as continuous-flowering types, and these are predominantly obscure tropical spe-cies not in cultivation. Some Sino-Himalayan species produce flower-bearing culms annu-ally but lose this characteristic when brought into cultivation and grown in less severe cli-mates. It would be highly speculative to sug-gest that any bamboos are actually sterile. More probably such bamboos are just undergoing a very long interval between proper flowerings, especially in view of the fact that good records only go back some 200 years.

Effects of Flowering

Although the event of a bamboo coming into flower is sudden and unexpected, there are often certain signs or clues given away by the plant shortly before. Many bamboos, in the year before a prolific flowering, will show un-usually vigorous growth of new culms, or in-creased activity in the rhizomes, followed sometimes by a slight yellowing of the foliage. The impending flowering of a bamboo is also heralded by a fattening of the leaf sheaths at the ends of the smallest twigs and at the ends of the culms, this usually happening toward late autumn or at the beginning of the winter prior to the spring whereupon the flowers will emerge and produce anthers and pollen. All the aforementioned signs were present on my clump of *Pleioblastus linearis* the year before it came heavily into flower in spring 1996. Dur-ing the summer of 1995 the plant grew lustily and the soil nearby swarmed with rhizomes. Yet just two years later the whole plant was vir-tually dead. I now have a seedling of that plant growing well in the same location; it is almost as big as its parent.

Bamboos are said to be monocarpic, mean-ing they flower once and then die, but this is not strictly true and in my experience is rarely the case. Most bamboos will survive a partial flowering with little or no permanent harm, al-though it is true that the effects of full, contin-uous flowering over an extended period can be extremely debilitating. Bamboos with a pachy-morph rhizome type, such as *Fargesia* species, do tend to be more prone to dying completely after prolonged gregarious flowering, but bam-boos with a leptomorph rhizome type often re-cover from a flowering bout, albeit very slowly if the plant is much weakened. While all the plant's strength is going into producing flow-ers, normal vegetative growth slows down or even ceases. Leaves may become yellow and drop off, and the rhizomes seem to lose their ability to make active growth. Meanwhile the bamboo becomes more and more unsightly, no longer an object of beauty and a joy to behold.

If a flowering goes on long enough, many gardeners understandably suffer a loss of pa-tience and dig out the plant. However, a well-established bamboo has considerable reserves of nutrients stored in the rhizomes. Eventually the flowering bout loses its force, and there is usually sufficient life left somewhere in the rhi-zomes to start new shoots and leaves. In their native environments, most bamboos growing in large colonies manage to regenerate them-selves after even a prolonged and profuse flow-ering. Occasionally a bamboo does die from flowering, but more often than not this is due to some other factor operating on the weak-ened plant, such as adverse weather, ill health, or being insufficiently established in its grow-ing quarters.

Causes of Flowering

Opinions differ as to what exactly triggers a bamboo's flowering. Physiological factors such

Fargesia nitida in flower.

as growing conditions and weather must be discounted, as bamboos of the same clonal origin may flower in several widely different environments simultaneously. There have been reported incidences of bamboos flowering after periods of severe weather or other stresses, but these might be coincidence. Once a seed is formed, there is presumably some time mechanism built into its botanical identity that will eventually trigger flowering and procreation. When a bamboo starts to flower, there is nothing we can do but wait for nature to take its course. Some authorities insist that the life of a flowering clump can be prolonged by systematically removing the flowering heads, or even by cutting down the flowering culms. In order to save a valuable plant, the laborious task of removing the flowers as they appear may be worthwhile, as this lessens the

drain on the plant's resources. However, cutting down the culms might be too extreme a step, as the bamboo could well die before it is able to grow any new culms, which may anyway still be afflicted by the inherent impulse to flower.

We can be reassured, however, by the fact that nearly all the bamboos introduced a hundred or more years ago can still be found in cultivation, despite having flowered at some time or other in the intervening period. Forms with colored culms or variegated leaves are at the greatest risk of becoming extinct, because any seed they produce will revert to their entirely green progenitor. This is balanced by the fact that such forms often occur in the first place either as variant seedlings or as mutations when bamboos regenerate after flowering.

This clump of *Himalayacalamus falconeri* at Penjerrick, in Cornwall, has flowered profusely and died, and yet is still attractive in its desiccated state.

Seeds

Bamboo seed is quite a scarce commodity. Fertile seed is rarely available, mainly because bamboos flower infrequently, often with very long intervals between flowerings. Moreover, bamboos grown outside their native environment do not always set fertile seed. When a bamboo does set seed, it can be produced in enormous quantities, and a year later the ground all around the plant, if not cultivated, can look like a miniature bamboo forest, with seedlings sprouting everywhere. Bamboo seed is very vulnerable to the depredations of birds, insects, and small animals, so if you are fortunate enough to find any seed on a flowering bamboo, it is best to harvest it quickly.

Bamboo seeds look like grains of cereals such as rice or wheat. There can be considerable variation in size, but most temperate bamboos produce seeds less than 2.5 cm (1 inch) long, and some seeds may be little larger than the grass seed used for making lawns. Such small seeds can be very difficult to distinguish from the dead and desiccated remains of the flowers and are best found by feeling and squeezing until a hard lump is detected. At the other extreme, some tropical varieties, such as *Melocanna baccifera*, produce a large, fleshy, fruit-like seed the size of a pear. In the case of bamboos, the seeds take the form of a grain or caryopsis, which is simply a hard one-seeded fruit, in common with other members of the grass family.

As a generalization, most bamboo seed found on plants growing outside in cool-temperate climates will be ripe enough to harvest approximately four to five months after the flowers have appeared, which, since bamboo flowers tend to appear at the end of winter, usually means that the seed can be harvested around midsummer. The seed tends to lose its viability rather quickly once harvested, and so it is best sown straight away. The growing of bamboos from seed is covered in more detail in chapter 5.

Seedlings

The seedling stage for a bamboo is properly defined as the period between germination and the point at which the full complement of vegetative structures is present. This period is

Chimonobambusa marmorea fully in flower and laden with conspicuous quantities of ripening purple seeds.

relatively short, sometimes lasting just a few weeks if the seedling is growing strongly in optimum conditions.

As the seed germinates, a single root appears. This is the primary root. The primary root comes directly from the seed capsule and is the only root of a bamboo that does not emerge from the node of a culm or rhizome. This first root orientates itself downward and begins to branch, but it is limited in its growth and never develops to any great length or complexity. It is soon overtaken by roots that develop from primordia on the lower nodes of the first culm.

Shortly after emergence of the primary root, the first culm emerges: the primary culm. The primary culm also never develops to any great size or height; it is usually short, only 2.5 to 8 cm (1 to 3 inches) for most temperate species. It is the first segmented stem of the new bamboo and usually has leaf blades at all of the main nodes aboveground. Occasionally a second culm may start to develop before the primary culm has attained its full height, but more often secondary culms are produced from buds at the basal nodes of the primary culm. These emerge in the form of tillering.

When several secondary culms have been produced, the seedling then develops its first proper rhizome: the primary rhizome. At this point the seedling should have all its main vegetative structures, although any culm branching may be immature or only partially char-acteristic of a more mature plant. Generally, in the first year of growth, seedlings have smaller leaf blades than mature plants, though con-versely, many seedlings in their second and third year of growth can have leaf blades that are much larger than typical.

As the seedling advances into more adult growth, so the rate of growth can be very rapid. This is known as seedling vigor and is typical of most plants, whether monocot-yledons or dicotyledons. Unless there is any check on the growth, there is soon a flourish-ing of more rhizomes and progressively larger culms, until the mature dimensions of the spe-cies for any combination of growing conditions and climate are attained. This period of devel-opment from seedling to mature specimen can take place over as little as three or four years for some tropical bamboos, but more typically occurs over six to twenty years for temperate bamboos.

Seedling of *Pleioblastus simonii* in various stages of development, at 10 days (left), 30 days (center), and 150 days (right).

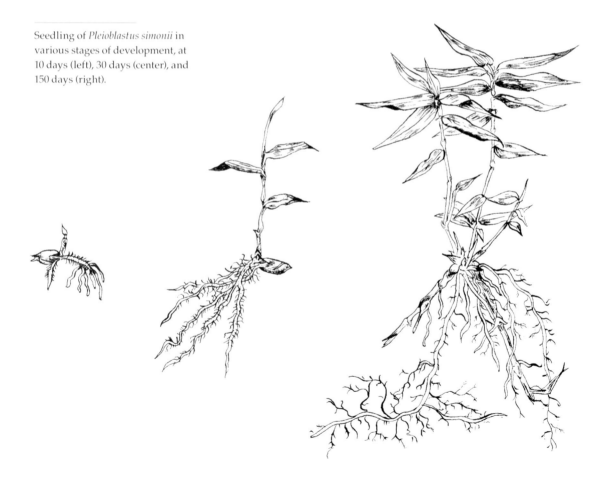

CHAPTER 3

The Horticultural Uses of Bamboo

Bamboos could well be described as the most underappreciated plants in horticulture. Even today, with bamboos enjoying greater popularity, their potential as garden plants is still largely untapped. I wonder how many gardeners realize that there are bamboos suitable for almost every conceivable site, situation, and use. Bamboos can be grown in the smallest town garden or the largest country estate. They are cold-resistant and surprisingly easy to grow. They have great ornamental appeal. Yet until recently these wonderful plants were largely ignored by all but a dedicated core of enlightened enthusiasts.

Why, then, are bamboos so largely underused as garden plants? Two reasons seem most likely. Firstly, there remains an unfortunate mixture of ignorance and misconception about the whole subject of bamboos, not just among the gardening public but also among professional gardeners and writers. The same fallacies about bamboos are repeated in countless articles in contemporary horticultural literature, the most typical statements being that all bamboos are very invasive and all bamboos die after flowering. The second reason why bamboos remain so underappreciated is that until the 1990s the selection available through nurseries was uninspiring. In the past, nurseries customarily offered the most common bamboos, or the most easily propagated bamboos, but not necessarily the most ornamental. Thus, bamboos acquired an unfortunate and unjustified reputation for being rampant scruffy weeds, worthy only of relegation to the remotest corners of the garden.

It is time for bamboos to take their deserved place in modern garden design. There are now many reputable sources for obtaining the choicer species and cultivars, including most of the newer introductions, and there are all sorts of ways to enjoy and make the most of these fascinating plants. The enthusiasts or collectors among us might simply wish to display the maximum number of species and forms that can be accommodated in the area available, to the exclusion of other garden plants, creating a purely bamboo garden. Botanists and taxonomists would perhaps wish to create an ordered display, in which adjoining bamboos are related in some way, giving a rather formal tone to the plantings. Those of us who are primarily gardeners, whose interest in bamboos developed out of knowledge and use of other plants, might try to create a more ornamental effect in the garden, contrived through harmony or contrast with nonbambusoid plants such as trees, shrubs, and perennials.

Garden Design with Bamboos

In selecting suitable species and forms for different uses in the garden, it is absolutely vital to know the maximum height for a given bamboo as well as its rate of invasion. Bamboos are available in such a vast range that there is nearly always a variety to be found with the appropriate height and spread for any particular purpose. In a restricted planting area, a clump-forming bamboo with pachymorph rhizomes might be a more realistic choice than a very invasive bamboo with leptomorph rhizomes. Ask yourself what the bamboo might look like in five or six years' time. A little research or foreknowledge can save much trouble in the longer term.

The character and atmosphere of a garden will be strongly influenced by the presence of bamboos. Bamboos generally impart a restful quality to a planting, and yet they draw attention to themselves because they are so different from other plants. Many have a strong structural element to their appearance. There is always movement with bamboos, for they respond to the slightest breeze. Those types with larger leaves often produce a distinctive, pleasant rustling noise when stirred by the wind. The taller species and cultivars have a definite architectural quality and can make impressive specimen plants in any garden design. Furthermore, many taller varieties can be used to create fast-growing hedges and screens that are attractively informal but very effective. Most of the bamboos with more architectural proportions, especially those with very thick culms or large leaves, can be used to create an exotic effect. This style of gardening is quite fashionable, and bamboos are an important and essential component of such a garden.

Most bamboos associate well with water, particularly those varieties with a very arching or fountain-like habit, and this association has a long tradition in gardens. Nothing could be more attractive than a clump of *Fargesia* cascading over the edge of a stream or lake. Of course, the real beauty of bamboos lies in their decorative evergreen foliage, especially in the dead of winter, when other plants are barren and leafless. The foliage of bamboos can make a pleasing background for other plants. Indeed, so long as they are given enough space and light to grow, bamboos fit in very well with other plants. Many shorter types make further use of the foliage effect by being excellent understory or groundcover subjects, often thriving under trees where other plants struggle to grow. Many bamboos also make good tub or container plants for the patio or terrace and are quite hardy enough to be left outside all winter.

In recent years there has been a surge of new introductions, raising the number of temperate bamboos in cultivation in Europe and the United States from little more than 70 in the 1960s to well over 200 currently. Many of these introductions have exciting colored culms or variegated leaves, providing an absolute rainbow of possibilities for the modern garden designer. As more and more garden-worthy types are introduced from the wild, the selection available will become vast. Culms are already available in colors ranging from the basic green to black, brown, golden yellow, red, and violet-purple, all in various combinations, whether entire, striped, blotched, or tinted. Colored-culm bamboos come into their own as specimen plants and can be used to give sudden contrast to a planting scheme or to draw attention. For this reason, it is often better to use bamboos with green culms for hedges and screens on boundaries to the garden, as these act as an innocuous background rather than a focal point. There are also a great many combinations of leaf color, usually in some form of white or yellow, the color either entire or

This specimen plant growing at Stream Cottage originated from seed collected in South America in the 1980s. It is a seedling variant of *Chusquea culeou* with an unusual habit.

striped with the basic green. Variegated leaves can be used to brighten up a dull corner or as a contrast to darker plants, fences, or walls.

Hard Landscaping

The term *hard landscaping* simply refers to features such as paths, walls, fences, and other permanent structures. The beauty of a bamboo can be enhanced by appropriate association with such features. The use of stone, for example, can mimic rock that might be found in the wild environment. Different types and textures of natural stone or reconstituted stone can be used for path surfaces or walls. And if the path or wall has a deep and well-made foundation of at least 45 cm (1½ feet), it also serves as a barrier to the spread of unwanted rhizomes. This can be very useful in keeping invasive bamboos apart from other plants or bamboos, or in just setting a limit on their possible expansion.

As a general rule, the smaller the garden, the more important and essential the hard landscaping. This is particularly true of small

I found this specimen of *Pleioblastus pygmaeus* growing on top of a dry-stone wall in Cornwall. No doubt it survives because of the wetter climate in this part of England. Indeed, this photograph was taken in pouring rain!

urban gardens, where hard landscaping features can create the effect of more space and emphasize the plants by isolating or enclosing them. Moreover, the smaller the garden, the more the plants and associated landscaping design will be scrutinized by visitors. In these circumstances, the gardener would be well advised to keep the plantings well tended and manicured at all times. In a larger garden the plantings are often viewed from longer distances, and the greater number of plants and landscape features has the effect of spreading and diluting the attention of visitors. In this way the larger garden is more forgiving

of mistakes or planting arrangements that are less well thought out. Less intense hard landscaping is needed here, and greater areas can be laid to lawn, with correspondingly larger planted borders.

The Small or Urban Garden
With increasing urban populations and the constant demand for more houses in towns and cities, gardens for newer houses are becoming progressively smaller. The smaller garden usually has a higher proportion of hard landscaping features in relation to beds and borders available for plants. Many smaller gar-

dens do not have any areas laid to grass, but merely paved areas, wooden decking, or other hard surfaces. These hard surfaces may be surrounded by narrow beds or borders that offer limited scope for planting, so that each plant must be carefully chosen. In gardens such as these, bamboos need to be considered very carefully. The most invasive types should be ruthlessly excluded unless they are to be grown in large containers, planters, or raised beds hemmed in by solid boundaries.

Although this might seem discouraging, there are many bamboos suitable for more restricted spaces. Indeed, one can often see well-grown bamboos squeezed into impossibly small beds and containers in town gardens, especially in the centers of large cities. The secret to success with bamboos in small gardens lies in selecting plants that can give the desired effect without taking up too much space. So often, the most appealing small gardens are those that seem greater in size and abundance due to the discriminating use of tall, airy, upright foliage plants with little girth or spread. Certain species of bamboo are a prime example of this type of plant.

Where space and design do allow for height, the most suitable taller bamboos for small gardens are the clump-forming types that come from high-altitude environments in the wild, such as *Drepanostachyum*, *Fargesia*, and *Thamnocalamus* bamboos. With their modest rate of invasion and their typical height of around 3 to 5 m (10 to 16 feet), they can be grown in quite restricted beds and borders and safely planted along roadside boundaries or as tall focal points in shrubberies. Where a little more height can be accommodated, *Borinda* bamboos can also be used. All of these bamboos usually have a cascading, fountain-like habit and small, delicate, paper-thin leaves. Such leaves will curl up if exposed to strong sunlight, so

these bamboos are often best planted where they will receive some shade. They are excellent subjects for planting under or near trees or in the shade of buildings. Moreover, with their thinner culms and smaller leaves, they look less exotic than other taller bamboos and so do not look out of place in a cottage-style garden.

Some of the less invasive species of *Phyllostachys* and *Semiarundinaria* can be grown with care in limited spaces, even near the walls of buildings. However, it is important to prevent their rhizomes from gaining access to weak, crumbling, or shallow masonry, as there is a

Fargesia robusta in a small suburban garden. This species has harder leaves that will not curl in full sun.

chance of penetration through cracks or holes. Little damage is likely to occur, as bamboos have no secondary growth and will not expand their diameter after having extended themselves. But rhizomes can sometimes gain access to drains and cause blockages. It is clearly unwise to plant the most invasive bamboos, which include many species of *Chimonobam-*

A well-grown specimen of *Phyllostachys viridis* 'Sulphurea' by the patio at Stream Cottage. This plant was the first bamboo to meet the eyes of visitors upon entering the garden, and set the scene for the many good things to come. In later years the rhizomes became a nuisance as they penetrated under the paving stones and greenhouse.

busa, *Pleioblastus*, and *Sasa*, in small gardens if their rhizome spread cannot be tolerated, or controlled in some way. Eager young rhizomes traveling urgently in all directions, under paths and into established shrubs, will be exasperating if not an unmitigated nuisance.

The Medium-Sized or Semi-Urban Garden

The slightly larger garden, often found on older properties or in a more suburban setting, usually has a greater proportion of beds and planted areas or lawns in relation to areas of hard landscaping. This allows for the planting of bamboos to a much greater extent, with a lesser risk of shutting out the available light or closing in the garden. The greater space available for planting tempts the use of larger bamboos or larger patches or groves of a single species or variety. A lawn specimen is appropriate here, perhaps one of the more impressive species of *Fargesia* or *Thamnocalamus*, or a well-chosen *Phyllostachys* with colored or thicker culms.

The medium-sized or semi-urban garden often has large shrubs or small trees that need to be underplanted or separated with vegetation, providing the perfect opportunity to use bamboos as groundcovers or infill plants. If a section of the garden needs to be partitioned off, or the view to the neighbor's garden excluded, or a roadside boundary planted, a bamboo hedge or screen could be used. Many bamboos are suitable for this work, and hedges can be created by using a single species or variety or by having a row of different bamboos, planted with generous gaps between them to keep their rhizomes apart underground.

The Larger or Country Garden

The larger rural garden offers the greatest possibilities for exploring all the various ways that bamboos can be grown. A large garden is more likely to have significant areas laid to grass and

A mature ornamental border at Stream Cottage, with various plants growing in association with *Phyllostachys aurea*.

wider borders planted with taller shrubs and trees. There may also be wilder areas of rough grass or even woodland, all of which provide ideal places to grow larger or more invasive bamboos. The larger garden may also have natural water features such as running water or lakes. In this setting, bamboos can offer cascading foliage over the water, or be used to stabilize the banks of streams or rivers with their network of rhizomes.

A much wider range of bamboos can be grown in a larger garden, and more scope and distance can be given to the plantings. Just being able to stand well back and view bamboos from a greater distance often enhances their appeal. Large infill plantings and groundcovers can be used in front of large shrubs or under trees. Specimen bamboos can be used to great effect as focal points or as accent plants within the overall design.

With greater space available, the bamboos with thicker culms, such as *Phyllostachys* species, can develop properly as specimen clumps or groves without the need for constant cutting back. This principle is most important if thicker culms are desired, because in a developing bamboo, the thickest culms usually emerge at the perimeter of the grove. Therefore, the more a bamboo is allowed to spread out underground, the greater the chance it will produce the tallest, thickest culms possible for the given climate and growing conditions. Constant cutting back to control spread will inhibit this process. This is particularly important if the bamboo is being used as an essential taller hedge or screen to hide some unsightly object or view.

With all of this in mind, we can now look in more detail at some of the different ways to grow or display bamboos. There are no clear-cut boundaries for how a particular bamboo should be used, for most bamboos can be grown in a variety of ways, and a species that is ideal as a specimen plant may also be suitable for use as a hedge or screen. For easy reference, see "Lists of Bamboos for Specific Purposes," located at the end of the book.

Specimen and Infill Plants

Most gardens have areas of lawn or paving surrounded by ornamental shrub borders, or perhaps a border next to a pond or other water feature. These are the principle places where bamboos can be grown as a specimen plant or infill plant.

A bamboo used as a specimen plant may be short or tall but needs to be distinct, impressive, striking, elegant, highly ornamental, and adaptable to growing either in isolation or as a focal point in combination with other plants. A specimen bamboo may be simply a single clump of closely packed culms, or it could be a moderately extended grove of more widely spaced culms, though in this case it needs to have definite boundaries, rather than meandering vaguely into surrounding grass or other plants. It is preferable that the bamboo cho-

sen as a specimen is not too invasive. In a cultivated border a little more invasiveness may be acceptable, but it is still advisable to refrain from using the most aggressive species, which can overrun established trees or shrubs. Additionally, the root systems of trees and shrubs can be damaged, as advancing rhizomes from invasive bamboos may have to be dug up. Grass or other plants can be grown almost right up to a specimen bamboo, although it is advisable to leave a small gap of at least 30 cm (1 foot) completely clear, for better appearance and ease of maintenance.

An infill plant is simply a specimen plant that covers a greater area as a block of vegetation, or serves the purpose of filling up a given space. The infill plant does not need to be so sharply defined, unless its boundaries are set by hard landscaping features or the edge of a grass area. Nor does it need to be quite so architectural or imposing. A good infill bamboo can be more invasive, since the concept is to create a mass of culms and foliage that is ornamental and pleasing but not necessarily demanding of visual attention. This mass could be impenetrable so as to exclude light from the soil surface and thus inhibit weed growth, or could be a more open grove of distinct culms. Infill plantings are ideal for those deserted or awkward corners found in most gardens. There is also sometimes a blank void under trees, and bamboos are often the only plants other than ivy (*Hedera helix*) that will thrive in such a situation.

Since all bamboos are invasive to some extent, most species and forms can be used either as a defined specimen or as a larger infill planting. The pachymorph clump-forming types or the very least invasive of the leptomorph bamboos are the preferred choices for specimen plants. Just about all other bamboos can be considered for infill work, depending on their individual merits and dimensions. If a less invasive bamboo is the choice for an infill planting because of its attractive foliage or culms, simply use several plants of the same variety in a group, with short distances between each plant so that they join together quickly. Many of the more low-growing invasive bamboos, particularly from the genera *Indocalamus*, *Pleioblastus*, and *Sasa*, are eminently suited to infill work but are also ideal for groundcover plantings.

Foliage Effect

Nearly all temperate bamboos can be grown for their attractive foliage, but some are much better for this purpose than others. If a specimen plant is required, and if it has to stay within prescribed bounds, any of the clump-forming bamboos of *Chusquea*, *Drepanostachyum*, *Fargesia*, *Himalayacalamus*, and *Thamnocalamus* will be a good choice for a fine foliage effect. These bamboos seldom grow much taller than 5 m (16 feet), with certain species and forms growing much shorter than that, and thrive in most positions but with a slight preference for partial shade. Many clump-forming bamboos have extremely delicate leaves that are prone to curling up toward their midrib in strong sunlight. This does them no harm, however; each leaf will open out again to its normal shape as soon as the sunlight is blocked by clouds.

All the clump-forming bamboos are characterized by having relatively slender culms in a tight clump and usually small, delicate-looking leaves. The slenderness of the culms almost always produces an arching, often cascading habit, particularly as the culms gain increasing amounts of foliage with each successive year. In this way the culms gradually become more arching, until a habit rather like a fountain or a giant mushroom ensues. This effect is ideal for

associating with a water feature of any kind, though of course the bamboo must be sited above the water table.

Perhaps the most impressive bamboo for foliage effect in a mild temperate climate is *Chusquea culeou*. Its culms are thick compared with most clump-forming bamboos, and it thrives best in a position with some overhead shade. Near water, *Fargesia utilis* will provide a magnificent specimen of small, delicate leaves, cascading almost to the ground. A similar effect, though less cascading, can be achieved with *Thamnocalamus spathiflorus* or one of the *T. crassinodus* group, or, in very mild localities, a *Drepanostachyum* or *Himalayacalamus* bamboo may be used. In a very open position in the middle of a lawn, the excellent *Fargesia robusta* makes a fine, tall clump of glossy, rich green leaves that do not curl up in sunlight. *Fargesia rufa* is very similar but much shorter, growing only to 2 m (6 feet). All of these bamboos make fine specimen plants for lawn or border, where their very modest rate of invasion is ideal.

Where more invasiveness can be tolerated, or where an infill is required, other excellent foliage bamboos may be used. Both *Pleioblastus gramineus* and the almost identical *P. linearis* have very long, narrow, grass-like leaves, often 25 cm (10 inches) long and only 1.5 cm (⅝ inch) wide, giving the effect of a tufted tree grass, especially where older culms arch under the weight of the foliage, and can be grown in sun or even quite heavy shade. An even more dynamic foliage effect can be given by *Yushania anceps*. This bamboo prefers shade and produces rich green culms with tumbling cascades of small elegant leaves. For a more open position the tougher *Y. maculata* is an excel-

Thamnocalamus spathiflorus associates well with a mixed border at Stream Cottage.

The delicate leaves of many high-altitude bamboos can curl in strong sunlight. This does no harm to the plant, and the leaves will quickly open out again once the sun goes behind a cloud.

lent choice, with its glossy dark green foliage and more upright culms. Perhaps the finest foliage bamboo is *Chimonobambusa tumidissinoda*, the walking stick bamboo. This species, which is grown for its disk-like nodes, also has wonderful, glossy, small, slender leaves, appearing like a huge fern moving gently on the slightest breeze. However, it compensates for its beauty by being undoubtedly the most invasive bamboo that can be cultivated in a temperate climate.

Large Leaves Effect

There are relatively few really attractive, taller, large-leaved bamboos that make good specimen or infill plants. The most suitable is the ubiquitous *Pseudosasa japonica*, which although very commonly planted and long cultivated, is a fine bamboo when well grown. The tough, glossy, deep green leaves are moderately large for a bamboo and are carried on strong, pleasingly upright culms, giving an architectural effect. The rate of spread is controllable in all but the smallest garden. ×*Hibanobambusa tranquillans* is a very fine taller bamboo with even larger leaves and is controllable enough to be used as a specimen plant, though it excels as infill. This naturally occurring hybrid bamboo, possibly a cross between *Phyllostachys* and *Sasa*, has tall, glossy culms that have a slight sulcus (probably from the *Phyllostachys* parent) and large, dark green leaves (probably from the *Sasa* parent). For a completely tropical effect with extremely large leaves, and where rampant rhizomes are acceptable, try *Sasa palmata* 'Nebulosa'. This long-cultivated species can be found colonizing vast areas in older gardens across Europe and the United States. The large glossy leaves are carried mostly at the tops of the culms, producing a palm-like effect.

Variegated Leaves Effect

All sorts of marvelous variegated bamboos are now in cultivation. Some do better in sunlight, while a few will keep their variegations in shade. The most spectacular variegated bamboo for an open position is the difficult but beautiful *Phyllostachys bambusoides* 'Castillonis Inversa Variegata', which has very bright, white-variegated leaves that have orange tints when young. It is very hard to obtain but well worth seeking out. The more invasive ×*Hibanobambusa tranquillans* 'Shiroshima' is equally spectacular but much easier to grow.

Its very bright, white-variegated, larger leaves are slightly pink-tinted when young, and it is the perfect variegated taller infill plant. Similar in height and spread but more subtle is the sought-after *Sasa kurilensis* 'Shimofuri', grown for the thin chalk-stripe effect of its white-variegated leaves.

A good variegated bamboo that makes a suitable compact specimen plant in an open position is *Phyllostachys aurea* 'Albovariegata', grown more for its almost clump-forming and fairly upright habit than for its variegations, which are pleasing but subtle. Unfortunately,

A colorful combination of banana leaves, the purple bracts of bougainvillea, and *Sinobambusa tootsik* 'Variegata'.

this cultivar came into flower in the early 1990s and is now scarce in cultivation. The subtropical *Sinobambusa tootsik* 'Variegata' is highly conspicuous in sun or partial shade but not completely hardy and inclined to be quite invasive once established. For a more shady position, try the pleasing *Pseudosasa japonica* 'Akebonosuji', which has creamy white striping in the leaves, or the closely related *P. japonica* 'Akebono', which produces almost completely white leaves in early summer, the coloration becoming gradually more creamy white as the season progresses.

Among the best of the shorter variegated bamboos is the delightful *Pleioblastus shibuyanus* 'Tsuboi', which, although somewhat invasive, seldom becomes a nuisance and can be grown in partial shade. Even less invasive is the charming *P. auricomus*, which has bright golden yellow leaves with thin green striping but needs a fairly sunny position for best leaf color. This species is not quite invasive enough to be a good groundcover, but it makes wonderful patches of infill at the front of a sunny border and in midsummer will be the brightest splash of yellow in the garden.

Thick Culms Effect

What could be more architectural than a grove of widely spaced thick culms reaching up to impressive heights? Height and thickness are closely related in bamboos, and it is impossible to have very thick culms on a bamboo that is very short, despite the fact that some gardeners new to bamboos seem to want this. The genus *Phyllostachys* offers the greatest possibilities for a taller specimen bamboo or an extended grove of larger plants where the effect of the culms is important. However, all species from this genus need to be grown in as open a position as possible; otherwise the habit suffers and their great appeal is lost. When it comes to choosing a *Phyllostachys* bamboo for a particular location, one is utterly spoilt for choice, as such a vast range of heights and habits are available. This genus contains the thickest culms of the hardy bamboos available for Western gardens, as well as the greatest variation of culm color.

Green-culmed *Phyllostachys* bamboos give an architectural but more restful effect, with each culm distinct and visible but not drawing the eye too dramatically. They are particularly useful for giving height to a planting. Ex-

Phyllostachys viridis growing in northern Italy, where the more warm-temperate conditions encourage many members of the genus *Phyllostachys* to produce thicker culms.

amples of worthy green-culmed varieties with reasonably thick culms are *P. aurea*, which has a compact upright habit and compressed internodes at the culm bases; *P. bissetii*, which is extremely hardy and has very dark green leaves and culms; *P. nigra* 'Henonis', which has magnificent foliage and an overall elegance; and *P. rubromarginata*, which has an impressive height and stature.

Three principal bamboos can be used to produce large groves with the thickest culms possible in cool-temperate climates. *Phyllostachys bambusoides* is one, although unfortunately it tends to lack vigor in cooler conditions and sometimes draws pests such as whitefly and aphids onto its rather coarse foliage. Much better for thick culms are the more elegant, more vigorous *P. dulcis* and *P. vivax*, bearing in mind that vigor and thicker culms go hand in hand with more active rhizomes. In more warm-temperate conditions or a favorable microclimate in cooler areas, use *P. edulis* for the supreme elegance of its foliage, habit, and culm thickness. This bamboo can be difficult to establish in cooler conditions but is well worth the trouble. Alternatively, *P. viridis* is almost as impressive and is somewhat easier to grow.

Colored Culms Effect

Specimen bamboos with colored culms can be used to strongly attract attention in a planting scheme, but they need to be sited with great care. Too many colored-culm specimens planted close to each other can have the effect of canceling out the impact that would otherwise be created by siting just one colored-culm specimen amidst completely green surroundings. Also, an infill planting with colored culms will sharply draw the eye and so is not always suitable where a background to other plantings is desired. In such a situation, a green-culmed variety might be a better choice.

Although colored-culm forms exist in many genera of bamboos, they are found in the greatest abundance in *Phyllostachys*. The most well known colored-culm bamboo is *P. nigra*, the black bamboo, whose culms are green at first but rapidly become a polished jet-black. This species is quite short for a *Phyllostachys*, usually growing to little more than 5 m (16 feet) tall, and it has a fairly minimal rate of invasion for a leptomorph bamboo, making it suitable for smaller gardens. Both *P. nigra* 'Boryana', with brown blotched culms, and *P. nigra* 'Megurochiku', with a black stripe in the sulcus, grow taller and are more invasive.

Many of the more recently introduced *Phyllostachys* bamboos have golden yellow culms, with or without green stripes, in various combinations. The most impressive of these are *P. bambusoides* 'Castillonis', which has rich yellow culms with a prominent thick green stripe in the sulcus, and *P. vivax* 'Aureocaulis', which has a few green stripes appearing here and there on bright yellow culms. *Phyllostachys bambusoides* 'Holochrysa' is very much worth growing for the almost orange-yellow color of its culms. All three of these bamboos can produce thick culms and need adequate space to develop properly. There are a couple of similarly colored alternatives more suitable for smaller gardens or gardens that are more exposed to cold winds: *P. aureosulcata* 'Spectabilis', with a green stripe in the sulcus, and *P. aureosulcata* 'Aureocaulis', which is completely deep yellow with hardly a green stripe to be seen anywhere.

Certain bamboos also have some of these colors reversed, such as *Phyllostachys bambusoides* 'Castillonis Inversa' and *P. aureosulcata*, both of which have culms that are green with a yellow stripe in the sulcus. Further developments in color can be found in *P. bambusoides* 'Kawadana', which has green culms with

many thin yellow stripes, and *P. violascens*, which produces stripes that are yellow at first, quickly becoming brown, and maturing to violet-purple. Be very careful, however, when using *P. violascens* as a specimen, because it can be extremely invasive.

Where a more compact, less open habit is required, try *Phyllostachys aurea* 'Holochrysa', which has completely yellow culms, *P. aurea* 'Koi', which has yellow culms with a green stripe in the sulcus, or *P. aurea* 'Flavescens Inversa', in which the colors are reversed. *Semi-*

The highly attractive "suntan" effect caused by strong sunlight on a young culm of *Phyllostachys aureosulcata* 'Aureocaulis' in midsummer.

arundinaria yashadake 'Kimmei' is a delightful introduction suitable for sun or partial shade, with slender, bright golden yellow culms and a fairly minimal rate of invasion. The completely clump-forming, colorful *Himalayacalamus falconeri* 'Damarapa' can be used in gardens with a mild climate. The yellow panels in its culms turn a conspicuous deep red when exposed to sunlight.

Upright Effect

Where a large, more erect specimen plant is required, try *Semiarundinaria fastuosa* or its richer green counterpart, *S. fastuosa* var. *viridis*.

An unusually upright clone of *Chusquea culeou* growing at Carwinion Garden.

Both produce very tall, ramrod-straight culms and can be grown in sun or shade. The effect is most architectural and can be used to give height to plantings or infill for narrow borders. The most impressive bamboo for an upright, architectural effect is the magnificent *Chusquea gigantea*, often considered the ultimate bamboo for maritime or cool-temperate climates. This species has thick, straight, light green culms in a nicely spaced formation, all surmounted with plumes of attractive small leaves. It deserves a prime position in the garden but also needs plenty of room to grow, for digging up the very deep rhizomes to control spread is arduous work.

Hedges and Screens

The need for a visual screen or hedge is common to all types and sizes of garden, whether to block the view of a neighbor, to screen an unsightly object, or simply to act as a division between different areas of the garden. A bamboo hedge has many advantages over other types of hedge or barrier, but most importantly, a solid barrier such as a wall or fence will reduce wind velocities effectively but can also create areas of turbulence that may be equally if not more damaging to plants. A hedge is preferable because it allows the wind to be filtered. Ideally the hedge should have 50 or 60 percent wind permeability.

Bamboos are an excellent choice for a hedge, with their propensity to establish easily and quickly increase in height. They can be expected to grow to a maximum height and to produce culms to about the same height thereafter, whereas conifers keep growing almost indefinitely. A bamboo hedge does not require annual pruning to increase density, and the tops of the culms need only be cut back if it is necessary to limit the height to an exact measurement. Older culms can be removed at ground level from time to time, as part of the maintenance needed to keep the hedge in good condition. Another less obvious advantage of a bamboo hedge is that the rooting system extends little further than the visible surface growth and does not impoverish nearby soil, as with privet or laurel. Bamboos are also much less formal than the traditional clipped hedges seen in many suburban gardens, giving an airy, relaxed atmosphere while being a distinctive feature in their own right. And when we take into account that useful garden canes and stakes can be cut from a bamboo hedge, it is clear that no other type of hedge has so many virtues.

While almost any bamboo can be used for a hedge, the more upright, denser species have the greatest merit. Species that are very invasive or that have an excessively open or excessively arching habit will be less satisfactory. Whichever species is chosen, it is advisable to select a bamboo that grows slightly taller than the area needing to be screened. This is because the very uppermost parts of a bamboo are more sparsely foliaged, and the densest parts, with the greatest screening potential, are in the middle two quarters.

For these reasons it is a good idea to use clump-forming pachymorph bamboos such as *Fargesia* species for short to moderately tall hedges of 1 to 5 m (3 to 16 feet) and the least invasive and more upright species of leptomorph bamboos such as *Phyllostachys* or *Semiarundinaria* for hedges above 5 m (16 feet). A pachymorph bamboo hedge will ultimately have the lowest possible maintenance regime for a bamboo hedge, requiring little more than keep-

A screening hedge of *Fargesia dracocephala* four years after planting.

ing it well watered during dry periods, while any leptomorph bamboo hedge will need occasional cutting back or controlling of unwanted rhizome activity around its edges.

A complete list of species and cultivars suitable for making hedges and screens can be found at the end of the book ("Lists of Bamboos for Specific Purposes"), but let us now review some of the better varieties.

Shorter Hedges

A shorter hedge up to 2 m (6 feet) tall is often useful as an internal partition in the garden or as a boundary screen that is neither too overpowering nor casts too much shade on the side without sun. At this height a hedge offers a token screening effect whereby it is possible to see over the top to some extent. By far the best varieties for such a hedge are in the clump-forming genus *Fargesia*. A *Fargesia* hedge will have small elegant leaves and densely packed slender culms, which are desirable characteristics in this height range. *Fargesia murielae* 'Simba' is the better choice for a shady situation, with its more delicate leaves, and *F. rufa* is the better choice for an open situation because of its harder leaves, which do not curl in sunlight. *Fargesia dracocephala* is slightly taller at approximately 2.5 m (8 feet) and is happy in sun or shade.

Moderately Tall Hedges

Where a greater degree of screening is appropriate, and where the view to and from whatever is on the other side of the hedge is to be blocked more completely when standing further away from the hedge, a height of 3 to 5 m (10 to 16 feet) may suffice. Excellent choices for this height range are the elegant and delicate-looking *Fargesia murielae* and *F. nitida* for more shady situations, and *F. denudata* or *F. robusta*, with their harder leaves, for more open situations.

In more sheltered or milder gardens, *Thamnocalamus crassinodus* 'Kew Beauty' and *T. crassinodus* 'Merlyn' make superb hedging bamboos, with their very small, elegant foliage. For a most impressive hedge of slightly thicker culms in this height range, try *Chusquea culeou*. Where a little invasiveness can be tolerated, and where a slightly more see-through effect is desired, *Pseudosasa japonica* and *Yushania maculata* make very fine hedges in sun or shade.

Maximum Height Hedges

When your neighbor is planning to build an upper-story extension that will overlook your garden, or when an eyesore is to be hidden or visually obliterated from view as quickly as possible and from as far away as can be achieved, a bamboo is needed that will provide the maximum possible height. In a cool-temperate or maritime climate, this means a hedge or screen reaching heights of 5 to 8 m (16 to 26 feet) or more. For hedges in this height range, the temperate pachymorph bamboos will simply not grow tall enough, apart from one or two of the newly introduced *Borinda* species, which may be difficult to find, so a leptomorph bamboo must be used. The favored choices for their more upright and less invasive habit are *Phyllostachys aurea* (and all its forms) for foliage density, *P. aureosulcata* (and all its forms) for a more filtered effect of sparser foliage, and *P. bissetii* for a superb and handsome dark green effect with medium density of foliage. All of these make first-class taller hedges in an open position.

Where the height of the hedge needs to be at least 8 m (26 feet) in an open position, try the slightly taller *Phyllostachys nigra* 'Boryana' or *P. nigra* 'Henonis', both of which have a pleasingly arching habit and fairly dense foliage, or try *P. parvifolia* or *P. rubromarginata* for a more upright habit but sparser foliage. In either a sunny or shady location, *Semiarundinaria fastuosa* and *S. fastuosa* var. *viridis* are absolutely without equal for a very tall, completely upright hedge or screen; both provide a wall of bamboo but are also prone to sending out long rhizomes occasionally.

For an extremely tall hedge, there are bamboos that grow to well more than 8 m (26 feet) in cool-temperate or maritime conditions, but these are inclined to produce very widely spaced culms when mature, thus somewhat defeating the object of providing a solid screen. This natural growth habit can be countered to some extent by restricting the bamboo's rhizomes with some sort of barrier. This works to concentrate culm production artificially within a given area, but it is far better to refrain from using the very tallest varieties with the thickest culms unless a hedge of considerable depth can be accommodated, or unless the more see-through effect is acceptable. With these considerations in mind, the very tallest bamboos for such a hedge are *Phyllostachys bambusoides*, *P. dulcis*, and *P. vivax*, all three needing an open position and lots and lots of room to grow.

Bed Widths

A bamboo planted for the purposes of making a hedge or screen needs adequate room to grow, just like any other planted bamboo. Because all bamboos invade at different rates and distances, the width of the bed needed for a bamboo hedge is determined more by the rhizome type than by the ultimate height of the hedge, as it would be with shrubs and trees.

Realistically, all clump-forming pachymorph bamboos, regardless of their maximum height, need an absolute minimum bed width of 60 cm (2 feet), and ideally at least 1 m (3 feet), to allow for six to eight years of clump expansion before the bamboo reaches the edge of the planting area. If the bed is too narrow, the bamboo will all too quickly fill it up and try to expand beyond its boundaries.

The same considerations apply to the more invasive leptomorph bamboos, but with an even greater absolute minimum bed width of 1 m (3 feet), or ideally at least 1.2 m (4 feet), needed to allow for adequate expansion. Once they reach beyond their boundaries, these bamboos are likely to need cutting back. Any attempt to grow a taller leptomorph bamboo hedge in a very narrow bed with solid boundaries will result in the plant becoming stunted and not reaching the desired height. To some extent, solid boundaries such as concrete or a rhizome barrier sunk in the soil will have the consequence of channeling the rhizomes along the length of the bed, but if the width is too narrow, a congested and pot-bound effect will soon result and the bamboos will not flourish. People new to bamboos often tell me that they wish to have a bamboo hedge growing to at least 8 m (26 feet) tall with really thick culms, and that the bed available for this is 50 cm (1⅝ feet) wide. I have to tell them that this is just not feasible. Giving bamboos adequate room to grow results in healthier, happier plants that are much more likely to reach their maximum height.

Planting Intervals

The distance needed between plants for a bamboo hedge depends mostly on the degree of invasiveness of the species selected, how quickly the plants are expected to join together to make a complete screen, and the initial size of the plants. As I say to visitors asking for a bamboo hedge in my nursery, it is a matter of your patience and your budget. Clump-forming varieties should be planted at intervals of 60 cm to 1 m (2 to 3 feet), and moderately invasive types such as *Phyllostachys* bamboos can be planted at intervals of 1 to 2 m (3 to 6 feet). Where you want the hedge to achieve density more quickly, use shorter planting intervals. Where you want the maximum height for a given species as quickly as possible, use bigger plants. Basically, the larger the plant and the smaller the planting interval, the quicker the hedge will reach maturity.

A note of caution, however. It is not a good idea to plant a long hedge with plants of just one variety, derived from one clone. Although flowering is an infrequent occurrence, should a clone come into flower, all plants of that clone can be expected to flower more or less at the same time. This could mean the disastrous loss of an entire hedge. To offset this risk, a long hedge can be broken up into blocks of different varieties. Or, if you are lucky enough to obtain seedlings or divisions of different seedlings of a particular bamboo, a hedge can be planted in which each plant is derived from a different seedling clone of the same species. This is the ultimate way to spread the flowering risk, because different clones can be expected to flower at different times.

Groundcover

A groundcover planting is very similar to an infill planting in the sense that a given space is filled up with vegetation, but it is usually shorter, with the main goal being to obscure or cover the soil surface. This type of planting is very desirable to busy contemporary gardeners who have less and less time to maintain their garden. A well-chosen bamboo groundcover can be visually satisfying, producing a neat and uniform mass of foliage at a low height. It is also evergreen, or nearly so, and thus provides year-round foliage interest.

Many of the dwarfer bamboos can be used to make an effective groundcover that will conquer even the most pernicious weeds. Varieties with rampantly invasive rhizomes are perfectly suited to this application, for they quickly spread out to form a pleasing low thicket of bamboos and a dense canopy of foliage that denies light to weeds. Very few plants can live underneath bamboos. Most of the shorter bamboos are vegetation of the forest floor in their native environments and are well suited to make groundcover in similarly difficult places, such as in the shade of garden trees.

Groundcover bamboos need to be used with great care in cultivated borders, where the searching rhizomes can rapidly become unmanageable. However, the rampant rhizome activity can be put to good use in stabilizing the soil on banks and roadside verges. Indeed, one of the safest places to take shelter during an earthquake is in a bamboo grove, because the rhizomes bind the soil together so effectively.

The ideal groundcover bamboo is short, dense, and very invasive. The invasiveness that is so often undesirable in taller bamboos grown as specimen plants is used here to best effect. In fact, it is an essential characteristic in any bamboo chosen for making a groundcover. The more quickly the bamboos spread out and knit together, the sooner the soil will be covered and the weed growth suppressed.

However, because of the highly invasive propensity of most of the shorter bamboos, this kind of groundcover is only practical where a large area needs to be covered with vegetation. A minimum area of 1 m (3 feet) square is recommended for even the least invasive groundcover bamboos. Otherwise the bamboo will quickly outgrow its prescribed area and overrun other plants unless the area has a solid boundary.

As a general guide, most of the shorter bamboos can be grown in any position, from full sun to heavy shade, though they are often visually at their best in a more open position. However, the more small-leaved dwarf species and varieties of *Pleioblastus* benefit considerably from a more open position for the sake of their habit, which can become less tight and dense and rather drawn in shade, and therefore less appealing. In very heavy shade, particularly under trees, *Sasa* bamboos are a better choice, except where extremely dry. In locations under trees that are too dry, it is hard to get any bamboo to grow properly, but *Sasaella* bamboos seem to have the best chance of survival where there is at least some moisture available.

Shorter Groundcover

A groundcover of bamboos less than 1 m (3 feet) tall may be appropriate in a large space at the front of a border or under much taller plants where there would otherwise be bare soil. Such a planting could also be used in circumscribed beds to relieve and interrupt the monotony of large areas of paved surface, or perhaps to occupy raised beds with low walls for a minimalist effect.

Ideal for this work are the very short *Pleioblastus pygmaeus* and *Pseudosasa owatarii*, both giving a neat appearance of miniature culms, usually little more than 30 cm (1 foot) tall if grown in the open, and topped by tiny leaves—rather like a dwarf bamboo forest! *Sasa quelpartensis* is also very short but with larger leaves that develop a marginal withering in winter.

Fairly short, at little more than 1 m (3 feet) tall and often less, are the excellent *Pleioblastus pygmaeus* 'Distichus', noted for the fern-like arrangement of its leaves, and *Shibataea kumasasa*, which is slower to spread and which has distinctively squat leaves, broad for their length

An attractive infill planting at the front of a large bed, using *Pleioblastus auricomus*.

and overall size, and carried on very short branches.

For a shorter, variegated bamboo, choose *Pleioblastus auricomus*, with its very bright golden yellow and green-striped leaves. This bamboo is most attractive when seen as a large patch or groundcover at the front of a sunny border, and it has a more minimal rate of invasion, seldom overpowering surrounding plants. In areas with at least some shade, the uncommon *P. akebono*, with its almost completely white younger leaves, could be used instead. *Sasaella masamuneana* 'Albostriata' is another very useful shorter, variegated ground-

cover bamboo. Its dense masses of dark green leaves are pleasingly striped creamy white when young, becoming less conspicuous with age. This cultivar is adaptable to almost any position and seldom gets so tall that it needs much trimming back. All three of these variegated bamboos seldom exceed 1 m (3 feet) tall unless grown in too much shade.

Taller Groundcover

Where more height is needed and the absolute obliteration of any view of the soil is not quite so important, some bamboos can be used for a groundcover of well over 1 m (3 feet) tall. Among the most suitable varieties is *Chimonobambusa marmorea*, which makes pleasingly arched tufts of foliage with smaller leaves and has attractively mottled new shoots. *Chimonobambusa marmorea* 'Variegata' gives the same

This extensive planting of *Sasa veitchii* at Cliveden in Hertfordshire shows how attractive and distinctive this bamboo can be in mass effect.

effect but with yellow culms that turn red is sunlight. *Pleioblastus humilis* var. *pumilus* is also superb as a taller groundcover, with leaves that look very fresh through winter in most gardens.

The outstanding *Indocalamus tessellatus* can be used to make architectural mounds of very large leaves. Although the culms of this species can reach heights in excess of 2 m (6 feet), they quickly bend down under the weight of the foliage so that the general height of the plant is seldom much more than 1.2 m (4 feet) in average growing conditions. The smaller, darker green leaves of *I. solidus* are carried on more upright culms that may occasionally need trimming down to reduce their height. For undulating mounds of medium-sized, apple green leaves, use *Sasaella ramosa*, one of the most satisfactory taller groundcover bamboos. In winter its leaves develop a slight marginal withering.

For a taller groundcover with attractive variegated leaves, try *Pleioblastus chino* 'Aureostriata', which has leaves with very variable amounts of creamy white striping, or *P. chino* 'Murakamianus', which has consistently bright creamy white striping. A rather grassy effect is given by *P. fortunei*, with its conspicuous white-variegated leaves. *Pleioblastus shibuyanus* 'Tsuboi' makes an ultimately taller, highly attractive, variegated groundcover that may need trimming back in later years to keep the height down.

For a dense, taller canopy of large leaves, or for planting in heavy shade, various species and varieties of *Sasa* are most useful. The dwarf form of *S. kurilensis* is excellent for its large, glossy leaves that become partially withered in winter. *Sasa veitchii* has very dark green leaves that become distinctively withered around their edges in winter and can look like variegation from a distance.

Pots and Containers

Many bamboos grow quite happily in pots or containers, making very attractive foliage features for the patio or terrace. Most of the shorter varieties are good for this purpose, particularly those with a cascading habit or variegated leaves, but even very tall species can be cultivated this way, as having them in a pot tends to stunt their height slightly and make their proportions manageable. Bamboos also associate particularly well with other potted plants that have exotic-looking foliage, such as phormiums, cordylines, and palms.

Growing bamboos permanently in pots or containers is completely different from growing them in the ground. It can be very rewarding but is more labor-intensive, mostly because of the increased watering regime but also be-

Fargesia murielae 'Simba' makes a fine specimen for a large container.

cause the bamboo will need repotting from time to time. However, this method of cultivation is relatively easy so long as a suitable variety has been chosen for the desired effect, the proper attention has been given to selecting an appropriate pot and potting compost, and the bamboo is watered regularly.

Most of the bamboos described in this book are hardy if planted in the ground, but when these same plants are grown in pots, the roots and rhizomes are much more exposed to winter frost. Therefore, in colder districts it is worthwhile giving additional winter protection to a valuable bamboo by wrapping the pot or taking it to a more sheltered location for the coldest months, unless the bamboo is extremely hardy.

Choosing Suitable Bamboos

Almost all bamboos can be grown successfully as permanent pot or container specimens. However, the most satisfactory choices are those that are clump-forming or only very moderately invasive. It is best to avoid very invasive species, as they will quickly fill the pot to overflowing with circling rhizomes that can eventually split even the strongest pot. If you wish to grow invasive varieties in pots, be prepared to repot them more frequently.

For smaller pots on the terrace or patio, try *Shibataea kumasasa*, with its pleasing masses of greenery, or *Pleioblastus auricomus*, which has bright gold-variegated foliage. *Sasaella masamuneana* 'Albostriata' gives a similar effect but has creamy white variegations. *Pleioblastus shibuyanus* 'Tsuboi', with its even more attractive variegations, is slightly taller and very suitable as a pot plant. *Fargesia rufa*, with its delightful fountain-like foliage effect, is probably the best all-round bamboo for a smaller pot and has the advantage of being both clump-forming and extremely hardy. *Fargesia murielae* 'Simba' is similar but slightly taller.

Where space or garden design permits a taller bamboo for a larger pot or container, most of the taller, clump-forming pachymorph bamboos such as *Fargesia* will be ideal. In milder gardens, *Thamnocalamus crassinodus* and its forms could be used instead. *Chusquea culeou* should not be selected as a permanent pot or container plant if possible, as it needs very good drainage and seems to dislike being in a pot at all, particularly in hot summer weather.

If a big enough pot is provided, some *Phyllostachys* bamboos make very fine containerized specimens for the larger terrace or patio. *Phyllostachys nigra* is the most popular choice for its polished black culms. Equally effective are *P. aureosulcata* 'Aureocaulis', with deep golden yellow culms, and *P. aureosulcata* 'Spectabilis', with lighter yellow culms streaked with green stripes on alternate sides. *Phyllostachys aurea* and its colored forms make very good, stiffly upright container bamboos and are useful for creating a dense screen as well. *Phyllostachys bissetii* is excellent for the handsome dark green effect of its leaf and culm.

Pot Size and Shape

Bamboos are not particularly suited for growing in very small containers, mostly because of their rapid growth, both above and often below soil level, but also because bamboos have a proportionately large total area of leaf surface transpiring water compared with other woody plants, and thus can dry out very quickly. Therefore, always use the largest pot possible. It is essential to choose a pot that is big enough to allow for at least some future expansion of the plant; otherwise the bamboo will fill its pot to overflowing after barely a year or two. A bigger pot also retains more moisture, providing a reserve when gardeners forget to water their plants, as even the best of us are prone to do. Furthermore, a bigger pot provides more weight against the effects of wind, for the up-right mass of culms and leaves acts like a big sail, and a taller bamboo can all too easily blow over in even the slightest gust if grown in too small a pot. Whatever size or shape of pot is chosen, make sure there are good drainage holes in the base of it, because a bamboo will soon resent poor drainage.

As a general guide, an ideal pot for a bamboo is wider than it is high, because bamboos form a "turf" of growth rather than having a central trunk. This means that a potted bamboo will require enough room in its pot to expand side-ways for at least a few years without reaching the edges of the pot. A pot that is wider than high is also more stable in wind.

The smaller bamboos, up to approximately 1 m (3 feet) in height, need a minimum of 20 li-ters (5¼ gallons) of pot volume, and ideally 30 liters (8 gallons) or more. Medium to moder-ately tall bamboos from approximately 2 to 5 m (6 to 16 feet) need a minimum pot volume of 60 liters (16 gallons), ideally more. Taller bamboos over approximately 5 m (16 feet) need a really large pot with a volume not less than 100 liters (26½ gallons) if they are to grow properly. It is worth mentioning that if a taller bamboo has been obtained as a smaller specimen, it is prac-tical to grow it on in a smaller pot for a year or two and then transfer it to the appropriately larger pot or other container.

Potting Compost

Ideally, potting compost for bamboos should not be too light, for this hastens drying out and reduces the weight of the pot, making the plant more likely to blow over. My suggested formula, based on many years of experience growing bamboos commercially in larger con-tainers, is 60 percent peat or something similar, 30 percent loam, and 10 percent sharp sand or grit, unless the loam is already very sandy. The acidity or alkalinity of the completed mix is not tremendously important for bamboos, but aim somewhere between neutral and slightly acid. To this mix, add a slow-release fertilizer that has a release period of at least a year. Bam-boos require copious amounts of food and can soon become starved and lackluster in a pot-ting compost in which all available food has expired. Add the slow-release fertilizer at the maximum strength prescribed on the bag or packet, and be prepared to add further quan-tities as a top-dressing in future years or after the initial release period has been completed.

Repotting

A bamboo can be maintained in a pot with reg-ular feeding for many years, but sooner or later it will need repotting. This will involve extract-ing the existing plant, with its mass of roots and rhizomes, from the container, so avoid pots with an inside rim or inwardly curving shape at the top that might make this difficult or im-possible. Once the plant is out of its pot it can be upgraded intact to a larger pot. If it has to

This is what can happen if a containerized bamboo is not repotted at regular intervals!

go back into the same pot, it will be necessary to chop out a piece of younger material from the edge of the clump to form the new plant, discarding any older material from the center of the clump. To do this effectively, follow the same criteria used when propagating a potted bamboo (see chapter 5). Keep the new plant well watered and protected from drying winds until reestablished.

Problems with Potted Bamboos

Where trouble occurs with a permanently potted bamboo, it is usually because of underwatering, overwatering, or problems with the potting compost. A potted bamboo needs constant monitoring to see if it has become too dry. Equally, a bamboo must not be allowed to become waterlogged for long periods because of poor drainage. If sudden or prolonged drying out occurs, the result is browning or loss of foliage, and in extreme cases, dying back of the culms. If this happens, all is not necessarily lost, for most bamboos are very hard to kill. Once the watering regime is resumed, most bamboos will recover, albeit gradually. If a bamboo has problems with its potting compost, this reveals itself through the foliage, which may become yellowed and less rich green in the case of starvation, or in the case of too much food, the youngest leaves may become whitish pale yellow. When a potted bamboo is utterly dead and beyond saving, all the roots and rhizomes will be brown and rotting rather than a healthy ivory color and firm.

A Purely Bamboo Garden

A garden comprising just bamboos, or where other plants are used minimally, is likely to appeal to only the most serious enthusiast. Although the concept seems simple, great care must be taken when planting different types of bamboo in close proximity; otherwise an impenetrable jungle may well be the end result. This is fine if an exotic, tropical effect is desired, with everything competing for light and space, but if created inadvertently through ignorance, great problems may ensue. I have seen many instances of people newly interested in bamboos just planting them at random in grass, or around an existing garden, with little thought as to their future growth. The effect may be satisfactory for a year or so, but the more invasive bamboos will rapidly take over, and a lot of effort will be required to keep the planting under control in order to avoid total chaos, with everything growing into its neighbor's territory. A little foresight and sensible planning are essential.

The most important principle in this type of garden, therefore, is to have a clear understanding of the rate of spread for each bamboo planted. Clump-forming bamboos such as *Fargesia* and *Thamnocalamus* species can be planted in close proximity, as they only spread at rates of a few centimeters or inches a year around the perimeter of the clump. Most *Phyllostachys* or *Semiarundinaria* species are capable of spreading 2 m (6 feet) or more per year in good growing conditions, although there will be relatively few rhizomes involved. At the furthest extreme, *Chimonobambusa* and *Sasa* species are capable of sending out a multitude of invading rhizomes to distances of more than 3 m (10 feet) in a good growing season.

Separation

If each bamboo is to be kept separate from its neighbor, it is vitally important to dig up any rhizomes that have invaded beyond their allotted space, just as soon as they are detected. Once rhizomes from different species have crossed over and become established, it can be very difficult to separate them without major disturbance to the whole planting scheme. An alternative to annually digging up stray rhizomes is to construct physical barriers to keep invasive species separate from each other. This method is not without certain drawbacks, however, and tends to create a pot-bound effect (as discussed in greater detail in chapter 4).

For those of us fortunate enough to have a larger garden, the best way to develop a purely bamboo garden is to begin with an expanse of ground that has been laid to grass, and to cut out island beds for the bamboos within the grass. Each island bed could contain combinations of bamboos, but maintenance will be far easier if there is only one variety of bamboo per island. The visual effect of this type of planting design is quite striking, the grass

forming wide pathways that snake or wend between each bed of bamboo. Mowing the grass helps keep the bamboos within their beds, but this is not a very satisfactory way to control bamboos in the longer term, since any mowed-off bamboo will keep trying to grow by sending up more shoots. A neater way of containing the growth is to set a rhizome barrier of some sort in the ground at the perimeter of each bed. Each pathway needs to be as wide as possible so that the shade from the overhang of bamboo growth does not impair or kill the grass.

An attractive grouping of taller- and shorter-growing species of *Fargesia*, *Pleioblastus*, and *Sasa*. When planted in such close proximity, these bamboos will soon grow into each other if not kept apart by assiduous work with a spade.

Part of Richard Broadhead's purely bamboo garden, which I designed. Each variety of bamboo is planted as a big group, with very wide expanses of grass between. On the left is *Yushania maculata* and on the right *Phyllostachys bambusoides* 'Holochrysa', both at two years after planting.

If bamboos are to be planted in close proximity without a boundary of grass or hard landscaping, it makes sense to associate plants with obvious differences. This helps distinguish varieties if one has crossed over underground with its neighbor. Also, associating obviously different bamboos with each other clearly creates greater visual interest, as opposed to a seemingly uniform and amorphous mass of bamboo. Taller bamboos can be underplanted with groundcover types, bamboos with colored culms can be alternated with bamboos with

green culms, those with big leaves can be associated with those with small leaves, and so on.

Whatever planting combinations are devised, it is still a good idea to make pathways of some sort to allow access to the plantings. This can be done simply by keeping corridors within the bamboo clear with a spade and secateurs, or by using a more simple form of hard landscaping such as stepping stones or gravel. Alternatively, more energetic gardeners, especially those with a liking for the jungle atmosphere, can keep a big machete by the house door and from time to time, when gardening friends arrive, lead forays into the bamboo, hacking impromptu passages at will!

Combining Bamboos with Other Plants

I have always been firmly of the opinion that it is best to associate bamboos with other plants whenever possible. Having visited countless locations containing bamboo plantings, I can assert with great conviction that bamboos are seen at their greatest advantage in a proper garden setting, along with lawns and other types of plants such as trees and shrubs. When a fine bamboo clump or grove is skillfully sited with plants of contrasting foliage or habit, its visual impact is intensified considerably.

Associating with Herbaceous Plants

Herbaceous plants can be used very effectively with many of the shorter bamboos. The clump-forming shorter bamboos provide contrasting structure and evergreen foliage as specimen plants within a herbaceous border, while the more invasive shorter bamboos can be used to make patches of leafy vegetation or an evergreen groundcover. Where bamboos are to be used in close association with herbaceous plants, it is important to consider that only the more hard-leaved and evergreen herbaceous plants are likely to withstand the shade often cast by a taller bamboo on its sunless side. Because of the shade and dryness under a clump or grove of bamboos, any underplanting with herbaceous plants is not easy, for the ground below a bamboo is nearly always just a carpet of the bamboo's own dead leaves. However, underplantings can be made with ivies (*Hedera* species), periwinkles (*Vinca* species), ferns, and all sorts of other herbaceous or subshrubby woodland plants that are adapted to shade.

Associating with Shrubs

Bamboos generally associate very well with shrubs so long as they are kept apart adequately. This requires growing any shrubs sufficiently far away that the bamboo cannot overrun or invade the territory occupied by the shrub, or in the case of a taller bamboo, cast a heavy shade over the shrub so as to exclude all the available light. Few deciduous shrubs

An attractive combination of culm and foliage colors in my garden. The bamboo is *Phyllostachys aureosulcata* 'Aureocaulis'. The dark leaves in front are *Ophiopogon planiscapus* 'Nigrescens'.

Part of my garden where bamboos are combined with shrubs and various spiky-looking plants such as phormiums and palm trees.

can compete successfully for light and moisture with bamboos, and most are likely to become drawn or stunted if grown too near an overpowering big bamboo. Some shade-loving evergreen shrubs with glossy foliage, such as *Aucuba* and *Sarcococca* species, can be grown under the overhang of taller bamboos, and woodland plants such as rhododendrons and azaleas will tolerate close proximity to bamboos to a degree.

Associating with Trees

When bamboos are to be planted in close association with trees, it is as well to remember that few plants, including bamboos, can be expected to thrive in the very dry conditions and heavy shade so often found under a mature evergreen tree. On the other hand, many bamboos are well suited to growing under most deciduous trees, particularly shorter bamboos such as *Indocalamus* and *Sasa*, and taller bamboos such as *Chimonobambusa*, *Chusquea*, *Dre-*

A riotous assembly of palms and bananas
combined with bamboo make an exotic effect
in the garden of Peter Jenkins.

panostachyum, *Fargesia*, *Himalayacalamus*, and
Thamnocalamus (with the exception of *T. tessel-latus*). If need be, these bamboos can be grown
successfully in fairly close proximity to the
trunk of deciduous trees, so long as there is ad-equate moisture available in the soil.

Exotic Effect

Bamboos are a principal component of any ex-otic-style planting. The urban environment
often contains buildings or settings that are
very modern or futuristic. Such locations lend
themselves to a more exotic planting scheme,
and bamboos fit in with this requirement ad-mirably. Nearly all bamboos look exotic, and

any bamboos at all in an exotic-style garden
will be complimentary to the effect. Several
species of *Indocalamus* and *Sasa* can produce su-perbly enormous leaves that impart a tropical
air to any garden. However, it is the effect of
thicker culms that most imparts an exotic fla-vor, particularly with use of the larger species
of *Phyllostachys* and *Semiarundinaria*.

Various spiky-leaved plants, such as *Phor-mium* and *Yucca* species, can be used with more
low-growing bamboos in sunny situations
to give an exotic effect. Large-leaved shrubs
such as *Fatsia japonica* or *Magnolia grandiflora*
and hardy palms such as *Trachycarpus fortunei*
combine well with most bamboos to establish

a more jungle-like feel. Many exotic-looking trees with attractive or colored bark such as *Eucalyptus* species also associate well with bamboos, so long as they do not deprive the bamboos of too much moisture.

This exotic style need not be confined to urban gardens. Almost any garden, large or small, can be designed and planted to evoke the atmosphere of a warmer climate, or even to create a subtropical effect. Bamboos comply with the essential need for a preponderance of evergreen plants in such gardens. This is not only due to the fact that many plants from warm-temperate and subtropical zones are evergreen, but also because too many deciduous subjects looking leafless or brown in winter are an unwanted reminder of colder climates.

Obtaining Bamboos for the Garden

Once the important decisions have been made as to which bamboos are appropriate for each desired use in the garden, the next matter to be addressed is how to obtain the plants. Of course, if you are fortunate enough to have a gardening friend who is growing bamboos that could be propagated, it is merely a case of asking for a piece and hoping the answer is in the affirmative! Otherwise the bamboos will have to be obtained as ready-grown containerized specimens from nurseries or other retail sources that sell plants.

General Nurseries
Larger nurseries or retail outlets that sell a range of plants can be expected to stock at least some bamboos, especially considering the upturn in interest in bamboos and other exotic-looking plants. This is the convenient way to get started for anyone new to growing bamboos. The selection, however, is likely to be limited to the most popular or most gaudy (and therefore most sellable) varieties. Any bamboos that have been left unsold for considerable periods may be in poor or neglected condition. Also, the sales assistants may not have much in the way of knowledge or advice to impart that will help with a prospective purchase.

Specialist Nurseries
A nursery that specializes in bamboos, or one that just focuses on a narrower range of plants than a general nursery, is more likely to have an extensive stock of different bamboos, including the less common varieties. The main advantage in purchasing from this type of source is the greater likelihood that the bamboos will be correctly identified and in better condition. The specialist grower can be expected to help with at least some information with regard to choosing varieties and should be able to provide advice on aftercare. Most specialist nurseries offer a mail-order service for customers too far away to collect the plants in person.

Not so long ago there were relatively few specialist growers of bamboos in Europe and the United States. Now they exist in profusion. Various publications exist to help those in search of specialist nurseries, listing virtually all plants in cultivation and where to buy them. Many growers also maintain a Web site, and Internet search engines can be used to locate these and other sources.

Evaluating Containerized Plants
I am often asked the question, "What should I look for when buying a bamboo?" To the uninitiated, the prospect of buying bamboos can be daunting, simply because the growth habit of bamboos is so different from other plants, and

the basic rules of what makes a purchase good or bad mostly do not apply. Here are the key points to consider when looking at a bamboo for sale in a container.

Firstly and most importantly, the plant should look generally healthy. Unless the leaves are meant to be variegated, they should be a rich green, not pale or yellowed. Some allowance must be made for the fact that a healthy bamboo can have brown-edged or partially withered leaves quite normally at certain times of year, especially in spring just before the new leaves are produced. Being healthy also includes the absence of any obvious pests or diseases on the foliage, and the absence of excessive dying back of twigs, smaller branches, or complete culms, with the exception of the occasional older culm that may be in the natural process of dying out.

Secondly, there should be evidence that the bamboo is likely to produce new rhizomes and new culms. This can be established by looking to see if the plant has any younger culms present or growing, or if there are signs of rhizome activity in the pot. As rhizomes grow within the pot, they are eventually forced to press against its sides, causing bulges and lumps, or may try to escape through the drainage holes at the base or even over the top rim. All signs of rhizome activity are good, up to a point. As a general rule, the best plant is the one with the most evidence of rhizome activity, and the more pot-bound the better. The exception is the plant that has remained unsold for much too long in its pot, which is now too small to hold the bamboo, and as a consequence has become so incredibly pot-bound and starved that it is stunted and not developing properly. Such a plant will not establish or grow normally until it is brought back to better health through repotting and feeding.

CHAPTER 4

Cultivation and Maintenance

It is not commonly realized just how easy bamboos are to grow. These plants have no exacting cultivation requirements. Ideal conditions include moist, light and free-draining (not heavy or waterlogged), open-structured, loamy soil, shelter from strong winds, and both sunlight and dappled shade. However, bamboos are incredibly tolerant of less favorable circumstances, and nobody should be deterred from growing them, for with little effort, suitable conditions can be contrived. Indeed, there is a saying among bamboo gardeners that we spend one year urging them to grow, and the rest of our lives cutting them back!

Wetter Sites

Bamboos can be grown successfully in virtually any situation that is not permanently waterlogged. Although they are often recommended for streamside plantings, they must be sited above the water table. It is commonly thought that bamboos are suitable for bog gardens, and yet, with one or two notable exceptions, a bog is the only place in the garden where bamboos cannot be grown. In fact, bamboos need conditions similar to those required for most trees and shrubs. If a bamboo is planted in a location where its roots and rhizomes are in boggy soil or water for longer than a few weeks, it will not grow properly, and before long the underwater parts will begin to rot.

If a bamboo is to be sited in close association with water, first determine the seasonal fluctuations of the water table, taking into account the possibility of heavy or prolonged rainfall and drainage from surrounding higher ground. Once this is known, any position above this point will be fine. Indeed, bamboos usually thrive when planted just above a stream or pond, as they can then draw all the necessary moisture for really lush growth. Such conditions can be created for planting bamboos within a boggy or wet area by simply building up the level of the soil into a mound. Any unwanted rhizome spread will then be regulated automatically by the water level, as the bamboos are effectively growing on an island.

Windy Situations

While it is accurate to say that bamboos are usually seen at their best in sheltered situations, few gardeners realize the degree to which most hardy bamboos can tolerate strong wind. Warm winds in Britain, northwest Europe, and the southern and western United States do little damage to foliage unless they are excessively dry or powerful or contain salt. Very strong cold winds are more harmful and usually cause at least some browning of the leaf tips and margins on all but the toughest bamboos by the end of winter. There are many exceptions to these guidelines, especially in places with variations in climate caused by altitude, landscape, large urban areas, or proximity to coastlines. Even in very exposed positions, including maritime gardens, most of the winter-damaged foliage on all but the most delicate bamboos should be replaced with new growth by midsummer. I know of a grove of *Pseudosasa japonica* that grows in dry sandy soil on the East Cliff at the seaside resort of Bournemouth, southern England, which despite extreme maritime exposure still manages to look pristine for most of the summer and autumn. When bamboos are given shelter from strong winds, whether by other plants, physical structures, or landscape features, they reward the gardener with an exuberance and lushness of foliage in the garden, and bring cheer and inspiration into even the gloomiest midwinter, recalling the lost days of summer.

Soil Type and Preparation

Almost any soil type will support the growth of bamboos, although some are much more desirable than others. An ideal soil will be light in structure, moist but well drained, and rich in nutrients. Anyone fortunate enough to have such soil need do very little beyond planting the bamboos. Less than ideal soils can still support bamboos, but more groundwork and preparation will be needed. Keep in mind, however, that bamboos are very shallow rooted, so any preparation of soil more than 50 cm (1⅝ feet) below the surface will be largely wasted unless it is specifically to aid drainage.

My early experiences with bamboos involved growing them on a heavy clay soil northeast of London. This type of soil will produce very healthy growth, because clay is usually rich in minerals and trace elements. However, this advantage is completely offset by the increased difficulty of getting bamboos to establish properly, and by the greater effort required to dig and cultivate the soil. Clay soils tend to waterlog easily in winter or during periods of heavy rain, and dry out to a concrete-like consistency with large cracks in hot summers. Heavy soils can always be improved, however, by working in sand (or other gritty material) or humus, which will increase aeration and drainage.

More lightly structured sandy soils are the easiest to cultivate and allow bamboos to develop their roots and rhizomes more easily, thus promoting quicker establishment. These soils are usually acid, which is ideal, since bamboos generally prefer neutral to slightly acid soils. The biggest disadvantage with sandy soils is their very free-draining nature, which means that they tend to dry out rapidly. Moreover, nutrients and humus are washed through to the subsoil quickly, leading to impoverishment. Regular top-dressings of fertilizer, compost, or well-rotted manure will compensate.

Although bamboos prefer acid soils, they can be encouraged to grow satisfactorily in more alkaline conditions, including the shallow clay soils often found over chalk or limestone. Occasionally the foliage will show signs of chlorosis after a few years of growth, indicating deficiencies of certain minerals. To remedy this, apply regular top-dressings of fertilizer, well-rotted manure, or garden compost. This will keep the foliage looking green and healthy and will also help increase the depth of the soil over time. In extreme cases, apply to the soil surface a preparation containing some form of iron, such as sulfate of iron, which will green the foliage more quickly.

Dry and Difficult Soils

If bamboos are to be grown on soils prone to rapid drying out, be sure to remain vigilant about watering, and since bamboos will only tolerate extremely arid conditions for a very short period of time, always provide extra water during periods of drought. Even if a bamboo was established when moisture was readily available, once the soil has become dry, the shoots and foliage will dehydrate and the plant will rapidly become lackluster and stunted.

Should you be so unlucky as to have really atrocious soil that defies cultivation, there is always the option of removing the topsoil completely and replacing it with something of better quality. Because bamboos are very shallow rooted, there is no need to excavate much deeper than 50 cm (1⅝ feet) or so, unless there is a hard pan of compacted subsoil that requires breaking up. Alternatively, a quantity of better soil could be imported and either mixed with the existing soil or added as a layer of better soil on top in which to grow the bamboos.

Establishing a New Plant

Once the site has been chosen and any soil preparation has taken place, planting can begin. Firstly, make sure weeds have been removed as much as possible. Bamboos will dominate most weeds once the clump or grove has become established, but initially it is best to have the planting site free of weeds, particularly perennial weeds. This is visually more attractive and prevents the bamboo from having to compete for light and water while it is still small.

When planting a bamboo, try to maintain the original soil level of the plant in its pot or previous position. If there is any doubt, this level can be recognized by the point at which the color of the culms aboveground changes to ivory-white belowground. Make sure the hole is sufficiently deep; it is better to slightly bury a new bamboo than have it planted to any extent proud of the surrounding soil.

If the bamboo to be planted has been growing in a pot, remove the pot by holding the plant firmly with one hand, or with help from another person if the plant is very big, and with the heel of the other hand or a piece of wood, firmly bang down onto the top rim of the pot until it falls away. The rhizomes and roots of the bamboo will now be revealed, and these must not be touched or teased out in any way as would normally be done to facilitate establishment with a shrub or tree. Any teasing out of bamboo rhizomes or roots is both damaging and a waste of time, for bamboos of course do not have a central trunk or root system.

Planting

Place the bamboo in its hole in as upright a position as possible, and check that it is at the right depth. Fill in the soil and tread down firmly all around the plant, making sure that any air spaces are properly filled. At all times be very careful not to step too closely to the bamboo, as this may damage any emerging shoots or rhizomes. Finish by making sure the soil around the plant is roughly level.

If the plant is somewhat top-heavy with culms or foliage, in proportion to the amount of root and rhizome attached at the base, it is a good idea to cut out at ground level a few of the older culms to prevent unnecessary wind rocking. Alternatively, strong stakes can be driven into the ground around the clump and tied to the larger culms, to be removed once the plant is established. Finally, add a top-dressing of humus or fertilizer. It is always best to add fertilizer to the soil surface, since bamboos are very shallow-rooted and any fertilizer added to the bottom of the planting hole may not be of much benefit to the plant. When all of this is completed, water the bamboo and the surrounding soil copiously. Be very attentive with regard to drying out by sun or wind over the next few weeks, always remembering that bamboos have a high proportion of foliage to root and can dry out very quickly.

Clear signs of new growth are evidence that the plant is becoming more self-supporting and can be gradually given less attention. Little else need be done during the first season other than keeping pernicious weeds at bay, making sure the bamboo does not suffer from want of water, and keeping an eye open for attack by insect pests or grazing from animals. In cold or very exposed locations, provide some winter protection for small plants during their first winter. This can be done by using simple screens to block prevailing cold winds or by covering bamboos with sacking, netting, or any other material that allows adequate air circulation.

When to Plant

The best times to plant bamboos are usually spring and early autumn. Planting in spring gives the new bamboo time to establish and root out into the surrounding soil before the main growing season commences in summer. Planting in early autumn can be even better, because some establishment will take place before the plant becomes dormant in winter, and by the following spring the plant will be well settled, rooted into the soil, and ready for a full season's new growth.

Container-grown bamboos, however, can effectively be planted at any time of year in temperate climates, because there is no root distur-

bance taking place, although in colder regions it is best to avoid planting in midwinter, as no useful growth will be made until the soil is warmer. Bare-rooted, transplanted material requires slightly different treatment because the disturbed roots and rhizomes will need more care and attention, at least until new growth is made and the plant is properly established in its new quarters. Unlike containerized material, bare-rooted transplants are more at risk from drying out if planted during hot summer weather. This is because their root systems have been disturbed and may not be able to take up enough water until development of new rhizomes and roots has commenced. If there is no alternative but to plant at this time of year, provide temporary shade for the foliage with netting or screens. It is worth bearing in mind that very small bare-rooted plants or divisions are often better established in a pot before being planting out in the garden.

Managing an Established Plant

Looking after an established bamboo is very simple. It will only need watering during extended periods of dry weather, unless the soil is very free-draining. In drought conditions a bamboo may need thorough watering every few days to prevent the plant becoming stunted. When leaves that are not in direct sunlight curl toward their midribs, this can be taken as evidence of dehydration, and water should be provided as soon as possible. Covering the soil around the clump with a mulch will help retain moisture by slowing down evaporation from the soil surface.

All bamboos benefit from regular top-dressings of compost or rotted manure. Grass cuttings can be used, but if they are fresh and heaped on too thickly, enough heat can be generated to damage emerging shoots. If your soil is highly fertile, as evidenced by bamboos having deep green foliage, a dressing every two or three years may be adequate. On poor soils, which lead to rather yellowish, dull foliage, a dressing once or even twice a year is advisable. Dressings or mulches can be applied at any time of year.

Fertilizer

In addition, fertilizer can be used to promote better growth of bamboos. The pachymorph clump-forming bamboos have a much lesser requirement for additional food and normally grow quite happily with the nutrients they get from the soil. In contrast, many of the more thick-culmed leptomorph bamboos, particularly *Phyllostachys* species, benefit enormously from the application of fertilizer. The best time to apply fertilizer with leptomorph bamboos seems to be midsummer, when the new shoots are maturing and rhizome growth is about to commence. This prevents the sudden arrival of extra plant food from causing the new culms to become drawn or overextended; instead the food goes into the rhizomes, thus promoting better general health and greenness of foliage, and larger shoots the following year. Almost any fertilizer intended for trees and shrubs will be suitable. Fertilizers with a higher nitrogen content, such as lawn food, will have even greater benefits, since bamboos are members of the grass family.

Thinning Out Older Culms

An important job to be undertaken with established bamboos is the regular removal of older culms. Nothing looks more unsightly than an otherwise thriving bamboo ruined by a congestion of expiring or dead culms, all for the want of a little maintenance. This work can be limited to a minimum of cutting out just the completely dead culms, which can be identi-

fied by their pale straw coloring and dry appearance. However, a mature grove of bamboo can be considerably improved by selective thinning out of older culms, even culms that are still alive and bearing leaves. This is because for the majority of bamboos, particularly the taller varieties such as *Phyllostachys* and *Semiarundinaria* species, culms are at their most attractive up to the age of three or maybe four years. After this point, the surface of the culm may discolor or deteriorate, and the branch structure will have developed to the point of congestion, causing the culm to arch increasingly under the weight of its foliage. It is neither practical nor necessary to remove older culms from the clump-forming pachymorph genera such as *Fargesia* or *Thamnocalamus* unless any dead culms are obviously visible. Usually, any very old or drying culms will be hidden and buried deep inside the clump, well out of sight.

Peter Addington and I dug up this unwanted rhizome of *Phyllostachys violascens* at Stream Cottage. This represents just one year's growth in the moderate climate of southern England!

With practice and experience, you can easily identify the older culms within a grove, not only by their more mature coloring and evolved branch complement but also by their size: the oldest culms in a developing bamboo tend to be smaller and thinner, the youngest culms taller and thicker. To do the job properly it is essential to sever culms as close to ground level as possible. This is not always easy if the culms are growing very close together. In such cases, it may be necessary to use special saws or secateurs that are adaptable to restricted spaces. Never attempt to snap or break culms with your bare hands; they will not break easily and are likely to split with razor-sharp edges that can inflict deep cuts if not handled with care.

Smaller bamboos, such as the shorter *Pleioblastus* species or *Sasa* and *Shibataea* species, can be cut to ground level every year or so. This practice of clearing away all the older material has the effect of allowing fresh new growth to be seen at its best. The ideal time to do this is early spring. By early summer the bamboo will have grown itself back again, although annual cutting down may result in the regrowth not reaching the normal maximum height for the species. An alternative approach, often used in Japanese-style gardens, is to trim regularly with shears or clippers to cre-

This specimen of *Shibataea kumasasa* in David Helliwell's Japanese-style garden in Oxford is regularly clipped to produce an attractive mound-like shape.

ate a mound-like effect. *Shibataea kumasasa* responds well to this treatment. Very attractive low shapes of greenery can be produced that can be kept tidy with only the occasional removal of an old or dead culm.

If it is possible to burn all the culms and cuttings removed from the clumps, the ash can be returned to the garden later. This useful top-dressing will provide plenty of silica in a form that can be readily taken up again by the roots. Alternatively, the same benefit can be achieved by shredding or finely chopping up all the cut material and composting it for later application as a mulch.

Controlling Spread

When a bamboo has become established in a given position, the need may arise to cut back the rhizomes to prevent unwanted spread. Clump-forming bamboos such as *Borinda*, *Drepanostachyum*, *Fargesia*, and *Thamnocalamus* species do not send out long rhizomes but remain in a fairly tight, closely circumscribed clump. This habit of growth makes them suitable for restricted spaces or as isolated specimen plants that will need little if any cutting back unless their original planting space was much too small. Invasive bamboos such as *Chimonobambusa*, *Phyllostachys*, *Pleioblastus*, *Sasa*, and *Semiarundinaria* species may send out long rhizomes, often rampantly so in lush growing conditions, and must be kept in check if the bamboo is not to invade beyond its allotted territory and become a nuisance.

It is better to remove unwanted rhizome spread on a regular basis than it is to allow a bamboo to extend itself undisturbed for consecutive seasons and become firmly established outside the permitted growing space, which will then necessitate extensive work to trace back and excavate all the unwanted rhizomes. For cool-temperate climates, it is usu-

ally sufficient to carry out this task once a year, either in spring or autumn, unless one has the enthusiasm and dedication to deal with surplus shoots and rhizomes as and when they become apparent.

Wherever possible, it is better to dig up rhizomes completely, tracing them back toward the parent plant, rather than just cutting them through with a spade at the point where they have spread too far. Any rhizome material left

Trench warfare! A deep trench has been cut round each grove of leptomorph bamboo to contain spread in part of the garden at Carwinion. This method is very effective, although a little unsightly, as rhizomes can be cut off as they appear on the inside edge of the trench.

in the ground may have dormant buds that could produce new shoots or fresh rhizome, leading to further colonies in unwanted places. As a less labor-intensive alternative, shoots can be broken off or mown at ground level as they appear. This has an inhibiting effect on spread but still leaves the rhizome in the soil with the possibility of further growth. A good method of control for large gardens is to thoroughly rotovate the soil around the bamboo on a regular basis, which will constrain growth to prescribed limits. However, this technique will also leave lots of small chopped-up sections of rhizome in the soil that may continue to grow.

For contemporary gardeners with busy lifestyles and less and less time to maintain their gardens, the most effective way to control spread is by using a solid boundary through which the rhizomes cannot penetrate. This effect can be accomplished most simply by sinking into the soil a purpose-made rhizome barrier made out of flexible plastic or metal. Such a barrier needs to be at least 50 cm (1⅝ feet) deep in order to contain the rhizomes of most bamboos adequately. A similar barrier could be created by casting a concrete wall into the ground that is of sufficient thickness so as to avoid cracking too easily and leaving gaps that rhizomes can pass through.

A rhizome barrier has been used to retain this grove of *Phyllostachys vivax* 'Aureocaulis'.

Moving an Established Plant

Depending on the invasiveness of the species concerned and the growing conditions in a particular location, most bamboos are fairly easy to dig up and move to a new location up to about three years after planting. This does not apply, of course, to a bamboo that was already very large to begin with. There can be many reasons for wanting to move an established bamboo. The most common occurs when the wrong bamboo was chosen in the first place and has proved to be too tall or invasive for its site.

I have found from long experience that the optimum times for moving existing big clumps or very large divisions are early spring and autumn, when the soil is warm enough to promote immediate new growth of roots or rhizomes. If an established bamboo is moved during the shooting season, from midspring to late summer, there will usually be much desiccating and dying back of any very young or partially developed shoots, unless the root and rhizome network can be lifted intact. Therefore this period should be avoided if possible.

If the bamboo is to be moved intact to a new site, the challenge is to cause the least amount of damage to the plant and to carry out the task with the least amount of work and effort. If the bamboo is to be eradicated and destroyed, it can be dug up in pieces, with no concern for any damage done to culms or rhizomes.

Realistically, an established bamboo clump or grove can only be moved in an intact state by manual labor if it has a girth or average width of no more than about 2 m (6 feet), and at this width, seriously hard work will be involved. Any clump beyond that in girth or width will need to be dug up in pieces or sections, or, if it is to be kept intact, a mechanical digger or excavator will need to be used. Or as an even more drastic alternative, the more fool-hardy and impatient gardener could place two or three sticks of dynamite under the bamboo, light the fuses, and stand well back!

Moving by Hand

Digging up a clump-forming bamboo with a girth of less than 60 cm (2 feet) is simply a matter of pushing a sharp spade into the soil about 10 to 20 cm (4 to 8 inches) all around the plant to a depth of about 30 cm (1 foot), unless the bamboo is an exceptionally deep-rooted species, and then just levering back with the spade until the bamboo comes free from the soil. If the bamboo is more invasive and has spread out, with culms growing at a distance from the original plant, a decision will have to be made whether these can be included in what is to be dug up or whether they need to be dug up separately; but otherwise follow the procedure for a clump-forming bamboo.

If the bamboo to be moved has a girth or width of greater than 60 cm (2 feet), it is best to dig a 30 cm (1 foot) wide trench all around the clump or grove to a depth of at least 45 cm (1½ feet) and at a proximity to the bamboo that will not directly damage the outer culms. Once the trench has been dug, start to undercut the bamboo with the spade, making sure to dig just below the lowermost rhizomes. When the bamboo has been undercut as much as possible and as far under as possible, try an experimental levering upward with a strong spade to see if there is any appreciable movement of the plant.

If not, the next step is to drive a long and very strong pole or piece of thick-walled pipe underneath the bamboo with a hammer. Using a piece of wood or a large stone as a fulcrum, push down on the pole to lift the bamboo out of the soil. If this is carried out properly, there will be a wonderful tearing sound as roots are broken and the bamboo is levered free! Moving a big bamboo without the aid of a lever and fulcrum is a quite unimaginably laborious task, and not for the faint-hearted.

Once the bamboo has been properly separated from the soil, drag or transport it to its new location, which should already have an appropriately sized planting hole ready and waiting. Plant it as for any bare-rooted bamboo transplant.

Moving with Machinery

For gardeners fortunate enough to have access to any sort of mechanical digger or excavator, digging up and moving a large bamboo is comparatively easy. It is important to insert the bucket or shovel of the digger into the ground fairly vertically near the bamboo, so as to scoop out an adequate depth of soil and get properly under the bamboo. This action may have to be repeated several times all around the plant until it is free of the soil, whereupon it can be carried to its new home.

Do consider that moving a big bamboo with machinery is a rather coarse, though very labor-saving method, and more damage to the bamboo's rhizomes and roots is likely. Therefore, give extra attention to proper replanting in the new location, and make extra sure the bamboo does not suffer from wind-rock or drying out.

Problems, Pests, and Diseases

In cool-temperate Western gardens, bamboos are remarkably free from serious pests and diseases. In fact, bamboos are so tough and vigorous that the only circumstances that might lead to their death are too much or too little water, exposure to fire, saturation with extremely toxic chemicals, and profuse or prolonged flowering. Too much or too little water is the most likely reason for a bamboo not establishing well. Problems with water usually reveal themselves with extremely pale or yellowing leaves, followed by loss of foliage generally, and in extreme cases, dying back of the whole plant.

Once a bamboo is growing and thriving, the trouble it is most likely to experience will be with insect pests living on the foliage, though this is only true of certain susceptible species. This usually occurs as a result of particular weather or growing conditions or from extended periods of neglect. These insect pests do the bamboo little actual harm but can cause the foliage to look unsightly. A few fungal diseases attack bamboos, but these are mostly encountered, albeit infrequently, in the warmer parts of the United States and only seem to occur in cool-temperate Britain and continental Europe when plant material has been imported in an already diseased state.

Damage can be done to soft young bamboo shoots by slugs and snails during the shooting season in spring and early summer. Bamboo seedlings are particularly at risk. Protection can be given by scattering bait and by clearing away plant debris and maintaining good plant hygiene. Various small rodents will occasionally nibble young growth but will be very reluctant to eat indigestible older material. Grazing animals, both large and small, can give unwanted attention to bamboos in rural areas but are not usually significant in urban gardens. Damage in urban gardens is more likely to result from cats and dogs using planted areas for toilet purposes or inadvertently breaking off new shoots.

Pests

The principal insect pests that affect bamboos in cool-temperate climates are whitefly, various types of aphids, scale insects, mealybugs, and mites. Most insect pests will have clear preferences over which bamboo species to infest, and their rates of infestation will be strongly influenced by climate, weather, and growing conditions. Severe frost in winter will usually eliminate insect pests living on the foliage, unless there are any pockets of air remaining above freezing in which insects may survive. Some insect pests are susceptible to natural predators, either those occurring in the landscape or those introduced as biological control. Unfortunately for the gardener, many pests have been introduced from other climates on imported plants and can only be controlled effectively with chemical insecticides or acaricides.

Whitefly. This is a slightly more troublesome pest in the mild maritime climates of Britain and western coastal Europe than it is in the United States. These insects feed by sucking sap from the foliage, but the actual damage this causes is slight. The greatest harm is caused by their secretions, known as honeydew, which keep the whitefly from drying out. The honeydew attracts sooty molds that can render a bamboo unsightly in a very short time if the whitefly is left untreated, due to this pest's very rapid rate of reproduction and infestation. Whitefly are at their most prevalent in weather conditions that are generally mild and cloudy, particularly during spring, autumn, and very mild winters. During long hot summers, whitefly are prone to drying out and are liable to be eaten by predators carried in by warm air masses, such as ladybird beetles. In the garden, whitefly is most likely to infest *Phyllostachys* bamboos (particularly the *P. bambusoides* group), *Semiarundinaria* bamboos, and the taller *Pleioblastus* and *Pseudosasa* bamboos. Under glass or inside the house, almost any bamboo is susceptible, although most high-altitude bamboos with small, fine leaves are less prone to infestation. Some years ago I took part in a heated debate among a group of bam-

boo enthusiasts in a garden in Devon, regarding the identification of a green-culmed *Phyllostachys* species. The issue was finally settled when we agreed that with such an intense infestation of whitefly it could only be *P. bambusoides*!

Aphids. Aphids seldom infest bamboos grown outside, as there are usually other more suitable host plants in the garden. Under glass or inside the house, aphids can be troublesome where there is high air humidity and constant warmth, usually in spring or autumn. They produce honeydew excretions and need to be controlled quickly if the bamboo is not to be disfigured. Very dry conditions normally discourage aphids, and so they often disappear completely in summer, even on plants that have not been treated with chemicals.

Scale. Scale insects are much more common on bamboo plants in the United States than in Britain and continental Europe. They consist of clusters of tiny, oval, shell-like domes that tightly adhere to culms and branches. They seem to do little harm unless the infestation becomes heavy due to neglect. This pest is most prevalent in the warm-temperate and subtropical parts of the United States and is best treated before the cosmetic appearance of the culms is jeopardized.

Mealybugs. These pests are seldom found on bamboo grown in Britain and continental Europe, but they are quite common throughout the United States, where they are usually "planted" on culms by ants. Mealybugs are difficult to treat with chemical sprays because they have a protective waxy covering. Therefore, prevention is better than cure, and control is best achieved by eradicating ants from bamboo groves wherever possible.

Mites. Bamboo mites are a serious pest of bamboos grown in more warm-temperate conditions. This particular insect pest has become increasingly prevalent in Europe and the United States, mainly due to larger amounts of plant material from the Far East being imported by commercial growers. Red spider mites are very similar and have long been a native pest of ornamental plants grown in protected conditions under glass or inside houses or conservatories in Europe and the United States. Any bamboo grown inside for a length of time is at risk from bamboo mites and red spider mites. Mites generally require very dry, warm environments and can reproduce at incredible rates when conditions are favorable. For this reason, centrally heated houses make ideal breeding situations.

The various mites usually choose to infest *Phyllostachys* species first but will quickly spread to related bamboos such as *Semiarundinaria* species. Most of the high-altitude bamboos such as *Drepanostachyum*, *Fargesia*, and *Thamnocalamus* species are liable to become infested. The main sasoid genera, *Indocalamus*, *Sasa*, and *Sasaella* species, seem to be less affected and are usually infested only when other more favorable bamboos have been colonized. If bamboos have become infested indoors and all attempts to control the infestation have failed, simply move the plants outside: colder or wetter conditions will slow the infestation down as if by magic! Under glass, any form of overhead irrigation or increased air humidity will slightly reduce the chances of attack.

Various types of mites can damage bamboo foliage, particularly when the bamboo is grown under glass or inside during hot weather. On the left, the rectangular patterns created by bamboo mites. On the right, the dotted patterns created by red spider mites.

In cool-temperate climates, mites will be found on bamboos in the garden only during extended periods of heat and drought or over a succession of mild winters. The mites live on the undersides of the leaves, where they make minute webs, and are very difficult to see with the naked eye. The damage they do to the foliage is more obvious, with leaves becoming pale, due to numerous tiny wounds from underneath, and eventually drying up. Unfortunately, mites are able to defy chemical sprays by reproducing rapidly, allowing resistant strains to evolve. There are acaricides available that will provide control, but nontoxic sprays containing oil or soap (fatty acids) will also be effective if applied regularly, as these either glue up or dissolve the mites.

Diseases

Once a bamboo has become established in a temperate garden, it is relatively secure from disease. The diseases that do affect bamboos are only likely to be seen if infected plant material has been imported and the disease has been allowed to spread. In Britain and continental Europe such diseases are very rare indeed. In the United States only bamboo rust can be regarded as relatively common. Bamboos even seem to be resistant to honey fungus, a scourge of ornamental gardening throughout the West. If you are unlucky enough to encounter any of the following diseases, eradication is the only satisfactory remedy. Rigorously cut or dig out and burn any damaged material and maintain good plant husbandry and hygiene. Control of some bamboo diseases by fungicides may be possible, but little information is available. Cleanliness of the original stock is essential.

Bamboo rust. This is a fungal disease that causes brown powdery spots on the foliage. The new leaves are most prone to attack; when affected, they eventually shrivel and dry up. Little long-term damage is done, however, and most bamboos recover. This disease seems to prefer species of *Phyllostachys* and can occur almost anywhere in the United States but is particularly prevalent in the South.

Bamboo smut. This disease is known in Japan and in tropical areas of India and Burma. The resulting effect cannot easily be mistaken. Young growth appears swollen, and later soot-like spore masses break through. Bamboo smut has appeared in the United States on several occasions on imported *Phyllostachys* bamboos. In each case it has been dealt with drastically, with the affected plants dug up, rooted out, and incinerated.

Melanconium culm disease. This is occasionally observed in Western gardens, occurring when young culms have been weakened or damaged. The internodes near the culm base turn brown or purplish black, and the discoloration extends upward from node to node until the culm dies and the leaves dry up. When examined afterward, the wood of the culm is found to be infiltrated with mycelial threads. Mature, healthy growth does not seem to be affected.

CHAPTER 5

Propagation

Most gardeners at some time or other wish to increase their stock of a particular plant by propagation. In the case of most woody plants, this is merely a matter of buying a packet of seeds or taking some form of cutting or start from the aboveground parts of the existing plant. Unfortunately, it is not that simple with bamboos. Because of the often very long periods between flowerings of most bamboo species, seed is rarely, or at best only erratically, available. And for the temperate bamboos, most species cannot be readily propagated by detaching pieces of the aerial parts of the plant and placing them in potting compost and expecting them to root.

In fact, nearly all bamboo propagation has to be carried out by some form of division, usually by separating or detaching pieces of plant material from the underground parts of the bamboo, which may or may not have any culms attached. Dividing is an ideal method for the amateur gardener, who, with a little practice and experience, can propagate most of the temperate bamboos in cultivation with relative ease.

While all bamboos can be propagated successfully by the various forms of clump division, only tropical or subtropical species can be increased by cuttings taken from the aerial parts of the plant, using sections of culm comprising one or more nodes. In the tropical regions of the world this method is commonly practiced and is the means by which most native bamboos are propagated, unless seed is available. The temperate bamboos seldom respond successfully to this treatment, and such a method should only be attempted out of a desire to experiment, if there is ample material to spare.

In recent years, micropropagation has occasionally been used successfully for large-scale commercial propagation. Unfortunately, bamboos are not ideally suited to this technique, because this method relies on isolating the meristem of a bamboo. This is not always straightforward, since the growing point of a bamboo is just a series of overlapping sheath scales. The amateur gardener is unlikely to have the facilities to even attempt this method, and so it will not be covered within this book.

Growing from Seed

When bamboos flower outside their native environments, they do not always set large quantities of fertile seed. There are frequent exceptions, however, such as the recent flowering of *Fargesia murielae*, during which large quantities of seed have been produced, and indeed, many self-sown seedlings have arisen around the bases of flowering clumps.

As explained in chapter 2, a bamboo seed resembles a grain such as rice or wheat, and its presence within a flower can be distinctly felt as a hard lump. Seed found this way in cool-temperate climates should be harvested when ripe and sown immediately; otherwise germination can be delayed for a considerable period, sometimes years. When a bamboo comes into flower, the greatest quantity of fertile seed is usually set in that first season of flowering. With each successive season of flowering, there is nearly always a decrease in the amount of seed produced and also a decrease in its fertility.

Seed should be sown in pots or trays using a light compost, either peat-based or using peat alternatives that are suitable for seedlings, such as coir. A loam-based compost intended for seedlings can be used, but this is not recommended because these composts are inclined to be too heavy and set like concrete when wet. Once the right compost has been chosen, fill the pots or trays with it to about 2.5 cm (1 inch) from the top rim, and firm gently. The next step is to examine the seed available and remove any obvious pieces of chaff, husk, or any other unwanted plant material that could rot in the compost. The seed is now ready to be sown.

Seed should be distributed evenly across the compost, with a little space between each one, and with each more or less horizontal. When this is done, spread an additional layer of compost over the seeds so that they are buried to about 1 cm (⅜ inch) deep. Again, firm down the top of the compost gently. Apply water so that the compost is moist but not saturated. Now place the pots or trays in a warm environment that is constantly above 10°C (50°F), such as a greenhouse or window sill, avoiding any direct sunlight if sowing during late spring or summer.

Germination time will vary from a few weeks to several months or even years, depending on the freshness of the seed when sown. Keep the compost moist until the seedlings begin to emerge, and then water more sparingly to prevent damping-off. Give more sunlight when the seedlings are growing strongly, and also increase the amount of water so that sudden drying out does not occur through transpiration from the rapidly expanding amount of leaf area of each seedling. Beware of damage by insects and birds at

Seedlings of *Fargesia dracocephala*.

this stage, as seedlings are very vulnerable. Do not disturb the seedlings until they are bigger and producing new culms and rhizomes. At this stage they can be carefully separated and teased apart, whereupon they can be potted individually and grown on until large enough to plant outdoors.

Division

Division is the most common method used for propagating bamboos, both commercially and by the amateur gardener, unless seed is available. All bamboos can be propagated this way, whether temperate or tropical. With just a little knowledge, plus some practice and experience, you can easily produce thriving new bamboo plants from carefully chosen pieces of living material taken from existing clumps or groves. And of course, the great advantage of propagating by division is that by skillfully taking larger divisions, you can shorten the timescale between propagation and having the new bamboo established and producing culms of a mature diameter.

Propagating by division can successfully be carried out at any time of year, but the optimum time is in early spring, just before new growth begins in earnest. At this time of year, bamboos have a strong urge to grow, and even very small divisions can survive, when at other times they might fail. Division need not be restricted to the spring period, although it is best to keep within the growing season from spring to autumn, even if such disturbance may result in a check to growth for the detached material and sometimes to the remaining plant. Avoid the depths of winter, as small divisions are prone to rotting unless kept very warm. If there is no alternative but to divide in winter, try to take as large a division as possible, because this will have a much greater chance of

survival, especially if it is placed in an environment with some extra heat provided.

Tools

To carry out the division of bamboos, whether they are growing in the ground or in containers, it is essential to be equipped with suitable tools. Most essential is a sharp spade with a strong handle that can sustain strong leverage. An ordinary spade will suffice for simple divisions, but I have found that a spade designed for digging trenches, which has a long but very narrow blade, is the most ideal for digging up bamboo divisions from the ground. It is also useful to have a big hammer and just the blade of an old trenching spade, which can be used together to chisel through very tough rhizomes. Other tools may be needed, such as an axe, a crow bar or strong pole or pipe for use as a lever, old saws, and secateurs and loppers of various sizes.

Divisions from the Ground

The main principle when dividing from a plant growing in the ground is to secure the best possible division while inflicting the least possible damage to the parent plant. With the more rampant types of bamboo, this is easy, as growth can readily be dug up from the edges of the colony, and long sections of connecting rhizome with dormant buds present may be used for rhizome cuttings as well. Dealing with mature clumps of thick, closely packed culms can involve considerable effort.

To select growing material that could make a satisfactory division, start by looking all around the edges of the clump or grove for any culms, either single or much more preferably in a group, that may be isolated enough to get a spade behind. The ideal division will comprise one or more culms that can be dug up or otherwise detached with plenty of healthy rhizome still connected. Do not be tempted by any soft culms less than one year old, as these will not have hardened or developed their roots sufficiently for propagation purposes. Culms between one and two years old make the best subjects for propagation, as they will have developed their roots properly and will have fresh dormant buds at their bases or on any attached rhizome, giving active sources of new growth. Older material can still be propagated, but with decreasing viability in proportion to increased age, as any underground dormant buds may have rotted.

If the material to be dug up is very small or likely to have any attached rhizomes close to the soil surface, it is merely a matter of inserting a spade into the ground about 10 cm (4 inches) away from the culm or culms and le-

vering the division free. For larger or more deeply rooted divisions, first dig a trench closely around the outermost culms and then excavate underneath as well, being careful at all times not to damage the proposed division by attempting to undercut at too shallow a depth. Once you are more familiar with bamboos, you will have some idea in advance of how deep a particular species is likely to be. For those of you who are new to propagating bamboos, take a blunt rod or poker made from stiff wire and try some experimental probing all around the piece of bamboo to be dug up, until you know roughly at what depth you will

This group of culms is well isolated from the parent plant and can be easily detached using a trenching spade.

need to undercut. Bamboos form a "turf" in common with other members of the grass family; their rhizomes and roots are seldom deeper than 45 cm (1½ feet) and are often much closer to the soil surface.

When the excavations are completed as best as conditions permit, cut downward with a chopping action between the division and the rest of the clump or grove, until all connections with the parent plant have been severed and the division can be pulled free. With very large divisions or very stubborn divisions that resist the digging-up process, much effort can be saved by driving a strong lever under the division, once a certain amount of undercutting work has been completed, and then, using a block of wood as a fulcrum, pushing down on the lever to wrench the division free of the soil. This is the same method used to move a large established plant. It has saved me countless hours of unnecessary struggle over the years, and I cannot recommend it highly enough.

The task of excavating and chopping free is fairly straightforward if the proposed division is already well separated in distance from the parent plant, but it may require labor on a herculean scale if a division is to be taken from a mature, densely packed pachymorph bamboo with little room for a spade. In this instance, get some rope and tie together, in separate groups, all the culms of the parent clump and all the culms of the proposed division, and then bend them away from each other and tie them to stakes driven into the ground. This allows better access and more room to cut downward with a spade, axe, or other chopping device between the division and the parent plant, which is always the hardest part of dividing mature pachymorph bamboos.

Once the divided material has reached the propagating bench, an important decision has to be made: whether to grow on the division whole or, if the division comprises a group of culms and attached rhizomes, to redivide it into smaller pieces. It is vital to bear in mind that a larger division grown on intact has a much greater chance of success than any redivided smaller pieces. One live division is better than two or three dead ones! If the decision is taken to redivide, it is a good idea to first wash off as much soil as possible from the roots and rhizomes. This reveals the relationship between the various culms and rhizomes and shows what is attached to what. Thus there will be less chance of accidentally cutting through in the wrong place.

Larger material comprising several well-rooted culms, all connected to each other by healthy rhizome, can be planted out directly into a nursery bed or even in the final growing position in the garden. Keep divisions adequately watered until established. All smaller divisions benefit from being established first in a pot or tray and kept warm and moist until new growth can be detected. When preparing the divisions for potting, discard any damaged or dead material and cut back culms and foliage only enough to make the propagation process manageable, as any surplus foliage will be shed by the plant anyway. A sure sign of a "good" division is when there is no yellowing, curling, or shedding of foliage in the days after propagation. This means that the division has adequate rhizomes and roots attached to support itself until new growth can be made, and will thus establish and grow away more quickly.

Dividing Containerized Bamboos

Any bamboo grown in a container, whether pachymorph or leptomorph, will sooner or later completely fill the container and need to be repotted or divided. The two great advantages associated with dividing a containerized bamboo are that there is no effort required in the way of digging, and as soon as the pot is removed, the outer edge of the rhizome and root network is revealed. Being able to see where any rhizomes have reached the edge of the pot is useful when making decisions about what and where to divide.

If the bamboo has produced culms around the edges of the pot, and there are obvious open routes between culms running across the plant where an old saw or spade can be inserted, the simplest way to divide is by cutting the entire root ball roughly in half, or in thirds, quarters, and so forth, depending on how many divisions are required. This can be likened to cutting a big cake into bite-sized segments. If it is less clear where to make the cut, begin by washing off as much of the soil or pot-

ting compost as is practicable, thus revealing the intricacies of the culm and rhizome connections. Unfortunately, washing off the soil is not a viable option if the bamboo has been in its pot a long time and is considerably root-bound. However, unless a root-bound bamboo has become excessively starved and neglected, it will most likely have a lot of rhizome present, and so any divisions will have a greatly enhanced chance of survival.

All the divisions of a potted bamboo can be treated the same way you would treat divisions made from bamboos growing in the open ground. Smaller divisions may need to be pot-

Use an old spade or other sharp implement with a small sledge hammer to chop the root ball of a potted bamboo into carefully chosen pieces.

ted individually, and the biggest and best division could be put back into the middle of the original container to make a new plant. Care and attention will be needed for several weeks or months, until the division or divisions are established and producing new culms and rhizomes.

Rhizome Cuttings

Propagating by rhizome cuttings is simply a finer form of division. It is a useful method when large numbers of propagules are required. Not all bamboos are suited to this method of propagation, and even with those bamboos that can be propagated this way, a higher failure rate must be expected. This method only works well with the leptomorph bamboos, which often produce long lengths of invading rhizome suitable for detaching for propagation. Pachymorph bamboos generally will not propagate readily from pieces of rhizome that do not have any portions of culm attached. Therefore, I would recommend only experimenting with this method on pachymorph bamboos if there is material to spare and success is not essential.

To make rhizome cuttings, select pieces of rhizome comprising at least two nodes and an internode, preferably a long series of nodes and internodes. Choose ivory-colored rhizome with obvious dormant buds present at the nodes. Cut off any dead or damaged material and discard any rhizome that is too old, as indicated by being more brownish or even blackish. Next, find appropriately sized pots in which the sections of rhizome can be curled round inside, or if the rhizomes are too inflexible, find long trays or rectangular containers in which the rhizomes can be laid out horizontally. Then carefully cover with potting compost and keep warm and moist until new growth emerges. If

this method is carried out during spring or in the main growing season, all of the more robust or stiffer sections of rhizome can instead be planted horizontally in a nursery bed outside. This process is much more successful when younger sections of rhizome no more than two years old are used, because they will have lots of fresh dormant buds. Also, the more invasive species will propagate this way much more easily than less invasive species.

Propagated material, whether potted or in a nursery bed, should be grown on until properly established, with new shoots and rhizomes having been produced. New bamboos created by this method will take longer to become mature clumps or groves, simply because the propagated material is so much smaller than a proper division that has culms attached. Once each rhizome cutting has produced new culms and rhizomes, it may then be transferred to its chosen site in the garden and planted.

Branch and Nodal Cuttings

Most species of pachymorph bamboo from the tropical or subtropical regions of the world can be propagated from sections of the aerial parts of the plant. The pachymorph species of tropical and subtropical bamboos often have the ability to produce roots and rhizomes from the branched nodes of their culms if the nodes are either in contact with or buried under the soil, or otherwise in a moist and enclosed environment. There have been occasional reported incidences of this method working with some temperate bamboos, but then only with species that have multiple or more prolific branch developments.

To attempt this method, detach either a whole culm, which would ideally be one or two years old, or cut some sections of a culm or even sections of any thicker culm branches comprising two or more nodes and internodes. These then need to be buried horizontally in the ground or in a nursery-type environment in long containers or trays, with the branches trimmed back so that just a few leaves and twigs remain above soil level. Alternatively, the sections can be placed in water so that, again, only a few leaves and twigs remain clear. After a few weeks or longer, look for signs of roots being produced, and hopefully some small new culms and rhizomes.

Once any such growth is more apparent, the sections can be lifted out of the soil or water and divided into individual plants, one for each rooted node of the original culm. Pot on or grow on until big enough to be planted permanently. I have seen this method in operation at a commercial nursery in northern Italy, where sections of culms from *Bambusa multiplex* 'Alphonse Karr' were placed in large vessels of water and after several weeks had rooted enough to be potted up into numerous new bamboo plants. The water was not changed in all the time it took for the pieces of culm to root and had become quite revoltingly stagnant and covered in green algae by the time the sections were rooted, but seemingly to no ill effect with regards to successful propagation.

Culm Layering

Certain bamboos can reproduce by bending their culms right down to the ground and rooting down at the nodes, thereby producing a new plant. In this way the bamboo can advance and colonize great areas very quickly. *Chusquea valdiviensis* is a good subject for amateur gardeners wishing to experiment with culm layering, since it is relatively easy to propagate this way. I have produced plants for sale of this species on various occasions by using this method. Of course, the great advantage of propagating tropical and subtropical bamboos by layering culms is that they are still receiving water and nutrients from the parent bamboo while the propagating process takes place, unlike completely detached material. This method is unlikely to work with the temperate bamboos, particularly the leptomorph species, which simply do not have the proper ability to make roots and rhizomes from the branched culm nodes.

CHAPTER 6

The Utilization of Bamboos

If bamboo can be described as the world's most underappreciated plant in horticulture, its use as a raw material is more than adequate compensation. The physical properties of the dry culms make them eminently suitable for an incredibly diverse range of applications, while the new shoots can be eaten as food and the foliage used for animal fodder.

An ancient elixir known as *tabashir,* or *tabasheer,* once believed to be an infallible cure for all ailments, is found in the internodal cavities of many tropical bamboos. Floyd Alonzo McClure (1966) describes it as consisting largely of amorphous silica in a microscopically fine state. It is still widely used for medicinal purposes in the Far East but has long been regarded as having little value in Western medicine. However, artificially produced amorphous hydrated silica has been used successfully to treat certain types of food poisoning, by absorbing toxins into its insoluble structure and thus rendering them inactive. *Tabashir* has also been found to have useful catalytic properties for certain chemical reactions.

In most Asian countries, bamboo has ancient associations with handicrafts and is comprehensively utilized for the material needs of daily life. Thicker culms can readily be worked with simple tools to manufacture vessels and implements for the home, and even to produce musical instruments. Colonel William Munro in his 1866 *Monograph of the Bambusaceae* includes a charming account of how the natives of Malacca would perforate the culms of living bamboos to produce musical tones as the breeze passed through them. Each culm could produce up to 20 notes by having a slit of varying size cut into each internode. These orchestras of the wind were called by the natives *bulu perindu* or plaintive bamboo.

Throughout history there have been many famous instances in which bamboo has come to the aid of humankind. Undoubtedly the most well documented example occurred in AD 552, when two Persian monks placed silkworm eggs in the hollow of a bamboo cane to smuggle the eggs from China to the court of Emperor Justinian at Constantinople. This led to the collapse of the Eastern silk trade and at the same time formed the foundation of the Western silk industry. More recently, the world's first incandescent light bulb, invented by Thomas Edison, had a filament made from carbonized bamboo. In 1882 Edison started a company to produce such lamps on a commercial scale. The original bulb is preserved in the Smithsonian Institution in Washington, D.C. In Japan it has been demonstrated scientifically that the charcoal from certain bamboos has superior properties for use in electric batteries, compared with charcoal from conventional sources. The silica-rich charcoal from bamboo is also used by jewelers in the Far East for polishing precious stones.

Bamboo as a Building Material

Where bamboo grows naturally in the world, particularly in many of the densely populated regions of the tropics, the culms often provide the only suitable source of material for housing, being both sufficiently inexpensive and available in abundance. Bamboo has often been called the timber of the poor, but this may be qualified by understanding that the wood from bamboos can be superior in certain fields of application. The long hollow cylinders have a favorable weight-to-strength ratio and have the useful attributes of flexibility and resilience, thus making them ideally suited for construction.

All the main structural parts of a house can be made from bamboo, except the fireplace and lower part of the chimney. The building of such dwellings requires considerable technical knowledge and manual skills, with usually more than 2000 individual components being required for a complete bamboo house. Culms can be used entire or split. When split very thinly, such material can be woven into matting for walls and floors, or twisted into strong cord for binding and fastening. Slender culms and branches can be made into "bamboo thatch" for the roof. Bamboo can also be bent or straightened by heating. Temperatures in excess of 150°C (302°F) will cause the culms to become pliable and malleable, and once cooled, the shape will be retained. Traditionally in Bangladesh and Burma, approximately 50 percent of all houses are built exclusively from

bamboo, and in the lowland regions of Ecuador, some 90 percent of all houses use bamboo in their construction. Bamboo was a popular choice of building material in ancient China and Japan, and the design principles established in these early dwellings can still be seen in the traditional architecture of both countries. One of the most famous constructional uses of bamboo in Japan is the "moonviewing platform" built at the Katsura Palace in Kyoto in 1650, where bamboo was used as an open floor surface.

Many other large structures can be made from bamboo, a remarkable example being the suspension bridge over the river Min in Sichuan, China. It is about 250 m (800 feet) long and 3 m (10 feet) wide, built of huge cables of woven and twisted bamboo fibers, spanning seven supports in the riverbed. This incredible feat of engineering is the largest of its kind in the world. Many types of bamboo bridges can be seen throughout India, China, and Malaysia, including floating bridges, using bamboo rafts as pontoons.

Bamboo is much favored for scaffolding against high buildings in the Far East. Not only is it much cheaper than steel, but it is considerably lighter and easier to erect. The poles are often bound together with woven bamboo string. Considerable research has been carried out in recent years to investigate the use of bamboo in reinforced concrete in place of steel. Concrete with bamboo can support loads of four or five times that of unreinforced concrete and is said to represent a cost savings of about 30 percent compared with steel reinforcement.

One of the most logical uses of bamboo has been the exploitation of its hollow culms as pipes. Circa 100 BC the Chinese piped natural gas in bamboo to provide fuel for salt production. Some of these lines extended over a couple of kilometers, and bamboo pipes may still be in

Demonstration of a house made from bamboo as might be found in native countries, with the walls removed to show the internal framework.

use today in the Sichuan salt industry. Marco Polo recorded in his journals that the Chinese had been using bamboo tubes to drill for oil at depths of more than 1000 m (⅗ mile) since at least 200 BC. In the tropics, one popular use for bamboo piping is to carry water in drainage and irrigation systems. In Tanzania, bamboo culms have been used as water pipes over a distance of 260 km (160 miles). A rather more refined approach to bamboo piping can be found in the famous bamboo organ in Las Piñas, Philippines. It was constructed from 950 separate culms in 1818 and still exists in working order.

On a smaller scale, various types of furniture can be manufactured from bamboo. In the past such products tended to be made from entire culms or splits, but today, with advanced technology, high-quality laminated bamboo is more frequently used. Bending is facilitated by the use of steam; however, microwave heating has now been successfully used in this respect, giving more even distribution of internal stresses. Bamboo is eminently suitable for glued laminates, as it is hard-wearing and strong and has greater elasticity than wood derived from trees, giving it more satisfactory bending properties. Plywood can also be made from bamboo and as such was used by the Chinese in the Second World War for the manufacture of aircraft skins.

Bamboo Paper Pulp

The industrial use of bamboo for paper pulp is relatively new, dating back to the early 20th century, but the Chinese were making paper from bamboo by hand some 2000 years ago. Before the advent of paper, the ancient Chinese kept records on thin strips of bamboo tied together with leather or silk, and many of these "books" were sufficiently durable to have survived in legible condition to the present day. The basic process of papermaking has remained largely unaltered over the centuries, although in recent history mechanization and industrialization have greatly improved the efficiency of the procedure and the quality of the final product.

Bamboo possesses certain natural advantages over many types of tree wood for use in papermaking. The fibers are much more slender, which gives a smoothness and flexibility to the finished paper. A high cellulose content makes bamboo particularly suitable for pulping and enables it to be used in rayon and cellophane production. In fact, bamboo can produce up to six times as much cellulose per hectare as can many softwoods; and, of course, bamboo can be repeatedly harvested, whereas trees can be harvested only once and then have to be replanted, taking some 30 years to mature. The principle disadvantages of bamboo for paper pulp are the increased transport costs, due to the higher size-to-biomass ratio, because the culms are hollow, and the greater number of impurities that have to be removed in the cooking process.

The global need for paper is incessant, and demand continues to exceed supply. It is estimated that world paper use is increasing by 5 percent annually. This, coupled with large-scale deforestation in the tropics, has provided considerable incentive for finding new sources of raw material as alternatives to trees. Bamboo is increasingly regarded as a feasible substitute. Within the next 50 years it is quite possible that bamboo could replace trees as the world's primary source of material for paper pulp.

Edible Bamboo Shoots

It is often assumed that pandas are the only animals that eat bamboo, but the plant is a principle source of forage and fodder for many animals, both domesticated and wild, in those parts of the world where bamboos are native. Also, wherever bamboos are cultivated as an economic crop for the harvesting of the culms, it is common practice to use the trimmings as fodder. Sheep and cattle eat it with relish, and bamboo forage is said to confer superior stamina in horses, compared with grass and hay. Many wild animals, including elephants, buffalo, and gorillas, will eat bamboo, though this is usually confined to grazing of the foliage. Pandas are thought to be the only animals that eat bamboo exclusively. An interesting secondary use of bamboo foliage has been found in Japan, where dried mature leaves are used for deodorizing fish oils.

Bamboo shoots are an important dietary component in most Eastern countries, especially China, Japan, Taiwan, and Thailand. Some of the shoots are taken from natural forests, but most are harvested from extensive commercial plantations. Much of the production is exported, but the home market for this delicacy is enormous. Taiwan and Japan each consume some 8000 tons of shoots every year. A properly managed plantation can provide 10 metric tons per hectare (4 tons per acre) annually, with harvesting carried out once or sometimes twice a year. In most parts of Europe and North America, commercial production of shoots is not viable. This is because the really thick shoots cannot be readily grown without very high temperatures and humidity, particularly in early summer, when the shooting season is at its peak for most species. Such production may be possible in the south of France and Italy, and various attempts have been made to exploit the warm, humid climate of the southeastern United States.

Although very thick shoots cannot be produced from bamboos grown outdoors in all except the most favored parts of Europe and the United States, the thinner shoots of virtually all the hardy species are edible and are often considered to be superior in flavor. Out of all the hardy bamboos, those belonging to *Phyllostachys* usually provide the thickest shoots, whereas most of the other genera tend to send up a greater number of shoots annually but of much smaller diameter. When harvesting shoots for consumption, it is important to remember that sufficient shoots must be left to grow into full-sized culms in order that the bamboo can perpetuate itself; only very vigorous, rampant varieties can be kept in check by eating them! As a general rule no more than half the number of shoots produced each year should be taken, and in colder districts, where growth is less rapid, no more than a third should be taken. Avoid removing shoots at all from newly planted clumps until such time as they are properly established and growing strongly.

When harvesting shoots, a similar method should be employed to that used for commercial harvesting. Select shoots that are just appearing through the surface of the ground. This event can often be anticipated a day or so beforehand, by a slight bulge in the soil where the shoot is pushing its way up from underneath, and also by a noticeable damp patch in dry ground, where the tip of the shoot exudes moisture to soften its passage upward. At this time, a little friable soil or similar medium should be used to cover the shoot, to allow it to increase in bulk without being exposed to daylight. Once light is allowed to reach a shoot, it starts to change from white to green and rapidly becomes fibrous and woody, marring the flavor and making it tough and indigestible. Do not remove shoots that have reached this stage. When the shoot emerges from the mound of covering medium, dig down and cut off just where the shoot joins the rhizome from which it has developed. Try not to damage the rhizome as this will be detrimental to future growth.

In terms of food value, bamboo shoots equate approximately with an onion, with the principal constituents being protein, carbohydrates, calcium, and phosphorous. Preparation and cooking are very simple: With a sharp knife, cut through the sheaths only, lengthways from tip to base. Starting with the basal sheaths, remove and discard all except the most tender sheaths at the tip, until the "flesh" is exposed. Pare away any discolored areas and cut off the tough basal section. The remaining core can be sliced across or down, or diced into various shapes, and then boiled for about 20 minutes with at least one heaped teaspoonful of salt added per half liter (1 pint). Some experimentation may be required here: the salt removes the bitterness or acridity from the flavor, and some species may require more salt than others. Alternatively, the water may be changed after the first 20 minutes of cooking. *Phyllostachys aurea* is notable for being singularly free from bitterness and usually requires much less salt. The shoots can be eaten at this stage, hot or cold, or can be prepared further by shallow frying for a few minutes. They can be eaten alone as a vegetable or combined in a recipe with other foods. They taste rather like sweet corn and have the texture and appearance of a raw potato.

Harvesting Bamboo Culms

Considerable quantities of bamboo culms are imported by Europe and the United States each year from the Far East, primarily for use as plant supports. These culms originate mostly from one species, *Pseudosasa amabilis*, commonly known as the Tonkin cane. This species is a native of southern China and will only grow satisfactorily in a warm-temperate climate, although I can grow it reasonably well in southern England, close to the sea. In common with bamboo shoot production, bamboo culm production usually takes place in large, commercially managed groves for reasons of economy and convenience. In warmer areas, where thick culms can be produced, much of the cut material is sold and used locally, mainly for building and construction, though also for paper pulp. Regardless of the end use, harvesting and curing methods throughout the Far East are very similar, and the same principles should be applied when cutting canes for use in Western gardens.

It is important to stress that while canes of satisfactory quality for garden use can be produced in the British Isles and similar cool-temperate or maritime climates, the high quality required for other uses is harder to achieve. This is due mostly to inadequate or improper ripening of the culms in such climates. Each culm that is to be cut must be properly mature. The process of lignification takes at least two years, ideally three years. Culms less than two years of age will not have ripened sufficiently to be of much use, being too soft and easily bent, as the silica content and consequently the hardness of bamboo culms increase with age. Very old and dead material should be discarded, as it will be brittle and easily broken.

With knowledge and experience it is possible to determine the age of a culm visually and with reasonable accuracy by examining the development of the branches and other age-related criteria applicable to the species. However, it is far easier to adopt a method used on many commercial plantations, which is to mark each year's growth on bamboos grown for harvesting culms by using a dab of paint or indelible ink, perhaps having different colors or numbers for each succeeding year. Avoid cutting too much material only from the periphery of bamboo clumps or groves; bamboo has a centrifugal growth habit, whereby the greatest proportion of new growth occurs at the outer edges of the clump, with the oldest and most suitable culms for harvesting left in the interior. The older culms are less valuable to the bamboo in terms of manufacturing and storing nutrients, and their removal tends to stimulate the plant into the production of new shoots.

Cutting can be carried out at any time of year but is best avoided during very cold weather

Making bamboo fencing in Japan using *Phyllostachys nigra*. Photo by David Helliwell

and during the shooting season in early summer, when any new shoots are easily damaged. Select culms that are reasonably straight (unless curved ones are specifically required). Using a robust pair of secateurs, or a fine-toothed saw for larger culms, sever each culm as close to the ground as practicable. It is not a good idea to cut midway between nodes, as this can sometimes lead to unwanted splitting. Trim off the branches with a sharp knife or saw, always cutting upward; branches cut downward tend to detach with a strip of culm wall. Finally, cut off the slender tip of the culm, whereupon the culm is now ready for the curing process.

Good technique is essential if garden canes are to be produced of any quality, and curing must be carried out with care and patience. Curing should take place in a dry, well-ven-

tilated shed or store, the culms preferably laid flat on racks, with adequate supports underneath to prevent sagging or bending, and turned periodically. The duration of the curing process can be calculated using a simple formula. In cool-temperate and maritime climates, curing will take at least three months per 1.25 cm (½ inch) of diameter; in warmer climates, it will take at least two months. As the culm dries, so it will change from green to straw-colored, and in so doing will become lighter in weight, whereupon its fibers shrink and tighten, giving strength and durability. A list of species recommended for garden canes can be found at the end of the book ("Lists of Bamboos for Specific Purposes").

Dried bamboo used to make an impenetrable fence in Japan. Photo by David Helliwell

CHAPTER 7

Descriptive List of Genera, Species, and Cultivars

This descriptive list includes the temperate woody bamboos in cultivation in Western gardens. It is intended to be a work of reference, providing helpful information to anyone wishing to grow bamboos or understand their individual characteristics in more detail. It is by no means fully comprehensive but is intended to cover those bamboos that can be obtained with reasonable ease from nurseries and other more specialized sources. Most if not all the bamboos described here can be obtained in Europe and the United States with a little perseverance.

The list describes various genera, species, and cultivars in alphabetical order, giving the essential information regarding dimensions, appearance, cultivation, and hardiness. It is important to note that such a list can only be used as a guide, for although bamboos can be broadly categorized for the purposes of making comparisons between different species and cultivars, they are inherently variable within certain limits, depending on their maturity and their growing conditions. For this reason I have not given an exact set of maximum or typical dimensions, or an exact hardiness assessment for each bamboo. Instead I have used a defined range or category for each aspect of a particu-

lar bamboo that is reasonably constant for cool-temperate or maritime climates worldwide.

Bamboo Nomenclature

The taxonomy of bamboos can be very confusing to the uninitiated. Botanists are constantly making changes or revisions. The bamboo enthusiast not only has to contend with some very long and complex names but also must be aware of a whole host of synonyms that may have been attributed to a particular bamboo. Indeed, it is often said in the world of bamboos that if a bamboo has had its name changed six times, the sixth name will be the same as the first! We must all accept that these constant name changes and revisions are part of growing bamboos. This is because it is the universal practice to name plants by the characteristics of their flowers. This is a simple matter for most other woody plants, because they usually produce flowers at least once a year. But for bamboos the long intervals between flowerings mean that a botanist attempting to identify and classify a plant may not have flowers available to study. For this reason, most bamboos that have been introduced from the wild have been named originally using vegetative characteristics such as leaves, branches, culms, sheathing organs, and so forth. In the time that has elapsed since bamboos began to be identified and cultivated, many species have since come into flower, whereupon botanists have been able to ascertain more precisely to which genus a bamboo rightly belongs. The taxonomy of bamboos is a complex subject, and we can expect changes and revisions of the specific and sometimes even the generic names for some time to come.

There has always been some controversy with regard to the way in which the various variegated and colored-culm bamboos should be named. In many cases, wild populations of these plants exist, so perhaps they should be regarded as a variety or form in the strict botanical sense. To balance this argument, it could equally be asserted that some of these colored bamboos are maintained only in cultivation and may not exist properly or to any great extent in the wild, in which case such bamboos would be more properly treated as cultivars. Rather than plunge into the battleground of formal bamboo taxonomy, I have elected to use in the descriptive list those names by which these bamboos are known in horticulture and by most bamboo enthusiasts. I have used the terms *form* and *variety* throughout in the loosest sense, meaning simply a version of a bamboo species that differs in some notable or distinct way. For example, among the forms of *Phyllostachys bambusoides*, 'Castillonis' is distinguished by its colored culms.

It is inevitable that any list of names will attract disagreement from some quarters, but of course there really is no such thing as a completely correct name. Any botanical name is only correct in the opinion of one or more botanists, and then only until such time as it is challenged by the publication of a new name by one or more other botanists!

Identifying Bamboos

The descriptive list can also be used as an aid to identifying any bamboos you may have or may have seen, where the correct name or correct identification is in doubt. When attempting to identify bamboos, it is of paramount importance to take into account the relative maturity of the plant and the effect of growing conditions.

Immature bamboos may not have their typical growth characteristics fully present, or may have larger leaves or much smaller culms than would be seen on an established plant of many years' successive growth. This can easily mislead the inexperienced bamboo grower into making a faulty identification. It is only when a bamboo is established and producing thicker, more mature culms that the vegetative characteristics can be regarded as being most typical for a given species.

Perhaps more misidentifications result from improper allowance being made for growing conditions than from any other factor. The combined effects of sunlight or shade, the moisture content of the soil, the fertility of the soil and the level of nutrients available, wind exposure or shelter, climate and vagaries of the growing season, and the general health of the bamboo—all play an incredibly significant role in determining whether the vegetative characteristics are typical for the species.

For example, a bamboo that is drought-stricken, starved, and stunted could be expected to have smaller and paler green leaves than usual, would probably have more slender and closely packed culms than usual, and a more constricted or poorly developed network of rhizomes. Conversely, the same bamboo growing in lush and fertile conditions would have larger and deeper green leaves, thicker and more widely spaced culms, and a more open and better developed network of rhizomes.

Using the Descriptive List

Each plant entry in the descriptive list begins with the bamboo's botanical name. This is followed by a list of any synonyms, the country or countries to which the bamboo is native, and a simplified combination statement about the plant's height and invasiveness. Height and invasiveness are the two most important pieces of information needed in order to decide the suitability of a species for any particular purpose in the garden.

The more in-depth description begins with a generalized discussion of any significant points regarding the history, appearance, characteristics, and relative merits and garden worthiness of the bamboo. Following this, each entry is divided into sections, one section for each aspect of the bamboo, including culms, culm sheaths, branches, leaves, rhizomes, cultivation, and hardiness.

Culms

Categories for culm dimensions are used that indicate the expected dimensions of the culms when the bamboo has reached maturity in average to good growing conditions. When starting with a small, immature plant, four to six years' growth may be needed before culms of mature dimensions are produced. Climate is an important factor in determining the mature culm dimensions of many bamboos. All the categories for culm dimensions assume that the bamboo is being grown in a cool-temperate or maritime climate. In cooler conditions the lower end of each category is more likely to be appropriate, and conversely, in warmer conditions the upper end of the category is more appropriate.

The stronger-growing leptomorph genera, in particular *Phyllostachys*, can be expected to produce much larger diameters and heights than are given here if grown in warm-temperate conditions.

Culm Sheaths

The relative persistence of the culm sheaths is a useful aid to identification for many species. Whereas some bamboos shed their culm sheaths very promptly as the culm extends upward, so other bamboos may retain their culm sheaths for much longer, often for many years. The color and characteristics of the sheaths when they are young is a sometimes invaluable means of determining the correct identification for certain similar and closely related bamboos, notably the various green-culmed species of *Phyllostachys*. The individual colorations of the culm sheaths of some species are an attractive feature in their own right.

Branches

Each genus of bamboos tends to have its own particular characteristics for developing the complement of culm branches. It is a useful aid to identification.

Leaves

Leaves can be extremely variable in size within a bamboo plant, with many terminal leaves at the ends of the culms and the main culm branches often being larger than those produced at the ends of the lesser branches. However, leaf dimensions generally are fairly consistent for a particular species regardless of climatic influences. It is the maturity of the plant and the growing conditions that can have the greatest effect on leaf size. For example, *Indocalamus tessellatus* may not produce its typically very large leaves while it is an immature plant, nor will it do so when growing in very dry or poor growing conditions. Always be very careful not to attach too much importance to leaf size when making evaluations for the purposes of identification.

Rhizomes

Knowing the nature and relative invasiveness of the rhizomes of any given bamboo is often the single most important piece of information needed when making decisions about suitability for the garden. This section comprises a simple description followed by a statement of the actual rhizome type in brackets. After this, there may be further information that is useful with regard to specific characteristics.

Cultivation

Most bamboos will grow healthily in sun or partial shade, but some species may have more particular requirements. The categories used in this section indicate the optimum position for cultivation, in order to get the best possible results. Any other specialized conditions that may be needed for successful cultivation are also given.

Hardiness

Categories for hardiness are used that give a broad indication of the lowest temperatures a bamboo may be expected to tolerate before it is killed completely. The whole subject of hardiness is probably the most contentious of all the aspects of growing bamboos, if not of plants generally. It is absurd to state an exact temperature to which a bamboo will be hardy. There are just so many variables to be considered. It is not just the general climate of the region in which the bamboos are being grown that must be taken into account, but more importantly such factors as localized microclimate, altitude, and wind exposure, and also the length of time that a bamboo is exposed to cold.

Most of the temperate bamboos we have available to grow in our gardens are surprisingly hardy. Even species that are known to be less hardy, such as members of the genera

Chimonobambusa, Drepanostachyum, Himalaya-calamus, and some species of *Thamnocalamus,* are seldom killed outright even in more severe winters. If their culms and foliage are cut back to the ground by prolonged cold, it is rare that there will not be regrowth from the rhizomes the following season, unless the cold has penetrated deep underground. The greatest likelihood of bamboos from these genera being killed completely is when they have been left outside in pots through very cold weather over a very extended period, and the cold has penetrated deeply into their roots and rhizomes. More harm is often caused to the bamboo when the rhizomes are frozen for long periods and water cannot be supplied to the foliage, which may still be transpiring water even in cold weather. The bamboo in this case actually dies from drought. However, an important motto in gardening is, "Nothing ventured, nothing gained," so it is always worth trying bamboos that are considered less hardy, because you might be pleasantly surprised!

The Descriptive List

Arundinaria

This genus once contained a large number of species, very diverse in size and habit. Since the 1970s, botanists have reclassified nearly all the species into other genera, leaving, somewhat controversially, the two North American bamboos described below, and perhaps a few other species not yet in widespread cultivation. In general habit, the plants of this genus resemble taller species of *Pleioblastus,* with round, smooth, upright culms lacking an obvious sulcus, and an invasive, dense, thicket-forming manner of growth.

Arundinaria gigantea

Synonym *A. macrosperma*
Native to North America
Medium bamboo—invasive

A very variable plant in the wild. This bamboo is found in the southern and southeastern United States, specifically the states bordering the Gulf of Mexico, where it is known as canebrake or canereed. Its natural habitat is mainly the low-lying areas on the margins of swamps or river estuaries, where it once formed vast thickets. Due to overgrazing and development, it is now rare in the wild. It is an interesting and unusual subject for the garden, remaining quite rare in cultivation. In appearance it is superficially like a shorter and much less elegant *Pseudosasa japonica* or *Pleioblastus simonii*.

Unless grown in warm-temperate conditions, it is reluctant to achieve any great height.

Culms Medium-tall and very slender, 2 to 3 m (6 to 10 feet) tall and less than 6 mm (¼ inch) in diameter. Light green at first, maturing to dull yellowish green. Internodes smooth. Very thin-walled. Nodes moderately prominent. Very lax in habit due to the size of the leaves in proportion to the thickness of the culm. New shoots appear in early summer. **Culm sheaths** Persistent. Purple-tinted and fringed near the tip with short hairs. **Branches** Multiple. Numerous and short, borne in dense upright tufts. **Leaves** Long and medium-broad, 18 to 25 cm

Arundinaria gigantea looking at its best in midsummer.

(7 to 10 inches) long by 1.5 to 3 cm (⅝ to 1¼ inches) wide. Pale green on the upper surface, softly downy and matte green on the lower surface, tapering sharply to a point at the tip. Generally coarse in appearance and liable to become brown-edged and ragged in winter. **Rhizomes** Invasive (leptomorph). Spreads rapidly once established in good growing conditions. **Cultivation** Sun or semi-shade. Best grown in an open position, since heavy shade is inclined to make the habit drawn and lax. Although fairly hardy, this bamboo is inclined to look scruffy in winter when too dry or exposed to strong winds. **Hardiness** −10°C to −20°C (14°F to −4°F).

Arundinaria gigantea subsp. *tecta*

Synonym *A. macrosperma* var. *tecta*

Short bamboo—invasive

Differs from the species by having a smaller stature and by other minor morphological characteristics of botanical interest only. Sometimes regarded as a variety rather than a subspecies. Like the species, it is very variable in the wild. It grows naturally in vast tracts along the swampy margins of river deltas and has rhizomes that are specially adapted to damper conditions. It has little horticultural merit and will be of interest only to enthusiasts or collectors. As a cultivated plant it tends to look shabby and scruffy for most of the year. Although supposedly shorter than the species, subsp. *tecta* usually attains much the same height. When grown in cool-temperate conditions, the two plants can be hard to distinguish.

Culms Short and very slender, 1 to 2 m (3 to 6 feet) tall and up to 6 mm (¼ inch) in diameter. **Culm sheaths** Even more persistent than typical *A. gigantea*. **Cultivation** Needs a sheltered and very lush growing situation to look acceptable as a garden plant.

Bambusa

A large tropical genus of bamboos having a typical clumping habit of growth. Some species will withstand a certain amount of frost, such as *Bambusa multiplex* and its forms, but most are very tender and need greenhouse or conservatory cultivation in cool-temperate climates. When grown indoors, they can produce new shoots at almost any time of year. Outside, they require a long, hot growing season with good light intensity. Even with a good growing position outdoors, they are inclined to produce the bulk of their growth very late in the season, and this often fails to ripen properly before the onset of colder weather. Plants that have been stressed by cold in winter, though not killed outright, often produce pale, whitened new leaves in spring, taking some time to become properly green again.

Bambusa bamboos can be distinguished by their pachymorph rhizomes, which are sometimes quite open in habit, and by their distinctive culm sheath blades, which are usually wide in relation to their overall length. The culms are very round in cross section, and the leaves lack any obvious tessellation. All culm dimensions given for members of this genus assume that the plant will be grown as a greenhouse or conservatory specimen in a cool-temperate climate. When a plant is grown outside in warm-temperate conditions, its culms will often be much larger.

Bambusa multiplex

Synonym *B. glaucescens*

Native to China

Tall bamboo—clump-forming

A very variable tropical bamboo, much cultivated in the United States, where it is often used to make hedges or screens. In Europe it is cultivated, along with its many forms, mostly as a pot or container specimen. The long arching culms with their masses of fine, luxuriant foliage are most elegant and pleasing.

Culms Tall and slender, 3 to 5 m (10 to 16 feet) tall and 6 mm to 2 cm (¼ to ¾ inch) in diameter. Bright green, maturing to dull yellowish green. Internodes smooth and circular. Nodes moderately prominent. Very arched in habit, with only the youngest culms being upright. New shoots appear from late spring onward in cool greenhouse conditions, but only after a sustained period of warm weather. In heated conservatory conditions, shoots may appear at any time of year. **Culm sheaths** Semi-persistent. Plain green, rather broad for their length, and covered with fine hairs. Small auricles. **Branches** Multiple. Absent during the initial growth of the culm, then produced in great profusion. There is one prominent central branch, surrounded by numerous smaller branches. **Leaves** Medium-long and medium-broad, 9 to 18 cm (3½ to 7 inches) long by 1.5 to 3 cm (⅝ to 1¼ inches) wide. Plain green on the upper surface, silvery green on the lower surface, bluntly tapering at the tip. No obvious tessellation. **Rhizomes** Clump-forming (pachymorph). Makes a dense, closely circumscribed clump. **Cultivation** Sun or semi-shade. Can be grown outside in mild areas; otherwise it makes an excellent pot specimen for the house or conservatory. Tolerates shade but is best grown in good sunlight; otherwise the habit becomes very lax. **Hardiness** −5°C to −10°C (23°F to 14°F).

Bambusa multiplex 'Alphonse Karr'

Synonym *B. glaucescens* 'Alphonse Karr'
Tall bamboo—clump-forming
Differs from the species by having yellow culms with variable green striping, and a slightly smaller stature. A beautiful yellow-culmed cultivar much sought after as a houseplant in cooler climates. It was named after Jean-Baptiste-Alphonse Karr, a horticulturist, writer, and pamphleteer of the 19th century.

Culms Slightly shorter than those of the species. Bright yellow, with random green stripes and panels, often almost completely yellow. When exposed to sunlight, the yellow parts of the culm temporarily turn orange-red, becoming a deeper golden yellow with age. **Culm sheaths** Often with creamy yellow variegations. **Leaves** A thin creamy yellow stripe may be found on a leaf here and there.

The brightly colored culms of *Bambusa multiplex* 'Alphonse Karr'. This plant is growing outside in northern Italy, but it is best kept inside the house or conservatory during the winter months in cool or maritime temperate climates.

Bambusa multiplex 'Fernleaf'

Synonym *B. glaucescens* 'Fernleaf'

Medium bamboo—clump-forming

Differs from the species by having smaller leaves and a smaller stature. Commonly known as the fernleaf hedge bamboo. This cultivar is like a scaled-down version of the species, with the leaves carried in neat rows, giving a fern-like appearance. It is widely cultivated in the United States. 'Rivieriorum' is very similar, though slightly smaller in culm and leaf, but it is much less common in cultivation.

Bambusa multiplex 'Fernleaf' used as a patio plant for the summer and taken inside for the winter.

Culms Medium-tall and slender, 2 to 3 m (6 to 10 feet) tall and 6 mm to 2 cm (¼ to ¾ inch) in diameter. Slightly more slender than those of the species. **Leaves** Very short and very narrow, less than 5 cm (2 inches) long by less than 1 cm (⅜ inch) wide. Held closely in ranks at the end of each twig.

Bambusa ventricosa

Synonym *B. tuldoides* 'Ventricosa'

Native to China

Tall bamboo—clump-forming

Commonly known as the Buddha's belly bamboo. This species is normally encountered either as a bonsai plant imported from the Far East or as a houseplant. It is too tender to grow outside in cool-temperate climates and is only suited to indoor conditions. When it is grown outside in warm-temperate conditions, the culms can attain dimensions two or three times those stated here. The whole plant gives an imposing, structural, architectural, very dark green effect, making this species well worth growing. The culms and their branches readily produce swollen, bottle-like distortions in their native environment, but these distortions can only be encouraged in cultivation by specialized treatment.

Culms Tall and medium-thick, 3 to 5 m (10 to 16 feet) tall and 2 to 3 cm (¾ to 1¼ inches) in diameter. Deep dark green, maturing to yellowish green. Internodes smooth and glossy, often slightly zigzag, and sometimes developing swollen, bottle-like distortions under more restricting or drier conditions. Nodes moderately prominent. Upright in habit at first, with an arch developing in older culms under the weight of the heavy foliage. New shoots can appear at almost any time when the temperature is sufficiently high. **Culm sheaths** Not persistent. Sometimes retained longer on the branches. Plain green becoming orange-tinted when drying. **Branches** In threes. Usually one prominent central branch, accompanied by two smaller branches, one on each side. The branch internodes can also develop swollen, bottle-like distortions. **Leaves** Medium-long and medium-broad, 9 to 18 cm (3½ to 7 inches) long by 1.5 to 3 cm (⅝ to 1¼ inches) wide. Dark green and glossy on the upper surface, dull and matte green on the lower surface, tapering gradually to a fine point at the tip. **Rhizomes** Clump-forming (pachymorph). Makes a fairly open clump. **Cultivation** Sun or semi-shade. Makes an impressive pot plant for the house or conservatory, where space permits. Can become drawn and lax in too much shade. To produce the distortions of the culms and their branches, this plant needs to be underpotted, dried out, underfertilized, and generally neglected. Given good, normal cultivation it will be very reluctant to display anything but the most minor distortions. **Hardiness** 0°C to −5°C (32°F to 23°F).

Bashania

A small genus of robust, invasive bamboos once included in *Arundinaria*. They are endemic to the mountainous forested regions of central China and are adaptable to a wide range of growing conditions. In general appearance, they resemble the taller species of *Pleioblastus*.

Bashania faberi

Synonyms *Arundinaria fangiana*, *B. fangiana*, *Gelidocalamus fangianus*

Native to China

Medium bamboo—very invasive

An obscure smaller bamboo useful as an understory planting among taller species or deciduous trees. It has a certain charm, mostly because of its unusual tufts of comparatively broad leaves and its rather ungainly habit,

which is not unattractive. Possibly useful as a low hedge if the active rhizomes can be contained. The foliage is inclined to look very scruffy when this bamboo is grown in positions that are too dry.

Culms Medium-tall and very slender, 2 to 3 m (6 to 10 feet) tall and up to 6 mm (¼ inch) in diameter. Deep green at first, becoming yellowish green. Nodes not prominent. Generally loose, leaning or arching in habit due to the heavy foliage. New shoots appear in early summer. **Culm sheaths** Semi-persistent. Light green. **Branches** Multiple. Fairly short and becoming congested in older culms. **Leaves** Medium-long and medium-broad, 9 to 18 cm (3½ to 7 inches) long by 1.5 to 3 cm (⅝ to 1¼ inches) wide. Rather broad for their length. Light rich green and moderately lustrous on the upper surface, matte green on the lower surface, tapering to a slender point at the tip. Held in dense tufts on the numerous short branches. **Rhizomes** Very invasive (strongly leptomorph). Can be slow to establish but then spreading rapidly. **Cultivation** Sun or shade. Adaptable to a wide range of situations but inclined to have a better habit when grown in the open. **Hardiness** −10°C to −20°C (14°F to −4°F).

Bashania fargesii

Synonym *Arundinaria fargesii*

Native to China

Tall bamboo—very invasive

This species is the only representative of the genus that is well established in cultivation. It is worth growing for its attractive healthy-looking foliage and grayish younger culms, but beware of the deep-rooted and far-reaching rhizomes, which will quickly colonize surrounding areas. Useful as a tough windbreak.

Culms Tall and medium-thick, 3 to 5 m (10 to 16 feet) tall and 2 to 3 cm (¾ to 1¼ inches) in diameter. Rather slender for their height.

Deep midgreen at first, the color completely obscured by a coating of waxy gray powder that persists well into the second year as a silvery stained effect, ripening to light midgreen and then yellowish green. Very thick-walled and strong. Internodes of thicker culms often showing a slight bulbous swelling just above the nodes, particularly in the midculm region. Nodes not prominent. Noticeably upright in habit and sturdy-looking despite their slenderness, with only a moderate arch on older culms. New shoots appear in late spring. **Culm sheaths** Not persistent. Midgreen. **Branches** Three to five main branches at first, becom-

Bashania fargesii.

ing multiple. Fairly short. **Leaves** Medium-long and medium-broad, 9 to 18 cm (3½ to 7 inches) long by 1.5 to 3 cm (⅝ to 1¼ inches) wide. Deep, rich, shining green on the upper surface, matte gray-green on the lower surface, tapering gradually to a drawn-out point at the tip. Very hard and tough. **Rhizomes** Very invasive (strongly leptomorph). Often deeper than many other temperate bamboos. **Cultivation** Sun or shade. Inclined to be less upright in heavy shade. **Hardiness** −10°C to −20°C (14°F to −4°F).

Bashania qingchengshanensis

Native to China

Tall bamboo—very invasive

A very recently introduced species likely to be rare in cultivation for some years to come. At present only immature plants are available to describe, but my impression is that this bamboo is likely to be less tall and less attractive and garden-worthy than *B. fargesii*. It can most easily be distinguished by the longer leaves and more persistent culm sheaths, which may still have their bases attached to the nodes even after the rest of the sheath has disappeared.

Culms Tall and slender, 3 to 5 m (10 to 16 feet) tall and 6 mm to 2 cm (¼ to ¾ inch) in diameter. Deep midgreen at first, with a moderate coating of persistent waxy gray powder, most noticeable under the nodes, becoming yellowish midgreen, with traces of the gray coating remaining well into the second year. Very thick-walled but not so rigid as the culms of *B. fargesii*. Nodes not prominent. Fairly upright in habit, with older culms arching moderately. New shoots appear in late spring. **Culm sheaths** Persistent. Deep green and covered in stiff hairs. Lacking auricles. **Branches** Multiple. Fairly short. **Leaves** Long and medium-broad, 18 to 25 cm (7 to 10 inches) long by 1.5 to 3 cm (⅝ to 1¼ inches) wide. Deep green and lustrous on the upper surface, matte grayish green on the lower surface, tapering gradually to a slender, drawn-out point at the tip. Inclined to wither at the tips in winter. Very hard and tough. **Rhizomes** Very invasive (strongly leptomorph). Spreads rapidly once established **Cultivation** Sun or semi-shade. Requires good growing conditions to look attractive. **Hardiness** –10°C to –20°C (14°F to –4°F).

Borinda

This is a genus of relatively hardy, high-altitude bamboos, comprising some 20 species that were previously assigned to *Fargesia*, *Thamnocalamus*, and *Yushania*. Further species are likely to be added due to ongoing research into bamboos growing in the wild and the continuing introduction of new species into cultivation.

A new genus, *Borinda* is still controversial and is not universally accepted by botanists. It was established due to the investigation of Himalayan high-altitude bamboos by Chris Stapleton in conjunction with the Royal Botanic Gardens, Kew, in the mid-1980s. It had become clear that certain species did not exactly fit the criteria for the existing high-altitude genera because of untenable conflicts between flowering, branching, and rhizome characteristics, and therefore a separate genus was required. The naming of the species is still highly provisional, and further changes will inevitably occur.

In general appearance, *Borinda* bamboos resemble the Himalayan species of *Thamnocalamus*, but they usually have up to seven branches in the first year, with the two outermost branches usually angled so as to reach back behind the culm. The culms of some species may curve outward slightly at the base before becoming perpendicular. Almost all species of *Borinda* have long culm internodes that are longitudinally ribbed-striate. These ridges

are only just visible but can also be felt with a thumb or fingernail. The pachymorph rhizomes of *Borinda* bamboos tend to have shorter necks than other high-altitude bamboos, thus giving a very tight clump habit. All of these characteristics are more apparent in plants of mature proportions.

The leaves of *Borinda* are generally thin and delicate, with a rather matte upper surface, and are liable to curl in strong sunlight. Although most species have clearly visible tessellation in the leaves, they can be less evergreen than other bamboos in hard winters, with some species more deciduous than others. Nonetheless, this characteristic does not seem to be to the detriment of their overall hardiness. *Borinda* bamboos have a definite preference for cool and humid growing conditions, and dislike heat. Many species of *Borinda* have a pronounced and highly conspicuous waxy white powdery bloom on the young culms, while some of the newer species have attained very large culm dimensions for temperate pachymorph bamboos, giving an almost tropical effect. *Borinda* is tentatively divided into two groups: the larger, more evergreen species and the smaller, more deciduous species from higher elevations in the wild. These bamboos can be found across a continuous chain of high mountain ranges from western Nepal and Tibet to the Yunnan province of China.

With the exception of *B. fungosa*, which has been in cultivation since at least the early 1990s, the descriptions of *Borinda* species are derived from often immature plants growing at the University of Liverpool's Ness Botanic Gardens and at various private gardens in Cornwall in southwestern England. The plants described originate from botanical expeditions to Tibet, Bhutan, and China made between 1995 and 2003 to collect a diverse range of plant material for genetic conservation. A number of new bamboos were collected, including species of *Borinda* new to cultivation. Various parties, including private collectors, had an interest in these expeditions, but it fell to the University of Liverpool to grow on most of the bamboos that were collected. Many of the bamboo species introduced into Ness are much duplicated, and so there are often plants that purport to be the same species but that seem to have different characteristics. All of this adds to the confusion surrounding this new genus.

The following descriptions should be regarded merely as a guide, rather than as an absolute set of statements about the various characteristics of each bamboo. As these plants become more mature, and as further research is carried out into the naming and classification of each species, so these descriptions may need revising. All of the following descriptions, with the exception of *B. fungosa*, are based on the most promising clone out of those introduced for each species. In other words, I have described the clone with the best or most pronounced or most colorful characteristics, and therefore the clone that is most likely to be propagated and introduced into wider cultivation. This is an exciting new group of clump-forming bamboos, many of which are outstandingly beautiful and of the utmost garden worthiness.

Borinda albocerea

Native to China

Tall bamboo—clump-forming

A superb new introduction, well worth growing for its graceful arching habit and fine, elegant foliage. The new culms will stand out in any situation, having an intense white bloom that is superior to that of any other bamboo so far in cultivation. This is a sought-after bamboo that is likely to be in scarce supply for some years to come.

Culms Tall and slender, 3 to 5 m (10 to 16 feet) tall and 6 mm to 2 cm (¼ to ¾ inch) in diameter. Dull green with a highly conspicuous thick covering of snow-white powdery bloom at first, the bloom gradually losing its intensity as the culm matures, and finally disappearing as the culm ripens to yellowish green. Internodes bearing slight longitudinal ridges. Nodes moderately prominent. Fairly upright in habit when young, with older culms arching gracefully. New shoots appear in early summer. **Culm sheaths** Semi-persistent. Midgreen, slightly purple-tinted and blotched where ex-

Borinda albocerea has intensely white young culms.

posed to light. Covered in fairly stiff brown hairs on the outer surface. **Branches** Multiple. Up to seven main branches in the first season, held more or less horizontally, with the outermost two reaching back behind the culm. **Leaves** Short and narrow, 5 to 9 cm (2 to 3½ inches) long by 1 to 1.5 cm (⅜ to ⅝ inch) wide. Bright green and slightly matte on the upper surface, grayish matte green on the lower surface, tapering to a fine point at the tip. **Rhizomes** Clump-forming (pachymorph). Makes a very tightly packed clump. **Cultivation** Sun or shade. Best in semi-shade. **Hardiness** −10°C to −20°C (14°F to −4°F).

Borinda angustissima

Synonym *Fargesia angustissima*
Native to China
Tall bamboo—clump-forming

A fine, slender-culmed species, introduced from seed as *Fargesia angustissima*, worth a place in any garden for its elegant arching habit and small leaves. The new culms have the attractive powdery bloom that is typical of *Borinda*, but in this species it is less obscured by the foliage of other culms due to the relatively sparse foliage.

Culms Tall and slender, 3 to 5 m (10 to 16 feet) tall and 6 mm to 2 cm (¼ to ¾ inch) in diameter. Slender for their height and usually emerging from the ground on an outward curve before becoming upright. Dull light green with a copious covering of grayish white powdery bloom at first, the bloom disappearing gradually, and the culm ripening to yellowish green. Internodes bearing slight longitudinal ridges. Nodes moderately prominent. Very upright in habit when young, with older culms arching gracefully. New shoots appear in early summer. **Culm sheaths** Semi-persistent. Midgreen, flushed purple-red where exposed to light. Covered in stiff brown hairs on the

outer surface. **Branches** Multiple. Up to seven main branches in the first season, held almost horizontally, with the outermost two reaching back behind the culm. **Leaves** Short and very narrow, 5 to 9 cm (2 to 3½ inches) long by less than 1 cm (⅜ inch) wide. Bright light green and slightly matte on the upper surface, silvery matte green on the lower surface, tapering to a fairly abrupt point at the tip. Inclined to be partially or completely deciduous in cold winters **Rhizomes** Clump-forming (pachymorph). Makes a tightly packed clump. **Cultivation** Sun or shade. Best in semi-shade. **Hardiness** −10°C to −20°C (14°F to −4°F).

Borinda frigida

Synonyms *Fargesia frigida, F. frigidorum*
Native to China
Tall bamboo—clump-forming

An extremely delicate-looking species that looks superficially like *Thamnocalamus crassinodus* 'Merlyn', but could prove to be hardier than *Fargesia murielae* and *F. nitida*. Of all the *Borinda* species currently in cultivation, this is the most elegant. The tiny leaves are carried in great profusion on the slender and gracefully arching culms. Unfortunately, this bamboo seems to be more or less deciduous in all but the mildest winters, but in spring it produces a brilliant mass of bright green new leaves. A superb new introduction, worthy of growing in any garden, unless a completely evergreen bamboo is essential. Likely to be in scarce supply for many years to come.

Culms Tall and slender, 3 to 5 m (10 to 16 feet) tall and 6 mm to 2 cm (¼ to ¾ inch) in diameter. Dull green with a copious covering of gray-white powdery bloom at first, the bloom gradually disappearing as the culm matures to yellowish green. Internodes bearing slight longitudinal ridges. Nodes moderately prominent. Fairly upright in habit when young, with

Borinda frigida produces
cascades of tiny leaves.

older culms arching gracefully to become almost cascading. New shoots appear in early
summer. **Culm sheaths** Semi-persistent. Yellowish pale green, streaked brownish purple
on the sunny side. Covered in very fine beige
hairs on the outer surface. **Branches** Multiple.
Up to seven main branches in the first season,
held more or less horizontally, with the outermost two reaching back behind the culm. The
branch complement becoming congested in
later years. **Leaves** Very short and very narrow, less than 5 cm (2 inches) long by less than
1 cm (⅜ inch) wide. Of noticeably uniform size
throughout and produced in great numbers.
Bright green and slightly matte on the upper
surface, grayish matte green on the lower surface, tapering fairly abruptly to a point at the
tip. Extremely soft in texture and delicate-looking. Deciduous in most winters unless grown
in a very mild locality. **Rhizomes** Clump-forming (pachymorph). Makes a very tightly packed
clump. **Cultivation** Semi-shade or shade. Best
in semi-shade. Dislikes sun and heat. **Hardiness** Below −20°C (−4°F).

Borinda fungosa

Synonym *Fargesia fungosa*
Native to China
Tall bamboo—clump-forming

An attractive bamboo suitable for a sheltered position. Introduced by seed in the 1990s to the United States and Europe, and not very hardy in the seedling stage. Distinctive for its leaves, which are large for a clump-forming temperate bamboo. Although this bamboo is fairly cold-tolerant in general, the foliage tends to be deciduous in all but the mildest winters, leaving the plant looking rather sad in late winter and early spring, until new growth commences. Much used for weaving in its native country.

Culms Tall and slender, 3 to 5 m (10 to 16 feet) tall and 6 mm to 2 cm (¼ to ¾ inch) in diameter. Midgreen with a moderate covering of grayish powdery bloom at first, the bloom soon disappearing, and the culm ripening to yellowish green. The upper parts of the culm and the culm branches can become red-tinted in strong sunlight. Internodes bearing faintly perceptible longitudinal ridges. Nodes moderately prominent. Loosely arching in habit from an early age due to the heavy foliage. New shoots appear in early summer. **Culm sheaths** Semi-persistent. Light green and tinted purplish red on the sunny side. Outer surface covered in blackish hairs. **Branches** Multiple. Up to seven main branches in the first season, held at an angle slightly above horizontal, with the outermost two sometimes reaching back slightly behind the culm. **Leaves** Medium-long and medium-broad, 9 to 18 cm (3½ to 7 inches) long by 1.5 to 3 cm (⅝ to 1¼ inches) wide. Rich green and slightly matte on the upper surface, matte grayish green on the lower surface, tapering to a fairly abrupt point at the tip. Held in heavy bunches. **Rhizomes** Clump-forming (pachymorph). Makes a very dense clump. **Cultivation** Sun or shade. Best in semi-shade. **Hardiness** −5°C to −10°C (23°F to 14°F). Hardiness seems to increase with maturity.

Borinda grossa

Native to China
Very tall bamboo—clump-forming

A distinctive and vigorous new introduction with bluish gray foliage. It is noticeably open in habit and somewhere between slightly coarse and moderately elegant. The young culms stand upright while the older culms arch to the point of being cascading, giving the impression of a huge flower in which the older petals are

Borinda grossa has sea green foliage and a distinct habit.

peeling back from the bud of petals in the middle. When this bamboo is grown in the open, an attractive reddish coloration quickly develops in the tops of the culms and the main branches. **Culms** Very tall and medium-thick, 5 to 8 m (16 to 26 feet) tall and 2 to 3 cm (¾ to 1¼ inches) in diameter. Darkish dull green at first and covered in a moderately conspicuous steel-gray powdery bloom that persists through the first season, the culm ripening to dull yellowish green, and the upper parts of the culms and main branches quickly becoming strongly tinted dull crimson-purple. Internodes bearing perceptible longitudinal ridges. Nodes not prominent. Upright in habit only when young, with older culms arching to beyond horizontal. New shoots appear in midsummer. **Culm sheaths** Not persistent. Pale green, tinted pinkish red where exposed to light. Outer surface covered in stiff golden brown hairs. **Branches** Multiple. Three to five main branches in the first season, held almost horizontally, with the outermost two not so obviously backward-reaching as in other species of the genus. **Leaves** Medium-long and narrow, 9 to 18 cm (3½ to 7 inches) long by 1 to 1.5 cm (⅜ to ⅝ inch) wide. May have noticeably broader terminal leaves. Matte bluish sea green on the upper surface, matte gray-green on the lower surface, tapering to a fairly abrupt point at the tip. **Rhizomes** Clump-forming (pachymorph). Makes a fairly open clump compared with other species of the genus. **Cultivation** Sun or semi-shade. Seems to thrive in an open position. **Hardiness** Below −20°C (−4°F).

Borinda lushuiensis

Synonyms *Fargesia edulis*, "Yunnan 4"
Native to China
Very tall bamboo—clump-forming
A magnificent and highly coveted new introduction likely to become very popular when freely available. This description is based on the now famous plant growing at Carwinion Garden in Cornwall that is tentatively identified as *B. lushuiensis*. "Yunnan 4" refers to the collection number under which this plant has been known and distributed for several years.

With its thick and closely packed culms, this remarkable species looks almost like a tropical bamboo. The foliage is superb, with clouds of faintly lustrous leaves cascading heavily from the tops of the impressive culms. Propagation is difficult once the plant becomes established, due the very tight clump habit.

Borinda lushuiensis in late summer at Carwinion.

Culms Very tall and medium-thick, 5 to 8 m (16 to 26 feet) tall and 2 to 3 cm (¾ to 1¼ inches) in diameter, often slightly thicker. Midgreen and covered in a conspicuous, thick, grayish white powdery bloom at first, the bloom almost disappearing by the beginning of the second season, and the culm ripening to yellowish green and then to deep orange-yellow, particularly in sunlight. Internodes bearing perceptible longitudinal ridges. Nodes moderately prominent. Fairly upright in habit when young, the older culms arching heavily with the myriads of small leaves. New shoots appear in early summer. **Culm sheaths** Not persistent. Light green, tinted crimson-carmine where exposed to sunlight. Outer surface covered in fine brownish hairs. **Branches** Multiple. Up to seven main branches in the first season, held nearly horizontally, with the outermost two reaching back behind the culm. **Leaves** Medium-long and narrow, 9 to 18 cm (3½ to 7 inches) long by 1 to 1.5 cm (⅜ to ⅝ inch) wide. Matte light green, becoming faintly lustrous on the upper surface, matte green on the lower surface, tapering to an acute point at the tip. **Rhizomes** Clump-forming (pachymorph). Makes a very tight and impenetrably dense clump. **Cultivation** Sun or shade. Best in semi-shade. **Hardiness** −5°C to −10°C (23°F to 14°F).

Borinda maccluriana

Native to China

Extremely tall bamboo—clump-forming

An incredibly strong-growing species that produces culms to an exceptional height for a temperate pachymorph bamboo. Undoubtedly the skyscraper of clump-forming bamboos. The effect is urgent and vital. At the Ness Botanic Gardens it just seems to keep getting taller! It is also distinctive for the larger terminal leaves at the ends of the culms and main branches.

This species is greatly sought after because of its size and vigor. For obvious reasons it is not recommended for smaller gardens or restricted spaces.

Culms Extremely tall and thick, more than 8 m (26 feet) tall and 3 to 5 cm (1¼ to 2 inches) in diameter. Olive green at first and covered in a whitish gray powdery bloom, gradually losing the bloom after the first year and ripening to yellowish green, the upper parts of the culms and main branches becoming tinted wine-purple. Internodes bearing perceptible longitudinal ridges. Nodes moderately prominent. Strongly upright in habit when young, with some older culms developing a gentle arch. New shoots appear in early summer. **Culm sheaths** Semi-persistent. Pale green and slightly purple-flushed when exposed to light. Outer surface covered in reddish purple hairs. **Branches** Multiple. Up to seven main branches in the first year, held nearly horizontally, with the outermost two reaching back behind the culm. **Leaves** Medium-long and narrow, 9 to 18 cm (3½ to 7 inches) long by 1 to 1.5 cm (⅜ to ⅝ inch) wide. Very variable, with some terminal leaves noticeably broader. Matte light green on the upper surface, grayish matte green on the lower surface, tapering to a fine point at the tip. **Rhizomes** Clump-forming (pachymorph). Makes a dense clump. **Cultivation** Sun or semi-shade. Seems to prefer a more open position. **Hardiness** Below −20°C (−4°F).

Borinda papyrifera

Synonym *Fargesia papyrifera*

Native to China

Very tall bamboo—clump-forming

A splendid but more coarse-growing species that appears to develop an upright habit akin to *Semiarundinaria fastuosa*. The larger leaves seem to suit the more open habit of this species. The stout and steel-gray young culms are

an impressive feature, and the overall impression is that of strength and vigor. Likely to be scarse in cultivation for some years to come. Seems to be more evergreen than most other *Borinda* bamboos. **Culms** Very tall and medium-thick, 5 to 8 m (16 to 26 feet) tall and 2 to 3 cm (¾ to 1¼ inches) in diameter. Tending toward the upper end of these dimensions. Deep midgreen and covered with a conspicuous and intense grayish white powdery bloom at first, losing the bloom by the end of the second year, the culm slowly ripening to deep yellowish green and then to ochre. Internodes bearing noticeable longitudinal ridges. Nodes prominent and distinctly swollen. Strongly upright in habit, with only the oldest culms developing a slight arch. New shoots appear in early summer. **Culm sheaths** Not persistent. Light green and flushed crimson where exposed to light. Sparsely covered in light brown hairs on the outer surface. **Branches** Multiple. Up to five bold main branches in the first year, held almost horizontally, with the outermost two reaching back behind the culm. Sparsely and openly branched compared to other species in the genus. **Leaves** Medium-long and narrow, 9 to 18 cm (3½ to 7 inches) long by 1 to 1.5 cm (⅜ to ⅝ inch) wide. Sometimes slightly broader for their length. Midgreen and slightly matte on the upper surface, matte green on the lower surface, tapering to a fine point at the tip. **Rhizomes** Clump-forming (pachymorph). Makes a more open clump than other species of the genus. **Cultivation** Sun or shade. Best in semi-shade. **Hardiness** −5°C to −10°C (23°F to 14°F).

Borinda papyrifera shows strong upright growth and conspicuous young culms.

Borinda perlonga

Native to China

Tall bamboo—clump-forming

An excellent new introduction that is distinctive for its larger leaves and cascading habit. Superficially it resembles *Thamnocalamus spathiflorus*, with slightly darker leaves. It could also be confused with *B. fungosa*, but it has a slightly more pronounced bloom on the young culms, and more persistent culm sheaths. The new shoots seem to be produced later in the season compared with other *Borinda* species in cultivation. So far it has proved to be hardier than expected.

Culms Tall and slender, 3 to 5 m (10 to 16 feet) tall and 6 mm to 2 cm (¼ to ¾ inch) in diameter. Dull green with a moderately conspicuous covering of grayish white powdery bloom at first, the bloom soon disappearing, the culm ripening to yellowish green. Internodes bearing slight longitudinal ridges. Nodes moderately prominent. More or less upright in habit when young, with older culms arching and cascading considerably with the weight of the foliage. New shoots appear mostly in mid to late summer. **Culm sheaths** Semi-persistent. Light green, slightly crimson-streaked where exposed to light. Covered in stiff beige hairs on the outer surface. **Branches** Multiple. Usually three to five main branches in the first season, occasionally seven, held more or less horizontally, with the outermost two reaching back behind the culm. All branches late to develop, with the new culms remaining unbranched for many weeks. **Leaves** Medium-long and medium-broad, 9 to 18 cm (3½ to 7 inches) long by 1.5 to 3 cm (⅝ to 1¼ inches) wide. Variable, with some leaves much smaller. Deep, rather grayish, dark green, and slightly matte on the upper surface, grayish matte green on the lower surface, tapering gradually to a sharp point at the tip. Carried in heavy bunches. **Rhizomes**

The heavily arching habit
of *Borinda perlonga*.

Clump-forming (pachymorph). Makes a tightly packed clump. **Cultivation** Sun or shade. Best in semi-shade. **Hardiness** –10°C to –20°C (14°F to –4°F).

Borinda yulongshanensis

Synonym *Fargesia yulongshanensis*
Native to China
Tall bamboo—clump-forming

This superb new introduction has an almost bluish coloration to the young culms and produces a fine foliage effect. There seem to be many bamboos in cultivation that purport to be this species but that are clearly something else, although their true identification is unclear. The true species is native to the Yunnan province of China and grows between 3000 and 4200 m (10,000 and 13,800 feet), the highest altitude for a Sino-Himalayan bamboo. As may be expected, it is proving to be very hardy. This description is based upon Mike Bell's plant, which is growing at his bamboo garden near Wadebridge, Cornwall, and which is believed to be correctly identified.

Culms Tall and slender, 3 to 5 m (10 to 16 feet) tall and 6 mm to 2 cm (¼ to ¾ inch) in diameter. Deep green with a conspicuous covering of almost bluish white powdery bloom at first, the bloom slowly losing its intensity as the culm matures, and finally disappearing as the culm slowly ripens to deep yellowish green. The tops of the culms and main branches de-

Borinda yulongshanensis.

Multiple. Up to seven main branches in the first season, held more or less horizontally, with the outermost two reaching back behind the culm. **Leaves** Medium-long and narrow, 9 to 18 cm (3½ to 7 inches) long by 1 to 1.5 cm (⅜ to ⅝ inch) wide. Very variable, with many leaves much shorter. Matte light green becoming slightly lustrous on the upper surface, silvery matte green on the lower surface, tapering to a fine point at the tip. **Rhizomes** Clump-forming (pachymorph). Makes a very tightly packed clump. **Cultivation** Sun or shade. Best in semi-shade. **Hardiness** −10°C to −20°C (14°F to −4°F).

Chimonobambusa

A Chinese genus containing some of the most invasive bamboos in cultivation. They are very suited to shady conditions and enjoy a high air humidity. Unlike most bamboos with a leptomorph rhizome, they tend to produce most of their culms late in the growing season. The culms of many species have partially developed roots appearing as rather thorn-like curved hooks emerging from the lower nodes.

Chimonobambusa marmorea

Synonym *Arundinaria marmorea*
Native to Japan
Medium bamboo—very invasive

This attractive and elegant small bamboo produces pleasing sprays of gently arching foliage. The culm branches are fairly short and upswept, giving a herringbone effect. The name *marmorea* means "marble-like," a reference to this bamboo's attractive culm sheaths. It was named by Bory Latour Marliac and introduced into France in 1889. A short time later it was introduced into the British Isles and the United States. Many plants in cultivation have been flowering from the late 1980s onward, and co-

velop a persistent rich wine-purple coloration when exposed to sunlight. Internodes bearing slight longitudinal ridges. Nodes moderately prominent. Strongly upright in habit when young, with older culms leaning or arching heavily with the great quantities of fine leaves. New shoots appear in early summer. **Culm sheaths** Semi-persistent. Pale green, flushed and flecked reddish purple where exposed to light. Copiously covered in reddish brown hairs on the outer surface. Although a ring of dense hairs at the node is often cited as an identifying feature of this species, this was not present on the plant here described. **Branches**

The effect of a dwarf bamboo forest is created using *Chimonobambusa marmorea*.

pious quantities of viable seed have been produced.

Culms Medium-tall and slender, 2 to 3 m (6 to 10 feet) tall and 6 mm to 2 cm (¼ to ¾ inch) in diameter. Typically seen at the lower end of these dimensions. Light green at first, becoming dark purple-green in sunlight, and maturing to purple-flushed yellow-green. Thick-walled for the size of the culm. Nodes prominent. Upright in habit only when the culms are very young, quickly becoming arched from midculm. New shoots can appear at any time from late spring to autumn. **Culm sheaths** Persistent. Pale green becoming mottled brown and white with a pinkish purple hue. The

sheath blade is very small. **Branches** In threes. One branch is often slightly longer than the others. **Leaves** Medium-long and narrow, 9 to 18 cm (3½ to 7 inches) long by 1 to 1.5 cm (⅜ to ⅝ inch) wide. Bright green on the upper surface, matte green on the lower surface, bluntly rounded at the base, tapering gradually at the tip to end in a tiny tongue. **Rhizomes** Very invasive (strongly leptomorph). Very active and far-reaching, even in poor growing conditions. **Cultivation** Sun or shade. Rather too overpowering for the smaller garden but a marvelous tall groundcover or understory plant where space permits. Grows happily in full sun and is tolerant of heavy shade, surviving well underneath deciduous trees. **Hardiness** −10°C to −20°C (14°F to −4°F).

Chimonobambusa marmorea 'Variegata'

Synonym *Arundinaria marmorea* 'Variegata'
Short bamboo—very invasive

Differs from the species by having completely yellow culms and a smaller stature. The name 'Variegata' is somewhat misleading, since the white striping in the foliage is not very conspicuous and is often entirely absent. The variegations exist because of the yellow culms, as can be said of any yellow-culmed bamboo; there is always some white or yellow-white striping of the foliage here and there. In this case, there is usually more striping than would normally be expected of a yellow-culmed bamboo. This cultivar grows a little shorter than *C. marmorea* but retains all the other attractive attributes.

Culms Short and very slender, 1 to 2 m (3 to 6 feet) tall and up to 6 mm (¼ inch) in diameter. Pale yellow at first, becoming tinted deep red in strong sunlight and later maturing to deep golden yellow. **Leaves** Bright green on the upper surface with variable amounts of thin white striping, the striping becoming more creamy white, then creamy yellow, as the season progresses. Matte green on the lower surface, with the color of the striping sometimes penetrating through. Striping is sometimes completely absent. **Cultivation** Plant in as sunny a position as possible to encourage the vivid red coloration in the culms.

Chimonobambusa quadrangularis

Synonyms *Arundinaria quadrangularis*, *Bambusa quadrangularis*, *Tetragonocalamus angulatus*
Native to China
Tall bamboo—very invasive

Commonly known as the square-stemmed bamboo. Although a native of China, it has

Young culms of *Chimonobambusa quadrangularis*. This bamboo is among the most invasive species in cultivation.

been naturalized in Japan and surrounding countries for a great many years. It was introduced into Europe, and then the United States, late in the 19th century. With its very upright culms and their short branches, *C. quadrangularis* is a very distinctive and easily recognized bamboo. On thicker culms, the lower nodes and internodes are noticeably four-angled, giving an obtusely square effect in cross section. Both the foliage and the culms are rich dark green, with the leaves being almost the same color on both surfaces. This coloration in combination with the distinctive habit produces a most architectural overall effect. The culms are very thick-walled and strong, and can therefore be cut to make useful plant supports.

Culms Tall and medium-thick, 3 to 5 m (10 to 16 feet) tall and 2 to 3 cm (¾ to 1¼ inches) in diameter. Matte dark green, maturing to grayish yellow-green, then brownish green. Internodes with longitudinal ridges and obtusely quadrate in cross section, particularly in the lower internodes. Nodes moderately prominent, also obtusely quadrate in cross section, and often having partially developed roots emerging as small, thorn-like hooks. Very upright in habit, developing a slight arch near the summit. New shoots appear from early summer onward, although most of the new culms emerge in late summer and autumn. **Culm sheaths** Not persistent. Beige-green with purple spots and flecks, purple-flushed on the inner surface when faded and dry. **Branches** In threes. Sometimes up to five, fairly short for the height of the culm. **Leaves** Long and medium-broad, 18 to 25 cm (7 to 10 inches) long by 1.5 to 3 cm (⅝ to 1¼ inches) wide. Dark green and slightly matte on the upper surface, slightly matte midgreen on the lower surface, tapering gradually to a fine point at the tip. **Rhizomes** Very invasive (strongly leptomorph). Incredibly far-reaching in good growing conditions. **Cultivation** Sun or shade. This bamboo thrives almost anywhere but is seen at its best in lush, shady woodland fringes. It is exceptionally invasive when given a sufficiently moist soil and should only be planted where its rapid spread will not cause problems. A good hedging or screening bamboo for the larger garden where winters are not too severe. **Hardiness** −5°C to −10°C (23°F to 14°F).

Chimonobambusa quadrangularis 'Nagamineus'

Tall bamboo—very invasive

Differs from the species by having yellow culms with variable green striping, and a slightly smaller stature. The yellow coloring of the culms is very stable and consistent, with reversions seldom occurring. This bamboo is a good garden plant, though rather invasive, and can be used to lighten shady corners or under trees. It was discovered in the garden of Tetsuo Nagamine in 1968 and later named after him. A similar but inferior form called 'Suow' has

Chimonobambusa quadrangularis 'Nagamineus'.

very irregular green striping and is much less stable. Reversions frequently occur, and in time many plants produce only green culms.

Culms Slightly shorter than those of the species. Bright yellow, becoming red-tinted in strong sunlight, quickly maturing to dull orange-yellow. Green striping often present, sometimes appearing regularly above each set of branches, sometimes randomly. Striping may also be completely absent. **Leaves** A thin creamy yellow stripe may be found on a leaf here and there. **Cultivation** The culms retain a better color where not exposed to strong sunlight. Sunlight may encourage the red coloration temporarily but tends to bring about premature ripening to brownish yellow, which is not desirable.

Chimonobambusa tumidissinoda

Synonym *Qiongzhuea tumidinoda*
Native to China
Tall bamboo—very invasive

Commonly known as the walking stick bamboo. A remarkable and distinctive bamboo introduced from the Kunming Botanical Garden in China by Peter Addington in 1987 and propagated for wider distribution by myself shortly after. This desirable species was presented to Peter as a special gift from the director of the gardens. It has grossly swollen, disk-like nodes and is much used in its native China for making walking sticks and umbrella handles. Although cultivated primarily for the effect of the distinctive nodes, it is also a very impressive foliage bamboo, giving masses of small, elegant, glossy leaves in cascading sprays. At the time of this bamboo's introduction, we assumed it would be too tender for all but the mildest gardens. Time has shown, however, that this superb species is quite tough and durable, and able to withstand all sorts of unfavorable weather conditions.

Culms Tall and slender, 3 to 5 m (10 to 16 feet) tall and 6 mm to 2 cm (¼ to ¾ inch) in diameter. Rich deep green at first, becoming olive green and finally maturing to yellowish green. Internodes smooth and slightly glossy, with a slightly flattened section above the branches at each node that has noticeable longitudinal ridges. Nodes prominent, disk-like, and often twice the diameter of the internodes. New shoots appear mostly in spring and early summer, unlike most other cultivated species of *Chimonobambusa*. **Culm sheaths** Not persistent. Beige-green, flushed purple when

Chimonobambusa tumidissinoda has distinctive nodes that are swollen and disk-like.

young, with fairly large blades. **Branches** In threes. The central branch is longer than the other two. **Leaves** Medium-long and narrow, 9 to 18 cm (3½ to 7 inches) long by 1 to 1.5 cm (⅜ to ⅝ inch) wide. Deep rich green on the upper surface when grown in shade, glossy and slightly yellowish green when grown in sunlight, grayish matte green on the lower surface, drawn out to a fine point at the tip. **Rhizomes** Very invasive (strongly leptomorph). Probably the most invasive bamboo in cultivation. The ground all around the plant quickly becomes a mass of searching rhizomes, which often come to the surface in sinuous loops, recalling impressions of the Loch Ness monster. Be warned! It can travel great distances in one season. **Cultivation** Sun or shade. The foliage effect is much better when the plant is grown in an open position. The leaves will be a lighter green and much more glossy, the habit more elegantly cascading. Too invasive to be planted anywhere but a large garden or woodland. In a small garden it will need to be grown in a big container. **Hardiness** −10°C to −20°C (14°F to −4°F).

Chusquea

An important large genus of North and South American bamboos, originating over an extensive area throughout the Andes and from Mexico to Argentina. These bamboos are distinctive for their solid culms and for their unusual branching habit, where the culm nodes have multiple branch buds, often reaching around nearly the complete circumference of the culm, instead of having branches emerging from the compressed basal node of the first or primary branch, as with most other temperate bamboos.

The temperate *Chusquea* bamboos so far in cultivation all originate from cool, humid, misty, high-mountain localities and have certain cultivation preferences. In general, they

have a dislike of high summer temperatures combined with excess moisture at the root. For this reason, they are best grown in cool, shady positions, even in cool-temperate climates, and should definitely not be left under glass during the summer months. A maritime climate suits these bamboos very well, and consequently many excellent specimens may be found growing in the British Isles.

Chusquea coronalis

Native to Central America, Mexico

Tall bamboo—clump-forming

An extremely beautiful but incredibly difficult and not very hardy bamboo, included here because it is often encountered as a container plant for the house or conservatory in temperate Western gardens. It can easily be recognized by its very delicate and narrow leaves and by the typical *Chusquea* whorl of branches almost surrounding the culm. Tends to look very scruffy and forlorn in all but ideal growing conditions, and inclined to drop almost all foliage in winter. This species is a rather temperamental subject, needing much care and perseverance, and is only suitable for the dedicated bamboo connoisseur.

Culms Tall and slender, 3 to 5 m (10 to 16 feet) tall and 6 mm to 2 cm (¼ to ¾ inch) in diameter. Rarely seen at more than half these dimensions unless given permanent warm greenhouse conditions. Rich deep green at first, maturing to yellowish green. Internodes completely solid with a pithy interior. Nodes not prominent. Loosely upright when young and quickly arching and leaning in all directions. New shoots appear when the temperature is constantly above 20°C (70°F). **Culm sheaths** Semi-persistent. Light green, quickly becoming white before fading. **Branches** Multiple. Fairly short and of uniform length, produced around more than half of the circumference of the node. **Leaves** Very short and very narrow, less than 5 cm (2 inches) long by less than 1 cm (⅜ inch) wide. Light green and slightly matte on the upper surface, matte light green on the lower surface, tapering fairly abruptly to a point at the tip. Extremely delicate and soft. **Rhizomes** Clump-forming (pachymorph). Makes a dense clump. **Cultivation** Semi-shade or shade. Needs warm and humid conditions with a moist soil to thrive. **Hardiness** 0°C to –5°C (32°F to 23°F).

Chusquea culeou

Native to Chile and Argentina

Tall bamboo—clump-forming

A magnificent species of distinctive appearance, unlikely to be confused with any other bamboo. It bears a superficial resemblance to *Thamnocalamus tessellatus*, but that bamboo is much less impressive. The thick, solid culms of *C. culeou* usually stand stiffly upright, only arching slightly at the top. The myriads of small leaves are carried on numerous short branches at each node, giving a bottlebrush effect. A well-grown specimen is a superb feature in any garden. The strong culms can be cut to make excellent stakes for the garden.

Chusquea culeou is very variable in the wild, since it occurs over a large area, mostly at higher altitudes in the Andes. It was introduced into England in 1890. A great many seedling clones in cultivation date back to this original introduction, all lumped under the specific name *culeou*. The various clones differ mostly in leaf size and culm dimensions. Many of the older clones have been in flower since about 1990, giving rise to further great numbers of seedlings. In my travels I have seen two older clones that stand out as the best forms of the species. The first is a form with very dark purplish young culms and very dark foliage, originating possibly from the famous Pitt

White garden in Devon, where it still grows. It can also be found at the Royal Horticultural Society's Wisley Garden in Surrey. The second fine form, noted for its very small leaves and very thick culms, was to be seen, until it flowered, at the Savill Garden, Windsor Great Park, in Surrey. All the seedlings from the Savill Garden clone seem to have the same desirable characteristics. Older clones of this species are very difficult to propagate, and division is best carried out when plants are in the seedling stage or else still very small. Nowadays there are many named seedlings in cultivation, most of which make fine garden plants.

Culms Tall and medium-thick, 3 to 5 m (10 to 16 feet) tall and 2 to 3 cm (¾ to 1¼ inches) in diameter. These dimensions represent an average and are very variable between seedling clones. Light green at first, quickly becoming a matte yellowish green. Internodes completely solid with a pithy interior. Nodes moderately prominent at shortish intervals compared with other bamboos. Generally upright in habit and of sturdy appearance, with a slight arch developing on older culms. New shoots appear from late spring onward. **Culm sheaths** Semi-persistent. The tattered remains finally pushed away by the emerging branches. Pale mauve becoming greenish and finally white before fading. **Branches** Multiple. The zone of branch emergence often extends halfway to two-thirds of the way around the node. Although branches are usually quite short, some seedling variations have longer branches, possibly 1 m (3 feet) or more in length. **Leaves** Short and very narrow, 5 to 9 cm (2 to 3½ inches) long by less than 1 cm (⅜ inch) wide. Very variable between seedling clones. Deep green on the upper surface, matte green on the lower surface, tough and hard, tapering to a fairly abrupt point at the tip. **Rhizomes** Clump-forming (pachymorph). Usually makes a very dense, closely

The distinctive tufted and foxtail-like branching habit of *Chusquea culeou* can be seen on this fine specimen in Oxford Botanic Garden.

packed clump, but some seedling variations can be more open in clump habit as they mature. **Cultivation** Semi-shade or shade. All the best specimens are usually growing on open, sandy soil in cool, shady locations. However, this species will grow satisfactorily in full sun so long as it is not exposed to very high summer temperatures and is not over-watered. Many gardeners in coastal regions of the United States report that *C. culeou* will withstand marine exposure. **Hardiness** Below −20°C (−4°F).

Chusquea culeou 'Tenuis'

Synonym *C. breviglumis*

Short bamboo—clump-forming

Differs from the species by having a much smaller stature. This dwarf form probably originated as a seedling variant introduced in the early part of the 20th century. It has suffered from considerable confusion as to its correct name. It once bore the name *C. breviglumis*, which is a synonym for a much taller species with which this cultivar is not to be confused. Until 'Tenuis' started flowering in the early 1990s, along with many clones of the species, there were clearly two different versions

Chusquea culeou 'Tenuis' in early autumn.

in cultivation. The more commonly found version would frequently have thin, faint yellowish stripes in the youngest leaves, giving the effect of slight variegation. The other version lacked the striping in the younger leaves but had a slight gray cast to the foliage, young and old, and was of tighter habit. A great number of seedlings have been raised from the flowerings, and dwarf clones now exist that have the characteristics of both versions to a greater or lesser extent.

Culms Short and slender, 1 to 2 m (3 to 6 feet) tall and 6 mm to 2 cm (¼ to ¾ inch) in diameter. **Branches** Slightly shorter than those of typical *C. culeou*.

Chusquea cumingii

Native to Chile

Medium bamboo—clump-forming

An interesting smaller species of reasonable hardiness. The culms have a semi-scandent habit, and the small glaucous leaves, which are distinctly sharp-pointed and prickly, are carried on short clustered branches. The overall effect is highly attractive and unusual. In the wild this species grows in alkaline soil in drier, more open conditions than most other *Chusquea* bamboos in cultivation. Potentially an excellent and sought-after garden plant that may prove to be hardier than expected. The rhizomes tend to have quite long necks and are inclined to be deep for a clump-forming pachymorph bamboo, giving a fairly wide spacing to the culms, although this is not always obvious, due to the congested foliage.

Culms Medium-tall and slender, 2 to 3 m (6 to 10 feet) tall and 6 mm to 2 cm (¼ to ¾ inch) in diameter. Dull midgreen at first, quickly ripening through dull yellowish green to almost light brownish ochre if grown in the open. Internodes completely solid with a pithy interior,

and fairly short. Nodes not prominent. Stiffly upright at first, with some outermost culms held stiffly at an angle to the perpendicular throughout. All older culms slowly developing an outward curve near the summit to become semi-scandent. New shoots appear mostly in early summer but also at other times of year when the weather is mild. **Culm sheaths** Semi-persistent. Grayish light green, soon becoming whitish green before fading. **Branches** Multiple. Very short and angled in all directions, extending two-thirds of the way around

Chusquea cumingii has prickly gray foliage and a distinctive branching habit.

the node. **Leaves** Very short and very narrow, less than 5 cm (2 inches) long by less than 1 cm (⅜ inch) wide. Narrow for their length. Light glaucous grayish green and slightly matte on the upper surface, matte grayish green on the lower surface, tapering to a sharp and prickly point at the tip. Hard-textured and tough, with very short pseudopetioles. **Rhizomes** Clump-forming (pachymorph). The rhizome necks are somewhat elongated, giving a rather open clump habit. **Cultivation** Sun or semi-shade. Best in an open position. **Hardiness** −5°C to −10°C (23°F to 14°F).

Chusquea gigantea

Synonyms *C. breviglumis, C.* aff. *culeou*
Native to Chile
Very tall bamboo—moderately invasive

A superb species for cool-temperate gardens, possibly the most magnificent bamboo that can be grown in such a climate. It may not be the largest or even the most elegant bamboo, but this species, when given enough space, makes a most imposing grove of straight, thick, widely spaced culms. It is too large a plant for the smaller urban garden, but when given a free run in a woodland or parkland setting, it has no equal.

The circumstances surrounding the introduction of this bamboo are somewhat vague, as is its exact identification. It was originally distributed from a nursery in Germany as *C. culeou*. Later, in cultivation at Stream Cottage, Peter Addington's old garden, we noticed that this plant was significantly different from *C. culeou*, due to its much larger dimensions and the long primary branch at each node. The late Gerald Bol, who had much experience with collecting *Chusquea* bamboos in the wild, thought that it might be the true species *C. breviglumis*, and this name stuck to the plant until the

French botanist Jean-Pierre Demoly renamed it *C. gigantea*. It is not within the scope of this book to investigate the finer arguments of what is the correct name for this bamboo. Suffice it to say that *breviglumis* is the name under which this plant is most often grown. It may yet prove to be the "most correct" name.

Culms Very tall and thick, 5 to 8 m (16 to 26 feet) tall and 3 to 5 cm (1¼ to 2 inches) in diameter. Easily attains the larger end of these di-

The magnificent grove of *Chusquea gigantea* at Stream Cottage, showing the strong upright habit and distinctive effect of the sheaths on the younger culms.

mensions. Bright green at first, rapidly maturing to dull yellowish green. Internodes completely solid with a pithy interior. Nodes moderately prominent. The habit is very upright and sturdy, with moderate arching on very old culms. New shoots usually appear in early spring onward but can appear at almost any other time of year, including winter if the weather is mild. **Culm sheaths** Semi-persistent. Usually remaining only for the first complete season, then pushed away by emerging branches. Pale reddish when emerging from the ground and very colorful, becoming greenish white with reddish streaks and margins, then turning whitish before fading. **Branches** Multiple. There is usually one primary branch present in each cluster, which may be very long and one-third as thick as its parent culm, with all the other branches much shorter. The zone of branch emergence can extend halfway to two-thirds of the way around the node. **Leaves** Medium-long and very narrow, 9 to 18 cm (3½ to 7 inches) long by less than 1 cm (⅜ inch) wide. Bright green on the upper surface and slightly glaucous, matte green on the lower surface, tapering to a slender point at the tip. Firm-textured and tough. **Rhizomes** Moderately invasive (pachymorph with extended neck). Makes an open grove where one can eventually walk between the culms. Rhizomes are very deep under the soil surface, sometimes 60 cm (2 feet) or more. **Cultivation** Sun or shade. This plant seems to thrive in open positions and tolerates high summer temperatures slightly better than *C. culeou*. Its deep rhizomes make it difficult to control in restricted spaces, so unless you are prepared for some effort-intensive digging each year, only plant it where there is adequate room for future expansion of the grove. Originally thought to be tender, it has proved surprisingly cold-tolerant. **Hardiness** −10°C to −20°C (14°F to −4°F).

Chusquea montana

Synonym *C. nigricans*
Native to Chile
Medium bamboo—clump-forming

A most attractive and easily recognized bamboo, useful in the garden for its vertical culms, which are thick for their height. Unfortunately, this bamboo has a highly confused nomenclature. In the United States, *C. nigricans* is an accepted synonym. However, there are seedlings of *C. culeou* in cultivation in both the United States and Europe falsely bearing the name *C. montana*; these can be identified by their lighter green leaves and unswollen nodes, and also by their culms, which do not develop the blackish purple coloration. There is a most attractive clone of American origin called *C. culeou* 'Caña Prieta', which is widespread in cultivation under the name *C. nigricans*, and which does develop darker culms.

The description below is based on a group of bamboos derived from seed collected by Fred Schlegel-Sachs in Chile from what is believed to be the true species. These plants are becoming mature and at least conform in broad characteristics to previously published descriptions of the correctly identified species in the wild, but of course, they may yet transpire to be merely another variant of *C. culeou*.

Culms Medium-tall and medium-thick, 2 to 3 m (6 to 10 feet) tall and 2 to 3 cm (¾ to 1¼ inches) in diameter. Light green at first, becoming strongly flushed blackish purple in the second year, particularly in strong light, and eventually ripening to darkish yellow-green. Internodes completely solid with a pithy interior, and fairly short. Nodes prominent, distinctly swollen. Upright and sturdy in habit unless grown in heavy shade, with only a slight arch developing in older culms. New shoots appear in early summer. **Culm sheaths** Semi-persistent. The tattered remains are finally pushed away by the emerging branches. Light green, becoming white before fading. **Branches** Multiple. Extremely short, with the zone of branch emergence often extending between halfway and two-thirds of the way around the node. **Leaves** Short and narrow, 5 to 9 cm (2 to 3½ inches) long by 1 to 1.5 cm (⅜ to ⅝ inch) wide. Narrow for their length. Deep dark green on the upper surface, with a dull shine, matte grayish dark green on the lower surface, acutely rounded at the base, tapering gradually to a fine point at the tip. **Rhizomes** Clump-forming (pachymorph). Makes a dense and tightly packed clump. **Cultivation** Sun or semi-shade. Seems to thrive in an open position, where a more attractive and upright habit will be produced. **Hardiness** –10°C to –20°C (14°F to –4°F).

Chusquea uliginosa

Native to Chile

Tall bamboo—clump-forming

This unusual but very attractive half-hardy species has a clambering, sprawling habit and is adapted to grow on the perimeter of seasonal wetlands in its native environment. It is more widely cultivated in the United States than in Europe. The arching culms with their whitened sheaths give the effect of a jumbled mass of greenery. A certain amount of judicious pruning may be needed to keep the plant to reasonable dimensions if grown in a limited area. In common with many other scandent or semi-scandent *Chusquea* bamboos, this species

Chusquea montana.

enjoys being grown in an open position, but is less tolerant of very dry conditions. It is noticeably more elegant than *C. valdiviensis.*

Culms Tall and slender, 3 to 5 m (10 to 16 feet) tall and 6 mm to 2 cm (¼ to ¾ inch) in diameter. Midgreen at first and slightly purple-tinted in sunlight, maturing to yellowish green. Internodes completely solid with a pithy interior. Nodes not prominent. Strongly arching in habit from an early age, with some culms reaching down to the ground unless support is available. New shoots appear in early summer or whenever the weather is warm and mild. **Culm sheaths** Semi-persistent. Light green, quickly fading to whitish green. **Branches** Multiple. Very short, angled in all directions but generally toward the highest incidence of available light, extending more than halfway around the node. **Leaves** Medium-long and narrow, 9 to 18 cm (3½ to 7 inches) long by 1 to 1.5 cm (⅜ to ⅝ inch) wide. Very variable but usually narrow for their length. Deep green and slightly lustrous on the upper surface, matte green on the lower surface, tapering to a fine point at the tip. Held in dense clusters. **Rhizomes** Clump-forming (pachymorph). Makes an impenetrable clump of only loosely circumscribed boundaries. **Cultivation** Sun or semi-shade. Seems to prefer a more open position. **Hardiness** −5°C to −10°C (23°F to 14°F). May withstand slightly lower temperatures when well established.

Chusquea valdiviensis

Synonym *C. ramosissima*
Native to Chile
Tall bamboo—clump-forming
This native of southern Chile is loosely scandent and tends to overwhelm surrounding vegetation. The extremely arching culms bend right to the ground and even root down in places if left undisturbed. Although very ornamental, it has a bramble-like habit of growth and is a very difficult bamboo to site in the garden. It is too tender to be grown outside in all but the mildest areas.

Culms Tall and medium-thick, 3 to 5 m (10 to 16 feet) tall and 2 to 3 cm (¾ to 1¼ inches) in diameter. Rich green, maturing to very pale yellowish green. Internodes of smaller culms are usually circular in cross section, with thicker culms showing a slight sulcus. Nodes mod-

The habit of *Chusquea valdiviensis* is distinctively arching, congested, and bramble-like.

erately prominent. More or less upright only briefly, then vigorously arching right over to the ground if there is no means of support. New shoots appear in early summer once the warmer weather has arrived. **Culm sheaths** Semi-persistent. Remaining until being pushed away by emerging branches. Greenish flushed with pale mauve, becoming whitish before fading. **Branches** Multiple. Fairly short and often angled backward to assist with supporting the culm when climbing into surrounding vegetation. There is usually a long primary branch at each node that can be almost as big as the mother culm, which in turn has a primary branch within each branch cluster at each node, giving rise to endless subdevelopments and a jungle-like mass of vegetation. **Leaves** Medium-long and narrow, 9 to 18 cm (3½ to 7 inches) long by 1 to 1.5 cm (⅜ to ⅝ inch) wide. Rich dark green on the upper surface, matte green on the lower surface, drawn out to a fine point at the tip. **Rhizomes** Clump-forming (pachymorph). Makes a dense, impenetrable clump. **Cultivation** Sun or shade. In its native environment this bamboo is something of a jungle-like weed, scrambling into trees and other vegetation to make an impenetrable thicket. Given a mild enough climate, it can do the same in cultivation, so beware. However, where it is cut back regularly each winter by frost, it is unlikely to ever resemble a wild specimen. To make the most of this remarkable species, choose a sheltered position and allow plenty of room for the very arching culms. **Hardiness** −5°C to −10°C (23°F to 14°F).

Drepanostachyum

A genus of tender bamboos from the high-altitude subtropical forest of the Himalaya. In their native environment, they often die down each year under the winter snows. When brought to lower altitudes with a sufficiently mild climate, they retain their culms through the winter.

Species of this genus can be identified by their circular, thin, arching culms bearing masses of elegant foliage, and by their extremely delicate appearance. They have multiple branches of more or less the same length, held in a fairly horizontal position, giving a distinctive tiered effect. The genus *Himalayacalamus* contains species once attributed to *Drepanostachyum*, but these can be distinguished by their fewer branches carried in a more upright formation.

Although able to withstand some frost, *Drepanostachyum* bamboos are still easily cut down by prolonged spells of cold weather. Plants that have been cut down in the winter will usually regrow quite vigorously the following summer, regaining about half their previous stature. *Drepanostachyum* species have an intolerance of very high summer temperatures. Additionally, like many other bamboos with delicate leaves that originate from high altitudes, the foliage curls up toward its midrib in response to exposure from strong sunlight. This does no harm to the plant but can make it appear as if it needs watering. To cultivate these bamboos successfully outdoors, a mild, shady, fairly frost-free environment is required.

Drepanostachyum falcatum

Synonym *Arundinaria falcata*
Native to Bhutan, Nepal, Sikkim, India
Tall bamboo—clump-forming

A bamboo of extreme elegance. The delicate, almost linear leaves are carried in fine masses on numerous branches emerging from the slender olive green culms. It is not very hardy but is nonetheless well worth growing for the foliage effect. Flowering seems to occur at fairly short intervals, though copious quantities of fertile seed are usually produced. This species has been much confused in cultivation with the hardier *Himalayacalamus falconeri*, which has broader leaves and culms that are a lighter green and less slender.

Culms Tall and slender, 3 to 5 m (10 to 16 feet) tall and 6 mm to 2 cm (¼ to ¾ inch) in diameter. Slender for the length of the culm. Deep rich green at first, developing a purple stain above and slightly below each node, the culm slowly maturing to brownish green. Nodes not prominent. The habit becomes gracefully arching with the development of the luxuriant foliage. New shoots appear in early summer. **Culm sheaths** Not persistent. Crimson-purple, striated and coarse, and slightly rough on the inner surface. The sheath blade and auricles are minute and almost imperceptible. **Branches** Multiple. Approximately the same length. Angled upright at first, becoming more horizontal with age. **Leaves** Medium-long and very narrow, 9 to 18 cm (3½ to 7 inches) long by less than 1 cm (⅜ inch) wide. Bright green on the upper surface, dull and slightly matte green on the lower surface, drawn out to a slender point at the tip. Extremely delicate in appearance and lacking any obvious tessellation. In winter the leaves tend to point downward. **Rhizomes** Clump-forming (pachymorph). Makes a tight, closely circumscribed clump. **Cultivation** Semi-shade or shade. Grows fairly well in open conditions, but the leaves curl readily in sunlight. Succumbs easily to cold and requires a very sheltered position outdoors. Much better growth will be achieved in a wind-free environment with some degree of shade and adequate moisture. Makes a superb container plant for the terrace or patio. **Hardiness** 0°C to −5°C (32°F to 23°F).

Drepanostachyum khasianum

Synonym *Arundinaria khasiana*
Native to Nepal, Bhutan, India
Tall bamboo—clump-forming

A delightful foliage bamboo with attractively colored mature culms. It will withstand a little frost and is seldom killed outright, even when cut down in the winter, and recovers vigorously the following summer. In general appearance it is very similar to *Himalayacalamus falconeri*; indeed, it is difficult to tell them apart when young. More mature plants of *D. khasianum* seem to have more branches and slightly smaller leaves. Also, the culms of *D. khasianum* usually have their purple stains more above the node, but still develop an orange-purple coloration similar to *H. falconeri*. Many plants grown in Western gardens under the name *D. khasianum* may well prove to be misnamed plants of *H. falconeri*.

Culms Tall and slender, 3 to 5 m (10 to 16 feet) tall and 6 mm to 2 cm (¼ to ¾ inch) in diameter. Light green at first, developing a purple stain above the node, the whole culm later becoming yellowish green and ripening in time to an attractive orange-purple. Nodes not prominent. Arches gracefully as the foliage develops. New shoots appear in early summer. **Culm sheaths** Not persistent. Crimson-green, with no obvious auricles and a very small blade. **Branches** Multiple. Angled upright at first, becoming more horizontal with age. **Leaves** Medium-long and narrow, 9 to 18 cm (3½ to 7 inches) long by 1 to 1.5 cm (⅜ to ⅝ inch) wide. Light green on the upper surface, matte light green on the lower surface, tapering quite abruptly to a point at the tip. Delicate in appearance and lacking obvious tessellation. **Rhizomes** Clump-forming (pachymorph). Makes a tight, closely circumscribed clump. **Cultivation** Semi-shade or shade. Requires a mild, shady, wind-free environment outdoors.

Makes a superb container plant for the terrace or patio. **Hardiness** −5°C to −10°C (23°F to 14°F).

Drepanostachyum microphyllum

Native to Bhutan, Nepal, India

Tall bamboo—clump-forming

An elegant foliage bamboo grown for its smaller leaves and purple-brown older culms. In most other respects it is very similar to *D. khasianum*. This is one of the very best bamboos for a large container, so long as it is not left outside during very cold weather.

Culms Tall and slender, 3 to 5 m (10 to 16 feet) tall and 6 mm to 2 cm (¼ to ¾ inch) in diameter. Deep green at first, becoming purplish green and finally suffused purple-brown. Nodes not prominent. The plant arches gracefully as the foliage develops. New shoots appear in early summer. **Culm sheaths** Not persistent. Purple-green, with no obvious auricles and a very small blade. **Branches** Multiple. Angled upright at first, becoming more horizontal with age. **Leaves** Short and very narrow, 5 to 9 cm (2 to 3½ inches) long by less than 1 cm (⅜ inch) wide. Slightly grayish bright green on the upper surface, dull green on the lower surface, tapering fairly abruptly to a point at the tip. Lacks any obvious tessellation. **Rhizomes** Clump-forming (pachymorph). Makes a tight, closely circumscribed clump. **Cultivation** Semi-shade or shade. Can be grown in a more open position but much prefers a mild, shady, wind-free environment outdoors. Makes a superb container plant for the terrace or patio. **Hardiness** −5°C to −10°C (23°F to 14°F).

Drepanostachyum scandens

Native to China

Tall bamboo—clump-forming

An interesting recent introduction with a bramble-like growth habit similar to *Chusquea valdiviensis*. It is worth growing for the very attractive foliage and conspicuous oral setae on the leaf sheaths. The scandent, heavily arching habit does make this bamboo difficult to site in the garden, but it is proving to be fairly hardy, at least in southern England.

Culms Tall and slender, 3 to 5 m (10 to 16 feet) tall and 6 mm to 2 cm (¼ to ¾ inch) in diameter. Light green and covered with a persistent, slight grayish powdery bloom at first, the bloom eventually disappearing as the culm matures to yellowish olive green. Nodes not prominent. Arching, leaning, and scrambling onto any surrounding support or other vege-

Drepanostachyum scandens.

tation from an early age, or else arching over to the ground. New shoots appear in early to midsummer and often also in late summer. **Culm sheaths** Not persistent. Pale green and tinted dark red on the sunny side, with prominent oral setae. **Branches** Multiple. Fairly short and angled in all directions, giving the effect of barbed wire. **Leaves** Medium-long and medium-broad, 9 to 18 cm (3½ to 7 inches) long by 1.5 to 3 cm (⅝ to 1¼ inches) wide. Very variable. Rich green and lustrous on the upper surface, matte green on the lower surface, tapering to a long and sharp point at the tip. Hard-textured for the genus and having conspicuous pinkish purple oral setae on the leaf sheaths. **Rhizomes** Clump-forming (pachymorph). Makes a dense and congested clump. **Cultivation** Sun or shade. Seems to thrive in most positions but makes a better habit in the open. **Hardiness** −5°C to −10°C (23°F to 14°F).

Fargesia

An important, large genus of bamboos from central China and the Himalaya. They occur naturally over a large area and usually at higher altitudes between 1000 and 4000 m (3300 and 13,000 feet). Members of this genus usually have slender, circular, arching culms and a dense, clumping habit. The culms usually have four to six main branches initially, later surrounded by ten or more shorter branches, which characteristically emerge upright to the culm and then bend outward at about a 45-degree angle. Most species have small leaves that are often more robust than those of other high-altitude genera such as *Drepanostachyum*, *Himalayacalamus*, and *Thamnocalamus*.

This genus provides some of the most useful and ornamental bamboos in cultivation. Most species grow to a height of less than 5 m (16 feet), and there are several dwarfer species

and variants. Some of the hardiest bamboos in cultivation are found here, making *Fargesia* species ideal subjects for colder gardens or for growing in containers to be left outside during severe winter weather. They are ideal subjects for shade, where their full beauty may best be appreciated.

There is much interest in this genus, both from the world of taxonomy, where *Fargesia* is under review, and from the world of gardening, with many new species being introduced from the wild. Many of the newer introductions are proving to be excellent garden plants, although some are not so reliably hardy as the more established species.

Fargesia denudata

Native to China

Tall bamboo—clump-forming

Introduced by Roy Lancaster in the early 1990s. This makes a fine clump of gracefully arching, slender culms, bearing bluntly pointed leaves that are shorter than those of most other bamboos of the genus. The foliage effect is somewhat sparse and less luxuriant compared with other *Fargesia* species, but this is in no way to this plant's detriment. A good species for small gardens.

Culms Tall and slender, 3 to 5 m (10 to 16 feet) tall and 6 mm to 2 cm (¼ to ¾ inch) in diameter. Slender for their height. Bright green at first, with a slight gray powdery bloom, quickly ripening to yellowish green. Nodes not prominent. Fairly upright in habit at first, then arching gracefully with the development of the foliage. New shoots appear in late spring. **Culm sheaths** Semi-persistent. Usually retained for the first season. Pale green and lacking any obvious auricles or blade. **Branches** Multiple. Initially four or five but quickly joined by numerous shorter branches alongside. **Leaves** Short and narrow, 5 to 9 cm (2 to 3½ inches) long by 1 to 1.5 cm (⅜ to ⅝ inch) wide. Broad for their length. Rich green and glossy on the upper surface, dull grayish green on the lower surface, tapering quickly from before midlength to a point at the tip, giving a shortened effect. The leaves are held to the same angle to the twigs that bear them and often overlap. **Rhizomes** Clump-forming (pachymorph). Makes a dense, closely circum-scribed clump when young but can be more open in maturity. **Cultivation** Sun or shade. Although very cold-tolerant, it can suffer some damage to the foliage from exposure to cold winds and therefore benefits from a sheltered position in the garden. **Hardiness** Below –20°C (–4°F).

Fargesia dracocephala

Native to China

Medium bamboo—clump-forming

An introduction by Max Riedelsheimer from collected seed. Its name means "dragon's head," and it is very similar to *F. murielae*, though shorter. Dense, leafy clumps are produced, the culms distinctively bending outward from about halfway up their length, and sometimes straightening up again, giving a rather vase-like habit. The seedling clones in cultivation vary slightly in terms of their culm coloration; some have a wine-purple tinting in their upper parts, while others are more yellowish green.

Culms Medium-tall and slender, 2 to 3 m (6

Fargesia denudata in heavy shade photographed using flash.

to 10 feet) tall and 6 mm to 2 cm (¼ to ¾ inch) in diameter. Typically seen at the lower end of these dimensions. Midgreen at first, with a light dusting of gray powder, quickly ripening to a dull yellowish green, some clones becoming wine-purple in their upper parts. Nodes not prominent. Rather vase-shaped in habit, with outer culms often emerging at an angle to become more upright and then arching moderately near the summit. New shoots appear in spring. **Culm sheaths** Semi-persistent. Usually retained for the first season. Ranging from pale green to greenish purple, depending on the clonal variation. **Branches** Multiple. Initially four or five main branches but gradually joined and surrounded by ten or more shorter branches. **Leaves** Short and narrow, 5 to 9 cm (2 to 3½ inches) long by 1 to 1.5 cm (⅜ to ⅝ inch) wide. Sometimes slightly longer than these dimensions. Dark, slightly matte green on the upper surface, dull grayish green on the lower surface, not as bluntly rounded at the base as with most other bamboos, tapering quickly to a point at the tip. **Rhizomes** Clump-forming (pachymorph). Makes a dense clump that can become more open in maturity or if grown in heavy shade. **Cultivation** Sun or shade. Can be grown in sunlight with minimal curling of the foliage except perhaps in midsummer. Among the best bamboos for use as a shorter to medium-sized hedge or screen. **Hardiness** Below −20°C (−4°F).

Fargesia dracocephala.

Fargesia ferax

Native to China

Tall bamboo—clump-forming

A recently introduced species of great horticultural merit, producing a wonderful foliage effect. It is distinctive for its rather narrow and elegantly drooping leaves and grayish white young culms. There is a tendency for the foliage to be somewhat deciduous in hard winters, and this, along with characteristics such as the faint ridges present on the culms, invites speculation that this bamboo may prove to be a species of *Borinda*. I have only very small and immature plants available to describe, so please take all main dimensions and colors as a guide only.

Culms Tall and slender, 3 to 5 m (10 to 16 feet) tall and 6 mm to 2 cm (¼ to ¾ inch) in diameter. Light green and covered in a grayish light powdery bloom at first, ripening to yellowish green. Internodes bearing perceptible longitudinal ridges. Nodes not prominent. Fairly upright in habit when young but soon developing a graceful arch under the weight of increasing foliage. New shoots appear in early summer. **Culm sheaths** Not persistent. Light green, spotted and flecked with purple-brown. Covered in stiff brownish hairs on the outer surface. **Branches** Multiple. Five to seven main branches in the first year, with the outermost two slightly angled behind the culm. **Leaves** Medium-long and very narrow, 9 to 18 cm (3½ to 7 inches) long by less than 1 cm (⅜ inch) wide. Rich green on the upper surface, slightly grayish matte green on the lower surface, tapering to a slender point at the tip. Rather delicate-looking and inclined to droop from before midlength. **Rhizomes** Clump-forming (pachymorph). Makes a dense clump. **Cultivation** Sun or shade. Seems to thrive in most positions. **Hardiness** −10°C to −20°C (14°F to −4°F).

Fargesia murielae

Synonyms *Arundinaria murielae, Sinarundinaria murielae, Thamnocalamus spathaceus*

Native to China

Tall bamboo—clump-forming

A long-cultivated species, introduced to the United States by Ernest Wilson in 1907 and brought to the Royal Botanic Gardens, Kew, for propagation in 1913. Until it started flowering in the late 1970s, *F. murielae* was probably the second most widely cultivated bamboo in European gardens, after *Pseudosasa japonica*. All the plants in cultivation derived from that original introduction and more or less came into flower together, giving rise to vast numbers of seedlings. From these seedlings, many forms have arisen, notably 'Jumbo', which has broader leaves and is slightly smaller in stature, and 'Simba', which has slightly lighter green leaves and is smaller in stature. This species is of very easy cultivation and is ideal for the novice. It is very tough and adaptable and has many uses in the garden.

Culms Tall and slender, 3 to 5 m (10 to 16 feet) tall and 6 mm to 2 cm (¼ to ¾ inch) in diameter. Fairly slender for their length. Pale green at first, with a slight gray powdery bloom, quickly ripening to rich yellowish green. Nodes not prominent. Upright in habit at first, quickly developing a gentle arch with the weight of the foliage. New shoots appear in spring. **Culm sheaths** Semi-persistent. Usually retained for the first season. Pale green becoming creamy green before fading. **Branches** Multiple. Usually four or five at first, with further developments of shorter branches alongside as the culm ages. **Leaves** Short and narrow, 5 to 9 cm (2 to 3½ inches) long by 1 to 1.5 cm (⅜ to ⅝ inch) wide. Very light green on the upper surface becoming slightly glossy with age, dull grayish green on the lower surface,

A graceful mature clump of *Fargesia murielae* at Stream Cottage. This plant has since flowered and died.

tapering quickly to a point at the tip. **Rhizomes** Clump-forming (pachymorph). Makes a dense, tightly packed clump, becoming slightly more open if grown in heavy shade. **Cultivation** Sun or shade. Can be grown in any position, but the leaves curl readily in strong sunlight. Among the best bamboos for very cold, exposed gardens. Possibly the best bamboo for use as a tall hedge or screen. **Hardiness** Below −20°C (−4°F).

Fargesia nitida

Synonyms *Arundinaria nitida*, *Sinarundinaria nitida*

Native to China

Tall bamboo—clump-forming

Another long-cultivated species, introduced to England in 1889 from seed by Messrs. Veitch of Exeter, and named by Algernon Bertram Freeman-Mitford. Although delicate in appearance, it is surprisingly tough and hardy, well able to withstand severe winters and wind exposure. The very slender culms arch in a most elegant fashion, borne down by the myriads of small, rather grayish green leaves. This is one of the best bamboos for growing in shade and will live happily under the canopies of deciduous trees. Very old clumps have a distinct mushroom-shaped appearance. *Fargesia nitida* has been frequently confused with *F. murielae* in cultivation, but that species has much lighter colors in the leaf and culm. It is of equally easy cultivation.

There are a number of clones in cultivation arising from the original seed, of which several have been named. Two of the most distinct are 'Eisenach', which has a smaller stature and smaller leaves, and 'Nymphenburg', which has longer, narrower leaves. 'Juizhaigou', a newly introduced clone, has very reddish culms if grown in sunlight. Many older clones of *F. nitida* have flowered since about 1990.

Culms Tall and slender, 3 to 5 m (10 to 16 feet) tall and 6 mm to 2 cm (¼ to ¾ inch) in diameter. Deep green at first, with a powdery gray bloom that persists longer if the plant is grown in shade, becoming purple-flushed, particularly in sunlight, very slender and whiplike. Nodes not prominent. Upright at first, becoming very arched with the weight of the foliage. New shoots appear in early spring. **Culm sheaths** Semi-persistent. Usually retained for the first season. Purple-green, lacking auricles. **Branches** Multiple. Usually devoid of branches in the first season, then with four or five main branches, and later with shorter branches developing alongside. **Leaves** Short and very narrow, 5 to 9 cm (2 to 3½ inches) long by less than 1 cm (⅜ inch) wide. Variable between seedling clones. Dark, slightly matte, rather grayish green on the upper surface, matte gray-green on the lower surface, tapering abruptly

A young clump of *Fargesia nitida*. There are many seedling clones in cultivation, and this is a particularly robust and strong-growing form.

to a point at the tip. **Rhizomes** Clump-forming (pachymorph). Initially makes a closely circumscribed clump but tends to become more open with age. **Cultivation** Semi-shade or shade. Among the best bamboos for growing in shade under deciduous trees. It will tolerate full sun, but the leaves curl up very readily. Can be used as a hedge or windbreak because it is very tough, despite its delicate appearance. **Hardiness** Below −20°C (−4°F).

Fargesia robusta

Native to China

Tall bamboo—clump-forming

This magnificent introduction has very glossy culms and foliage, giving an impression of intense greenness. Its name is very apt, for this species stands up to exposure remarkably well, retaining its foliage almost intact through the winter months. As a mature plant, it is often slightly taller than most other *Fargesia* bamboos in cultivation. The cultivar known variously as 'Ming Yunnan' (a name first published in my 1997 nursery catalog) and 'Red Sheath' has slightly but distinctly broader leaves and distinct reddish culms and branch sheaths; it will probably be found, after further investigation, to be more closely related to *F. rufa*. *Fargesia robusta* 'Wolong' is very similar but has slightly bigger leaves still.

Culms Tall and slender, 3 to 5 m (10 to 16 feet) tall and 6 mm to 2 cm (¼ to ¾ inch) in diameter. Very rich, deep green and slightly glossy at first, maturing to a glossy, rich yellowish green. Nodes not prominent. Very upright in habit at first, becoming moderately arched with the weight of increasing foliage. The new shoots are produced prolifically in flushes; they are often the first shoots to appear in the bamboo garden, sometimes as early as late winter, and are an attractive feature of the plant. **Culm sheaths** Semi-persistent. Usually retained until the end of summer. Brownish mottled green and covered with stiff hairs as the culms emerge from the ground, later becoming intense pale green, then creamy white. **Branches** Multiple. Four or five branches initially, later becoming slowly surrounded by ten or so shorter branches. **Leaves** Medium-long and narrow, 9 to 18 cm (3½ to 7 inches) long by 1 to 1.5 cm (⅜ to ⅝ inch) wide. Rich, dark green and glossy on the upper surface, dull grayish green on the lower surface, fairly parallel-sided, tapering to a long point at the tip. **Rhizomes** Clump-forming (pachymorph). Makes an impenetrable clump at first due to the large numbers of new shoots produced each year. Can become considerably more open in maturity or if grown in shade. **Cultivation** Sun or shade. Since its robust leaves will take full sun without curling, this species can be grown successfully in a wide range of locations. It also seems to tolerate drought slightly better than most *Fargesia* bamboos. Ideal for use as hedges, screens, and windbreaks. **Hardiness** Below −20°C (−4°F).

A young clump of *Fargesia robusta* in my garden.

Fargesia rufa

Native to China

Short bamboo—clump-forming

This bamboo was introduced in the mid-1990s and promises to become very popular. Its ultimate height is not yet known, but it shows signs of being fairly dwarf. In general appearance it is rather like a scaled-down *F. robusta*, smaller in culm and foliage. Both the culms and their branches have conspicuous reddish sheaths.

Culms Short and very slender, 1 to 2 m (3 to 6 feet) tall and up to 6 mm (¼ inch) in diameter. Bright green and slightly glossy at first, becoming yellowish green and glossy. Nodes not prominent. Fairly upright when young, developing a moderate arch in later years. Very im-

mature plants will be arched from near the base. New shoots can appear very early, often from the end of winter. **Culm sheaths** Semi-persistent. Usually falling before the end of summer but retained longer on the branches. Distinctly reddish, retaining color for a time even after becoming dry. **Branches** Multiple. Usually four or five at first, becoming more multiple as the culm ages. The branch sheaths have the same reddish color as the culm sheaths. **Leaves** Short and very narrow, 5 to 9 cm (2 to 3½ inches) long by less than 1 cm (⅜ inch) wide. Glossy, rich green on the upper surface, dull gray-green on the lower surface, tapering gradually to a long point at the tip. **Rhi-**

Fargesia rufa.

zomes Clump-forming (pachymorph). Makes a fairly open clump considering the rhizome type and plant height. It is common to see the rhizomes at or even above the soil surface. **Cultivation** Sun or shade. The leaves will tolerate full sun without curling. Happily grows almost anywhere and makes a fine subject for container growing on a patio or terrace in full sun. Can also be used to make an attractive low hedge. **Hardiness** Below –20°C (–4°F).

Fargesia scabrida

Native to China

Medium bamboo—clump-forming

A first-class new introduction, immediately recognizable for its slender but rigid dark culms with their orange sheaths, and for its darker and elegantly shaped leaves. *Fargesia scabrida* looks a bit like *F. rufa* or a more elegant *F. dracocephala*, two species with which it may be superficially confused, but it is far better looking. A sought-after bamboo destined to become very popular.

Culms Medium-tall and very slender, 2 to 3 m (6 to 10 feet) tall and up to 6 mm (¼ inch) in diameter. Tending toward the upper end of these dimensions. Midgreen and with a faint gray bloom at first, quickly developing a persistent, almost blackish purple coloration with any exposure to sunlight, and eventually ripening to deep yellowish green. Nodes not prominent. Fairly upright in habit when young, developing a moderate arch with age. New shoots appear in spring. **Culm sheaths** Semi-persistent. Light green tinted with light orange, quickly developing a lasting rich orange-red coloration. **Branches** Multiple. Usually five main branches in the first year, with the outermost two slightly angled behind the culm. **Leaves** Short and narrow, 5 to 9 cm (2 to 3½ inches) long by 1 to 1.5 cm (⅜ to ⅝ inch)

wide. Tending toward the upper end of these dimensions. Deep, rather dark green on the upper surface, slightly lustrous grayish matte green on the lower surface, acutely rounded at the base, tapering to a slender point at the tip. Fairly hard-textured and tough. **Rhizomes** Clump-forming (pachymorph). Makes a dense and closely circumscribed clump. **Cultivation** Sun or shade. Seems to be very adaptable to a wide range of situations, but best in an open position. **Hardiness** –10°C to –20°C (14°F to –4°F).

Fargesia scabrida.

Fargesia utilis

Native to China

Tall bamboo—clump-forming

Perhaps the most imposing *Fargesia* bamboo in cultivation, this vigorous species can become too large for small urban gardens. The culms are thick compared with most *Fargesia* species, and within their first year begin to arch heavily, in time reaching almost to the ground. This habit is ideal near water or where space permits, but can swamp other plants growing alongside or underneath. The foliage closely resembles that of *F. nitida*, with which this species can be confused as a very young plant.

Culms Tall and medium-thick, 3 to 5 m (10 to 16 feet) tall and 2 to 3 cm (¾ to 1¼ inches) in diameter. Pale green at first with a light and very temporary dusting of gray powder, becoming purple-flushed in the upper parts when in sunlight. Nodes not prominent. Emerging from the ground often at an angle and soon arching heavily to become cascading by the second year. New shoots appear in spring. **Culm sheaths** Persistent. Lasting for at least the first season and often persistent at the culm bases for much longer. Pale green becoming creamy green. **Branches** Multiple. Usually four or five quite strong branches, often attaining con-

The older culms of *Fargesia utilis* can arch right to the ground, making this species one of the best bamboos for a cascading habit.

siderable length for a fargesia, becoming surrounded by several shorter branches. **Leaves** Short and narrow, 5 to 9 cm (2 to 3½ inches) long by 1 to 1.5 cm (⅜ to ⅝ inch) wide. Very variable within the plant. Rather dull grayish green on the upper surface, matte grayish green on the lower surface, tapering abruptly to a sharp point at the tip. **Rhizomes** Clumpforming (pachymorph). Despite the stoutness of the culms, retains a fairly closely circumscribed clumping habit. **Cultivation** Sun or shade. The leaves curl moderately in strong sunlight. A fine specimen plant where the overhang is acceptable. Always seen at its best cascading over water. **Hardiness** Below −20°C (−4°F).

×*Hibanobambusa*

A naturally occurring bigeneric hybrid bamboo thought to have originated when *Phyllostachys nigra* 'Henonis' and *Sasa veitchii* f. *tyugokensis* flowered simultaneously in the same locality. The leaves are large and resemble those of the *Sasa* parent, while the culms have a discernable sulcus and resemble those of the *Phyllostachys* parent. ×*Hibanobambusa* bamboos make attractive garden plants, keeping their foliage in fresh condition through the winter months, and have a useful medium-sized habit in cool-temperate conditions.

×*Hibanobambusa tranquillans*

Synonyms ×*Phyllosasa tranquillans*, *Phyllostachys tranquillans*

Native to Japan

Tall bamboo—invasive

Perhaps the most handsome bamboo in cultivation for a large-leaved effect. It is a better bamboo in this respect than *Sasa palmata* 'Nebulosa' and is less invasive. Both the foliage and the culms are an attractive dark green, making a good background or contrast to colored or variegated bamboos. It is relatively slow to put on height and with occasional cutting out of bigger culms can be used as an understory plant with taller bamboos.

Culms Tall and slender, 3 to 5 m (10 to 16 feet) tall and 6 mm to 2 cm (¼ to ¾ inch) in diameter. Tending toward the larger end of these dimensions. Culms are a shining dark green, retaining this color well as they age, but eventually ripening to dull yellowish green. Internodes with a clearly recognizable sulcus where branch buds are present. Nodes moderately prominent. Culms often emerge from the ground in a curve, then straighten to be-

×*Hibanobambusa tranquillans*.

come almost upright, with an occasional slight curve or zigzag, to then become very upright. Older culms develop a lean or a moderate arch under the weight of heavy foliage. New shoots appear in late spring. **Culm sheaths** Not persistent. Faintly purple-flushed when emerging from the ground, quickly becoming green, and coarsely striated on the outer surface. Has a small, linear sheath blade. **Branches** In pairs. Rather stout-looking for the diameter of the culm and of unequal size, fairly long and soon arching downward with the weight of the large leaves. **Leaves** Long and broad, 18 to 25 cm (7 to 10 inches) long by 3 to 6 cm (1¼ to 2½ inches) wide. Terminal leaves can be distinctly broader. Dark green and shining on the upper surface, matte grayish green on the lower surface, obtusely rounded at the base, tapering from midlength to a drawn-out tip. When young, the leaf sheaths have conspicuous, long oral setae. **Rhizomes** Invasive (leptomorph). Less invasive than *Sasa* and thus more suitable for small urban gardens. **Cultivation** Sun or shade. Very tough and durable, and able to withstand strong wind better than most large-leaved bamboos. Happily grows in a wide range of locations, including under deciduous trees. **Hardiness** Below −20°C (−4°F).

×*Hibanobambusa tranquillans* 'Shiroshima'

Tall bamboo—invasive

Differs from the species by having white-variegated leaves and a slightly smaller stature. It is among the most spectacular variegated bamboos, at its brightest in early summer when new growth appears, and when standing out strongly against any darker background. The new leaves are very colorful, often more white than green. The plant is slightly smaller than ×*H. tranquillans*, although the difference is not great, but it compensates for this with much more active rhizomes. This cultivar is probably too invasive for very small gardens, where it is best confined to a big container.

Culms Slightly smaller than those of the species. **Culm sheaths** Purple-tinted when emerging from the ground, becoming green with varying amounts of white striping. **Leaves** Often slightly less broad for their length than the leaves of ×*H. tranquillans*. Dark shining green with variable amounts of conspicuous white striping and bands on the upper surface,

The variegations of ×*Hibanobambusa tranquillans* 'Shiroshima' are always brighter and more reliable when the plant is grown in an open position.

the white parts of the leaf often pink-tinted when young, the colors appearing dull and grayish matte on the lower surface. All variegations becoming slightly less intense and more creamy white as the season progresses. **Rhizomes** In good growing conditions, inclined to spread more rapidly than ×*H. tranquillans*. **Cultivation** Sun or semi-shade. The variegated effect is considerably better when the plant is grown in a more open position.

Himalayacalamus

Various species once included under the genus *Drepanostachyum* are now listed here. Although very similar to *Drepanostachyum* bamboos, members of the genus *Himalayacalamus* differ in the formation of the branch complement, which develops more gradually and more upright to the culm, and which extends less far around the circumference of the culm. The culm sheaths are smooth and glossy inside, whereas those of *Drepanostachyum* are slightly rough inside. All *Himalayacalamus* species in cultivation lack obvious tessellation in the leaves and are not very hardy, withstanding only a few degrees of frost before being cut back. In common with *Drepanostachyum* bamboos, the leaves have a very delicate appearance and curl up readily if exposed to strong sunlight. A mild, sheltered position is needed for satisfactory cultivation.

Himalayacalamus falconeri

Synonyms *Arundinaria falconeri, A. nobilis, Drepanostachyum falconeri*
Native to Bhutan, Nepal, Sikkim, India
Tall bamboo—clump-forming

A bamboo of exceptional elegance for foliage effect. It forms dense clumps of arching, very thin-walled culms bearing multitudes of delicate light green leaves. This species is distinct from others in the genus because of its peculiar jelly-like secretions on the new shoots. It was introduced in 1847 from seed sent to the Royal Botanic Gardens, Kew, by Colonel Madden. Plants were later distributed across Europe and elsewhere. This species seems to come into flower at fairly regular intervals of about 30 years, with the most recent flowering having occurred in Britain and other parts of Europe in the early 1990s. On each occasion, copious quantities of seed have been produced to continue the species in cultivation.

Culms Tall and slender, 3 to 5 m (10 to 16 feet) tall and 6 mm to 2 cm (¼ to ¾ inch) in diameter. Bright green at first, with a slowly developing purple stain at the nodes, maturing to yellowish green and finally to an attractive orange-purple. Nodes not prominent. Very upright at first, then arching heavily with the weight of the foliage. New shoots appear in early summer, often coated at the tip with a jelly-like secretion. **Culm sheaths** Not persistent. Crimson-green becoming green and lacking auricles and oral setae. **Branches** Multiple. Angled upright at first, becoming more horizontal with age. **Leaves** Medium-long and narrow, 9 to 18 cm (3½ to 7 inches) long by 1 to 1.5 cm (⅜ to ⅝ inch) wide. Light green on the upper surface, matte light green on the lower surface, tapering fairly abruptly to a point at the tip. Delicate in appearance and lacking any obvious tessellation. **Rhizomes** Clump-forming (pachymorph). Makes a tight, closely circumscribed clump. **Cultivation** Semi-shade or shade. Requires a mild, shady, wind-free environment outdoors. Makes an impressive container plant for the patio or terrace. **Hardiness** −5°C to −10°C (23°F to 14°F).

Himalayacalamus falconeri is the perfect bamboo for a woodland garden in a mild climate.

The culms of *Himalayacalamus falconeri* 'Damarapa' can develop an intense red coloration when exposed to strong sunlight.

Himalayacalamus falconeri 'Damarapa'

Synonyms *Arundinaria hookeriana*, *Drepanostachyum hookerianum*

Tall bamboo—clump-forming

Differs from the species by having green culms with variable yellow striping. This distinctive and colorful bamboo was once regarded as a separate species and named *Arundinaria hookeriana*, which must now be considered a synonym. Where it occurs naturally, *H. falconeri* 'Damarapa' is known as *praong*.

Culms Bright green with stripes and panels of light yellow, which vary in width and may sometimes be almost absent. When exposed to sunlight the yellow parts of the culm turn deep red for at least the first season, and often for several seasons, later becoming golden yellow. This cultivar often sends up further shoots very late in the season. **Leaves** Occasionally, sometimes frequently, a thin creamy white stripe may be found on a leaf here and there. **Cultivation** Sun or semi-shade. Needs a sheltered, wind-free location outdoors with some exposure to direct sunlight so as to develop the red coloring on the culms.

Himalayacalamus hookerianus is known
as the blue bamboo because of its
distinctively colored younger culms.

Himalayacalamus hookerianus

Native to Bhutan, Nepal, Sikkim, India

Tall bamboo—clump-forming

Commonly known as the blue bamboo. This attractive and unusual species has been in cultivation for some time at the Royal Botanic Garden Edinburgh and Royal Botanic Gardens, Kew, where due to its most recent flowering it has been correctly identified. The seed produced has been distributed, enabling this wonderful bamboo to become more widely grown, although it is still not widespread in cultivation. The common name refers to the bluish coloration of the young culms. Unfortunately, it is not very hardy and can only be grown outside in very favored localities.

Culms Tall and slender, 3 to 5 m (10 to 16 feet) tall and 6 mm to 2 cm (¼ to ¾ inch) in diameter. Rich green at first, copiously covered in thick, waxy gray powder and becoming temporarily flushed dark purple, giving a grayish blue effect, maturing to yellowish orange. Nodes moderately prominent. Fairly upright at first, quickly becoming gracefully arching under the weight of the foliage. New shoots appear in early summer. **Culm sheaths** Not persistent. Deep green slightly flushed with purple, very long and tapering to end in a minute narrow blade, lacking auricles and oral setae. **Branches** Multiple. Sometimes flushed purple where older culms have been exposed to sunlight. **Leaves** Medium-long and narrow, 9 to 18 cm (3½ to 7 inches) long by 1 to 1.5 cm (⅜ to ⅝ inch) wide. Bright green on the upper surface, dull green on the lower surface, tapering to a narrow point at the tip. **Rhizomes** Clump-forming (pachymorph). Makes a fairly closely circumscribed clump, becoming more open in maturity. **Cultivation** Sun or semi-shade. The blue coloration seems to be more pronounced when this bamboo is planted in an open position, although sunlight causes the leaves to curl. Requires a sheltered, wind-free, almost frost-free location outdoors; otherwise makes a superb specimen for a large container to be taken inside in winter. **Hardiness** 0°C to −5°C (32°F to 23°F).

Indocalamus

A genus of leafy, mostly low-growing bamboos once ascribed to *Sasa* but differing from members of that genus by their usually longer leaves and less swollen nodes. Some species in cultivation have very large leaves indeed, and some shorter forms make excellent tall groundcovers. Their leaves are often a slightly lighter shade of green than those of *Sasa* species and are retained through winter in fresher condition. While very invasive, they are very slightly less so than *Sasa* bamboos when grown in cool-temperate climates.

Indocalamus hamadae

Native to China

Medium bamboo—very invasive

Not always the most garden-worthy bamboo because of the rather lax habit and slightly withered foliage in winter. This species is grown primarily for the size of the leaves, which are possibly the largest of any cultivated bamboo. When grown lushly, it can sometimes produce leaves up to 50 cm (1⅝ feet) long and 10 cm (4 inches) wide.

Culms Medium-tall and slender, 2 to 3 m (6 to 10 feet) tall and 6 mm to 2 cm (¼ to ¾ inch) in diameter. Usually seen at the lower end of these dimensions. Dull olive green at first, becoming slowly dull yellowish green with age. Nodes not prominent. Arching moderately from an early age with the weight of the enor-

The enormous leaves of *Indocalamus hamadae*. The snail on the left part of the main leaf is 1 cm (⅜ inch) in diameter.

mous leaves, with older culms becoming very lax. New shoots appear in late spring. **Culm sheaths** Persistent. Often very persistent on the culm branches. Purple-tinted at first, becoming greenish. **Branches** Solitary. Most larger culms have one main branch that is sometimes accompanied by two or three smaller branches. **Leaves** Very long and very broad, more than 25 cm (10 inches) long by more than 6 cm (2½ inches) wide. Can be up to twice these dimensions. Rich green with a dull shine and distinct longitudinal ridges on the upper surface, dull grayish green on the lower surface, tapering gradually to a point at the tip, which can wither during winter. Tough and leathery in appearance. **Rhizomes** Very invasive (strongly leptomorph). Spreads rapidly even in poor growing conditions. **Cultivation** Sun or shade. Although this bamboo is quite happy in an open position, where it will have a more erect habit, it produces its biggest leaves when grown in lush conditions with some shade. **Hardiness** –10°C to –20°C (14°F to –4°F).

Indocalamus latifolius

Native to China

Medium bamboo—very invasive

If grown well, this species has architectural proportions and imparts a tropical effect to the garden. Although slightly smaller in all parts than *I. hamadae*, it is a superior species. The leaves do not quite reach the length of *I. hamadae* but are often nearly as broad. The habit is much more erect, and the leaves are usually retained through winter in better condition.

Culms Medium-tall and slender, 2 to 3 m (6 to 10 feet) tall and 6 mm to 2 cm (¼ to ¾ inch) in diameter. Usually seen at the lower end of these dimensions. Dull olive green, becoming slowly yellowish green. Nodes not prominent. Upright in habit despite the weight of the foliage, and only slowly developing a moderate arch in later seasons. New shoots appear in late spring. **Culm sheaths** Persistent. Reddish purple when first emerging from the ground, becoming green. **Branches** Solitary. Stout for the size of the culm, sometimes accompanied by one or more shorter branches. **Leaves** Very long and very broad, more than 25 cm (10 inches) long by more than 6 cm (2½ inches) wide. Can be up to twice this width. Rich green with a dull shine and slight longitudinal ridges on the upper surface, dull grayish green on the

This commercially grown specimen of *Indocalamus latifolius*, seen in a nursery in Germany, well demonstrates the more upright habit and broader leaves typical of this species.

lower surface, obtusely tapered at the base, tapering fairly abruptly at the tip. Most leaves are broad for their length compared with other species in the genus. **Rhizomes** Very invasive (strongly leptomorph). Spreads rapidly once established. **Cultivation** Sun or shade. Quite happy in a wide range of situations but will produce bigger leaves when grown in lush conditions or where some shade is present. **Hardiness** −10°C to −20°C (14°F to −4°F).

Indocalamus longiauritus

Native to China

Short bamboo—very invasive

A reasonably garden-worthy species that is uncommon in cultivation. In general appearance it is similar to *I. tessellatus*, with which it is most likely to be confused. The name *longiauritus* refers to the elongated auricles found on the culm sheath. However, it is easier to identify this species by its inferior leaves, which are a slightly less rich green and often shorter than those of *I. tessellatus*, and are kept through winter in less pristine condition. In cool-temperate climates *I. longiauritus* seems reluctant to reach any great height compared with other members of the genus.

Culms Short and very slender, 1 to 2 m (3 to 6 feet) tall and up to 6 mm (¼ inch) in diameter. Dull grayish olive green becoming slowly yellowish green. Nodes not prominent. Arches slightly with the weight of the foliage as the culm ages. New shoots appear in late spring. **Culm sheaths** Persistent. Green slightly flushed with purple when young, becoming green. Its elongated auricles distinguish it from

Indocalamus longiauritus.

other members of the genus. **Branches** Solitary. Often later accompanied by one or two shorter branches. **Leaves** Very long and very broad, more than 25 cm (10 inches) long by more than 6 cm (2½ inches) wide. Long for their breadth and sometimes up to one and a half times the length given here. Dull midgreen with a very dull shine and slight longitudinal ridges on the upper surface, dull green on the lower surface, tapering from midlength to the tip, which often becomes withered during winter. **Rhizomes** Very invasive (strongly leptomorph). Slightly less invasive than other members of the genus in cultivation, but the difference is minimal. **Cultivation** Sun or shade. Suitable as a groundcover in a wide range of locations. Not so ideal as a specimen plant unless rigorously kept under control. **Hardiness** –10°C to –20°C (14°F to –4°F).

Indocalamus solidus

Native to China

Short bamboo—very invasive

This attractive species is most easily distinguished from other *Indocalamus* species by its smaller, darker leaves and by its more open habit, which results from the smaller leaves. The foliage is retained in good condition through winter unless the plant is grown in a very dry position, where there will be some tip and marginal withering. This bamboo can be used to make pleasing mounds of lush greenery under deciduous trees and other taller plants.

Culms Short and very slender, 1 to 2 m (3 to 6 feet) tall and up to 6 mm (¼ inch) in diameter. May become slightly taller in later years. Dull olive green at first, maturing to dull grayish purple-green. Internodes often solid for most of their length. Nodes not prominent. The habit is fairly upright, only arching slightly with age. New shoots appear in late spring. **Culm**

sheaths Persistent. Very persistent on the culm branches. Green slightly flushed with purple, with prominent auricles. **Branches** Solitary. Usually one shortish main branch, sometimes with one or more shorter branches on each side, developing later. **Leaves** Long and broad, 18 to 25 cm (7 to 10 inches) long by 3 to 6 cm (1¼ to 2½ inches) wide. Dark green and fairly lustrous on the upper surface, with slight longitudinal ridges, matte dull green on the lower surface, tapering to a slender point at the tip. May develop slight tip and marginal withering in winter. **Rhizomes** Very invasive (strongly leptomorph). Forms a dense thicket quite quickly,

Indocalamus solidus.

even in poor growing conditions. **Cultivation** Sun or shade. Very adaptable to almost any position but needs adequate moisture to keep the foliage looking fresh. **Hardiness** –10°C to –20°C (14°F to –4°F).

Indocalamus tessellatus

Synonym *Sasa tessellata*
Native to China
Short bamboo—very invasive

An architectural and very exotic-looking bamboo much used for foliage effect and for groundcover. The very large leaves are an attractive, rich lime green when grown in the open and are usually retained through winter in very good condition. Although the culms can sometimes be comparatively tall, the weight of the leaves bends them down, giving the pleasing appearance of a congested leafy mound. This species was introduced into the United Kingdom in 1845 and was included in the genus *Sasa* until it flowered in the 1980s, thus enabling an accurate identification to be made, whereupon it was transferred to *Indocalamus*. It still produces flowers sporadically.

Culms Short and very slender, 1 to 2 m (3 to 6 feet) tall and up to 6 mm (¼ inch) in diameter. Bright green at first and sometimes becoming purple-tinted where exposed to sunlight, maturing to dull yellowish green. Nodes not prominent. Culms quickly arch right to the ground with the weight of the very large leaves. New shoots appear in late spring. **Culm sheaths** Persistent. Very persistent on the culm branches. Deep purple when first emerging from the ground, becoming pale green. **Branches** Solitary. Long for the size of the culm, occasionally accompanied by one shorter

Indocalamus tessellatus.

branch. **Leaves** Very long and very broad, more than 25 cm (10 inches) long by more than 6 cm (2½ inches) wide. Long for their breadth and often up to twice the length given here. Rich green with a dull shine and prominent longitudinal ridges on the upper surface, dull and slightly grayish green on the lower surface, obtusely tapered at the base, slenderly tapered at the tip. **Rhizomes** Very invasive (strongly leptomorph). Much less invasive in poor growing conditions. **Cultivation** Sun or shade. Makes superb tropical-looking mounds of groundcover or a shorter specimen plant for foliage effect where space permits. **Hardiness** –10°C to –20°C (14°F to –4°F).

Otatea

A very small genus of tropical and subtropical pachymorph bamboos from Mexico and Central America. The foliage on most culms is carried only in the uppermost parts, producing a rather palm-like effect.

Otatea acuminata subsp. *aztecorum*

Synonym *O. aztecorum*

Native to Mexico

Tall bamboo—clump-forming

A very tender but exceptionally beautiful bamboo, much favored as a pot or conservatory plant in cool-temperate Western gardens. The slender arching culms are topped by masses of very delicate narrow leaves that almost obscure the culms. This, the only representative of the genus in common cultivation, needs constantly warm and very light conditions throughout the year. There seems to be considerable variation in the leaf size from plant to plant in Europe and the United States, possibly indicating that there are several clones in cultivation. I have given leaf dimensions below as an average that might be expected.

Culms Tall and slender, 3 to 5 m (10 to 16 feet) tall and 6 mm to 2 cm (¼ to ¾ inch) in diameter. Slender for their height and usually encountered in cool-temperate countries at much less than these dimensions. Deep green at first, ripening to yellowish green. Nodes not prominent. Loosely upright at first, quickly developing an elegant arch and becoming cascading

Otatea acuminata subsp. *aztecorum* in the early stages of coming into flower. This tender species made a very fine container specimen at Stream Cottage for many years. It was used as a patio plant during the summer months and taken into the greenhouse for the winter. The flowering seen here became so profuse that just a year after this picture was taken, the plant was completely dead.

with age. New shoots can appear at any time of year when conditions are warm and humid. **Culm sheaths** Semi-persistent. Light green. **Branches** Multiple. Often arched downward by the weight of the foliage. Developed only in the upper parts of the culm. **Leaves** Long and narrow, 18 to 25 cm (7 to 10 inches) long by 1 to 1.5 cm (3/8 to 5/8 inch) wide. Generally narrow for their length. Deep green and slightly matte on the upper surface, matte green on the lower surface, tapering to a slender point at the tip, with very short pseudopetioles. **Rhizomes** Clump-forming (pachymorph). The rhizome necks are fairly long, giving an open clump habit. This feature is less apparent if the plant is grown in a pot. **Cultivation** Sun or semi-shade. Needs very well lit conditions to thrive in cool-temperate latitudes. Best kept in a warm and frost-free environment. **Hardiness** 0°C to −5°C (32°F to 23°F).

Phyllostachys

An important large genus, invaluable to the gardener for its wealth of fine forms and attractive colored culms. The culms are produced in smaller numbers each season than those of other temperate bamboos, but are usually of much greater diameter. Most species develop an open grove-like habit, making it possible to walk between the culms. They are bold, impressive, and architectural, ideally suited to use as a specimen plant or as a tall screen.

Phyllostachys bamboos are found mostly in the lowland regions of China, although they occur to a lesser extent in Nepal and India. They have long been cultivated in Japan, where many species have become naturalized to the extent that they form a significant feature of the landscape. Within these wild populations or in cultivation, many variations have occurred spontaneously, often with colored culms, variegated leaves, or fascinating distortions, thereby providing a veritable painter's palette of exciting choices for gardeners. There is considerable argument between botanists as to the exact origin of these variants and whether they should be regarded as proper forms and varieties or merely cultivars that exist primarily as garden plants.

The genus can be distinguished easily from other bamboos by the presence of a clearly defined sulcus on the branched parts of the culm. This feature is also present on the culm branches and on the rhizomes. Below the point where there are branches or dormant branch buds, the culm is cylindrical. Any forms that have culms with a regular stripe of a different color in the sulcus will produce the stripes randomly in the completely cylindrical part of the culm. Nearly all species produce culms with branches in unequal pairs at the nodes, rarely having a third, weaker branch, which is usually poorly developed. Also, the number of main branches does not increase as the culm ages. Most species have prominent nodes, which may also be inclined, swollen, or distorted. Largely due to the big number of similar-looking species and their many variants, it is often difficult to make an accurate identification of a *Phyllostachys* bamboo, even to the practiced eye. Growing conditions and other factors greatly influence those vegetative characteristics that are the usual aids to identification. Often the only reliable means of confirming an identification is an inspection of the color and finer morphological features of the culm sheaths.

As natives of continental temperate climates, where the larger annual temperature variation produces cold winters and hot summers, *Phyllostachys* bamboos respond to cultivation in milder, maritime temperate climates by developing their open growth habit more slowly, sometimes remaining in a tight clump for many years. All species of *Phyllostachys* in cultivation prefer an open, sunny situation in the garden. This will produce the typical growth habit of sturdy, upright culms that only arch slightly in their upper parts. When these bamboos are grown in too much shade, their growth becomes drawn and lax, much to the detriment of their appearance. Adequate moisture is needed during the main growing months, as they are prone to aborting new shoots if there is sudden drying out or too great a fluctuation in the water table. *Phyllostachys* bamboos are greedy feeders, and an abundant annual dressing of compost or fertilizer will ensure strong, healthy growth.

Phyllostachys arcana

Native to China

Very tall bamboo—invasive

A useful species for general planting. The name means "hidden" or "mysterious," a reference to the original difficulty in finding distinguishing characteristics for identification purposes. Its culms are prone to interesting geniculations but otherwise stand reasonably straight and strong, with a slight arch near the summit. This species is very tough and hardy, maintaining its foliage through winter in fine condition, and can be used to make a good windbreak.

Culms Very tall and medium-thick, 5 to 8 m (16 to 26 feet) tall and 2 to 3 cm (¾ to 1¼ inches) in diameter. Dark green with a light powdery covering at first, maturing to glossy yellowish green. Nodes prominent. Upright in habit, with a slight arch to older culms, and prone to be geniculate in the lower parts. New shoots appear in spring. **Culm sheaths** Not persistent. Grayish green with a slight blue tint and occasional purple-brown spots. The blade is linear and wavy, auricles or oral setae are absent, and the ligule is prominent. **Branches** In pairs.

Unequal and fairly long, occasionally with a weakly developed third branch between them. **Leaves** Medium-long and medium-broad, 9 to 18 cm (3½ to 7 inches) long by 1.5 to 3 cm (⅝ to 1¼ inches) wide. Glossy, rich green on the upper surface, matte grayish green with a lighter strip on one side on the lower surface, tapering abruptly to a point at the tip. **Rhizomes** Invasive (leptomorph). Fairly slow to spread in cooler conditions. **Cultivation** Sun or semi-shade. Best in an open position. **Hardiness** −10°C to −20°C (14°F to −4°F).

Phyllostachys arcana 'Luteosulcata'

Very tall bamboo—invasive

Differs from the species by having green culms with regular yellow striping, and a slightly smaller stature. One of the better *Phyllostachys* bamboos with this coloration. The contrast between the colors of the culms is well defined, the yellow contrasting strongly against the surrounding dark green. It can sometimes be confused with *P. aureosulcata* but is easily distinguished by its smoother internodes.

Culms Slightly smaller than those of *P. arcana*. Dark green with a yellow panel in the sulcus, the contrast between the colors reducing as the culm matures to glossy yellowish green.

Phyllostachys atrovaginata

Synonym *P. congesta*

Native to China

Tall bamboo—invasive

This species has been widely grown for many years in the United States under its synonym, *P. congesta*. In Europe it is much less common. The culms are distinctive for their rapid taper from a relatively thick diameter at the base, giving the effect of a large bamboo, but without the corresponding height. The culms are also unusual for their tendency to age to grayish rather than to yellowish green. This bamboo can be used to make an open grove quickly.

In common with *P. heteroclada*, this species can tolerate wetter conditions than most bamboos, due to air canals being present in the rhizomes. The new shoots also resemble *P. heteroclada* but lack auricles and oral setae on the culm sheaths. This bamboo is commonly known as the incense bamboo, a reference to the attractive scent given off by the surface of the younger culms if rubbed lightly with a finger.

Culms Tall and thick, 3 to 5 m (10 to 16 feet) tall and 3 to 5 cm (1¼ to 2 inches) in diameter. Thick for their height. Bright green at first, ripening to grayish green in the lower parts and more yellowish green in the upper parts. Nodes prominent, particularly the nodal ridges. Very upright in habit, with some older culms developing a slight arch. New shoots appear in early summer. **Culm sheaths** Not persistent. Dark green tinted with wine. Auricles and oral setae usually absent, the blade noticeably wavy. **Branches** In pairs. Unequal and fairly long, occasionally having a weakly developed third branch between them. **Leaves** Medium-long and narrow, 9 to 18 cm (3½ to 7 inches) long by 1 to 1.5 cm (⅜ to ⅝ inch) wide. Light rich green and glossy on the upper surface, matte green on the lower surface, tapering fairly abruptly to a fine point at the tip. **Rhizomes** Invasive (leptomorph). Fairly slow to spread unless given lush growing conditions. **Cultivation** Sun or semi-shade. Best in an open position. **Hardiness** Below −20°C (−4°F).

Phyllostachys aurea

Synonym *Bambusa aurea*
Native to China, Japan
Very tall bamboo—invasive

Commonly known as the golden bamboo or fishpole bamboo. This species is believed to be the first *Phyllostachys* introduced into the United States, in 1822, and it remains widely cultivated there. It was introduced to Europe in the 1870s. The specific name *aurea*, which means "golden," confuses the uninitiated, for the culms are really just plain green, ripening to a yellowish green only over time, as with other green-culmed species. Unlike most green-culmed *Phyllostachys* bamboos, this species is fairly easy to recognize. The habit is stiffly upright, with the branches held at an acutely upright angle to the culms. The nodes are distinctive, usually having a discernable swelling underneath, and may also be clustered near the bases of the culms due to a pronounced shortening or compression of the internodal distances. The foliage is a slightly lighter green than most other species of the genus.

This species is a mainstay plant of the landscaping industry and is used extensively as a specimen plant or tall screen. While it is able to withstand exposure and low temperatures, it does not tolerate drought as well as other *Phyllostachys* species, and becomes stunted and lackluster. Given very warm, moist conditions, it can be invasive, but in a cool maritime climate it is almost static, with only an occasional runner.

Culms Very tall and thick, 5 to 8 m (16 to 26 feet) tall and 3 to 5 cm (1¼ to 2 inches) in diameter. Bright green and smooth, maturing to yellowish green. Nodes prominent, with a distinctive swelling underneath, and often crowded or clustered in the lower parts of the culm. Stiffly upright and sturdy in habit, with only a very slight arch on older culms. New shoots appear in early summer. **Culm sheaths** Not persistent. Pale green to buff and slightly rose-tinted. The blade is long and slightly crinkled, auricles and oral setae are absent, and the ligule is very short. **Branches** In pairs. Unequal

A mature grove of *Phyllostachys aurea* will freely produce culms that have compressed lower internodes, giving a highly ornamental effect.

and fairly long, occasionally with a weakly developed third branch between them, and held at an acute angle to the culm. **Leaves** Medium-long and medium-broad, 9 to 18 cm (3½ to 7 inches) long by 1.5 to 3 cm (⅝ to 1¼ inches) wide. Light green on the upper surface, matte midgreen on the lower surface, tapering fairly abruptly at the tip. **Rhizomes** Invasive (leptomorph). Fairly slow to spread in cooler conditions. **Cultivation** Sun or semi-shade. Needs a very open position and will grow poorly in shade. **Hardiness** –10°C to –20°C (14°F to –4°F).

Phyllostachys aurea 'Albovariegata'

Tall bamboo—invasive

Differs from the species by having white-variegated leaves and a smaller stature. A wonderful form that unfortunately came into flower in the early 1990s. Many plants died out or recovered to produce only green foliage. However, a few seedlings raised in America have produced variegation, and this form should gradually return to cultivation.

Culms Tall and slender, 3 to 5 m (10 to 16 feet) tall and 6 mm to 2 cm (¼ to ¾ inch) in di-

Phyllostachys aurea 'Albovariegata'.

ameter. Usually seen at the larger end of these dimensions. **Culm sheaths** Sometimes with white variegations. **Leaves** Light green with variable amounts of white striping and bands on the upper surface. Some young leaves almost completely white and often slightly orange-tinted. The white parts of the leaves reduce in intensity as the season progresses to become dullish white, the colors more matte on the lower surface. **Rhizomes** Much less invasive than typical *P. aurea*. Makes a tight clump in all but the warmest conditions. **Cultivation** Much more satisfactory in an open position. Some all-white leaves may scorch in very strong sunlight. Grows poorly in shade, with reduced intensity of variegation.

Phyllostachys aurea 'Flavescens Inversa'

Very tall bamboo—invasive

Differs from the species by having green culms with regular yellow striping, and a slightly smaller stature. A pleasing form that makes an ideal specimen plant for the smaller garden. The contrast between the green and the yellow in the culms develops slowly and is not as great as in other *Phyllostachys* bamboos with this coloration, but the habit is more refined.

Culms Slightly smaller than typical *P. aurea*. Bright green at first, slowly developing a yellow panel in the sulcus, the yellow parts taking at least one season to develop their color properly, then in much later seasons the contrast reducing as the culm eventually matures to yellowish green. **Rhizomes** Less invasive than *P. aurea*. **Cultivation** Best in an open position, although strong sunlight can reduce the contrast of the culm colors more quickly.

Phyllostachys aurea 'Flavescens Inversa'.

Phyllostachys aurea 'Holochrysa'

Very tall bamboo—invasive

Differs from the species by having completely yellow culms and a slightly smaller stature. A fine yellow-culmed form that deserves to be more widely grown. The color is not particularly apparent at sheath fall but improves with ripening, a process hastened by exposure to sunlight.

Culms Slightly smaller than those of *P. aurea*. Mustard green at first, the color deep-

This containerized plant of *Phyllostachys aurea* 'Holochrysa' in a nursery in France clearly shows the deep golden yellow mature coloration and the shortening of the internodes at the bases of the culms typical of the *P. aurea* group.

Phyllostachys aurea 'Koi'.

ening with age to golden yellow and finally to orange-yellow. Occasionally there is a thin green stripe present at random on an internode. **Leaves** A thin creamy yellow stripe may be found on a leaf here and there. **Rhizomes** Slightly less invasive than *P. aurea*. **Cultivation** Requires a very open position with good sunlight to help deepen the color of the culms.

Phyllostachys aurea 'Koi'

Very tall bamboo—invasive

Differs from the species by having yellow culms with regular green striping, and a slightly smaller stature. A choice form well worth seeking out. In common with 'Flavescens Inversa', the contrast between the yellow and the green is not as strong as in other *Phyllostachys* bamboos with a similar coloration, but the habit is more refined.

Culms Slightly smaller than those of the species. Greenish yellow at first, slowly developing a contrasting green panel in the sulcus that in much later seasons becomes less contrasting as the culm matures, while the other parts of the culm become more golden yellow. **Leaves** A thin creamy yellow stripe may be found on a leaf here and there. **Rhizomes** Less invasive than *P. aurea*. **Cultivation** Best in an open position, although strong sunlight can reduce the contrast of the culm colors more quickly.

Phyllostachys aureosulcata

Native to China

Very tall bamboo—invasive

Commonly known as the yellow groove bamboo. In 1907 this species was introduced into the United States, where it remains fairly widespread in cultivation, but it has only been grown widely in Europe since the 1980s. Phylogenetically, it is a mutated form of *P. aureosulcata* 'Alata', but since 'Alata' was discovered and named after *P. aureosulcata*, under the rules of nomenclature 'Alata' must be regarded as a cultivar. *Phyllostachys aureosulcata* and its cultivars are easy to distinguish from other *Phyllostachys* bamboos because of the rough surface of their young culms and their tendency to extreme sinuous or zigzag geniculations. They all have a useful, fairly upright habit unless grown in shade, where they can become very lax, and are liable to bend at the base. As a group they are very tough and hardy, and are among the best bamboos of *Phyllostachys* for cold or exposed gardens.

   Culms Very tall and medium-thick, 5 to 8 m (16 to 26 feet) tall and 2 to 3 cm (¾ to 1¼ inches) in diameter. Dark green at first, with a contrasting yellow panel in the sulcus, the contrast between the colors reducing as the culm matures to yellowish green. Internodes rough to touch when young. Nodes prominent. Upright in habit and very prone to geniculations in the lower parts of the culm. New shoots appear in early summer. **Culm sheaths** Not

persistent. Pale olive green with wine and cream streaks. The blade is lanceolate to narrowly triangular, auricles are well developed with small oral setae, though sometimes lacking on lower sheaths, and the ligule is large and convex. **Branches** In pairs. Unequal and fairly long, occasionally with a weakly developed third branch between them. **Leaves** Medium-long and medium-broad, 9 to 18 cm (3½ to 7 inches) long by 1.5 to 3 cm (⅝ to 1¼ inches) wide. Bright green and glossy on the upper surface, matte grayish green on the lower sur-

Phyllostachys aureosulcata. Culms of this species are prone to pronounced zigzag geniculations in their lower parts.

face, tapering gradually to a point at the tip. **Rhizomes** Invasive (leptomorph). Fairly slow to spread in cooler conditions. **Cultivation** Sun or semi-shade. Best in an open position. **Hardiness** Below –20°C (–4°F).

Phyllostachys aureosulcata 'Alata'

Very tall bamboo—invasive

Differs from the species by having completely green culms and a slightly larger stature. Phylogenetically, 'Alata' is really the typical form of the species, but since it was discovered and named after *P. aureosulcata*, under the rules of nomenclature it must be regarded as a cultivar. It grows more strongly than *P. aureosulcata* and quickly attains a more impressive stature. Occasionally 'Alata' may be found as a spontaneous reversion appearing within colonies of the colored-culm variants, and if not removed it will begin to dominate. It is a very tough bamboo indeed, well tolerating cold, exposure, and drought, and can be used to make a shelter belt for other plants.

Culms Slightly larger than those of *P. aureosulcata*. Dark green at first and often purple-tinted when very young and when grown in sunlight, maturing to yellowish green.

Phyllostachys aureosulcata 'Aureocaulis'

Very tall bamboo—invasive

Differs from the species by having completely yellow culms and a slightly smaller stature. Perhaps the best yellow-culmed *Phyllostachys* for smaller gardens. The upright culms are tidy, compact, and deep golden yellow, becoming almost orange-yellow in an open position. Strong sunlight will turn the young culms red temporarily, a most pleasing effect that disappears after the first season. An obscure clone called 'Lama Tempel' more or less resembles this cultivar, only with deeper colors, and can

sometimes have culms with the characteristics of other forms.

Culms Slightly smaller than those of *P. aureosulcata*. Bright yellow at first, with those parts of the culm exposed to sunlight becoming temporarily red-tinted in the first season, the culm maturing to deep golden yellow, almost orange-yellow. May occasionally have a thin green stripe or panel present at random on an internode. **Leaves** A thin creamy yellow stripe may be found on a leaf here and there. **Rhizomes** Less invasive than *P. aureosulcata*. **Cultivation** An open position in good sunlight will ensure better colors in the culms.

Young culms of *Phyllostachys aureosulcata* 'Aureocaulis'.

Phyllostachys aureosulcata 'Harbin'

Very tall bamboo—invasive

Differs from the species by having green culms with variable yellow striping, and a weaker constitution. An interesting form discovered growing in a garden in the United States. It has longitudinal ridges on the culm internodes, which often have yellow stripes between the ridges as well. Unfortunately it originated from a clone of *P. aureosulcata* that is less robust in culm and foliage and not very garden-worthy. The culms are short-lived and often die after only one or two seasons. My plant has produced an occasional flowering culm for some years, with little apparent harm. A bamboo for collectors only.

In 1992 in the garden of John Vlitos in Oxford, I discovered within a clump of the species, a culm that was yellow with thin green stripes at random around the circumference. This was propagated successfully, though with great difficulty, for these things always seem to occur in the middle of a clump—never at the edge! It grew into a plant that was clearly a new form. Later I gave it the name 'Harbin Inversa' as a temporary measure, because the striping seemed the opposite way round, the culm being more yellow than green. Since then, it has got into cultivation under that name, but it is not the proper inverse of 'Harbin' because it lacks the internodal ridges.

Culms Dark green with variable amounts of yellow striping that is usually present at random around the circumference of the culm, the culm often nearly yellow and green in equal proportions. Internodes longitudinally ridged. Culms mature very quickly to dull yellowish green with the striping almost inconspicuous, and to brownish orange-green by the end of the second season. More stiffly upright in habit than *P. aureosulcata* and less prone to geniculations in the lower internodes.

Phyllostachys aureosulcata 'Spectabilis'

Very tall bamboo—invasive

Differs from the species by having yellow culms with regular green striping, and a slightly smaller stature. An excellent colored-culm bamboo for general planting. The culms remain a fairly light yellow if grown in shade and attain a deeper color in full sun, though not as good a color as in 'Aureocaulis'. Strong sunlight will turn the young culms red tem-

Phyllostachys aureosulcata 'Spectabilis'. Like 'Aureocaulis', the young culms of this form can develop a temporary reddish "suntan."

porarily, a most pleasing effect that disappears after the first season.

Culms Slightly smaller than those of *P. aureosulcata*. Bright yellow at first, with a contrasting green panel in the sulcus. The yellow parts of the culm exposed to sunlight become temporarily red-tinted in the first season. The contrast between the main colors is retained well as the culm ripens to golden yellow. **Leaves** A thin creamy yellow stripe may be found on a leaf here and there. **Cultivation** An open position in good sunlight will ensure better colors in the culms.

Phyllostachys bambusoides

Synonym *P. quilioi*

Native to China

Extremely tall bamboo—invasive

Commonly known as the giant timber bamboo. A species native to China and long cultivated in Japan, noted for the size of its culms in good growing conditions. It is thought that the first introduction to Western cultivation was by French Admiral Du Quilio in 1866, but some authorities assert that the first introduction occurred later. In any case, by the late 1880s this bamboo was established in cultivation in the United States, where it became extensively planted.

Phyllostachys bambusoides and its forms are relatively easy to recognize. Apart from obvious differences such as colored culms or variegated foliage, the main distinguishing characteristics are the strongly spotted culm sheaths, the smoothness of the culms, and the large terminal leaves with their stiff oral setae. As a garden plant, the typical green form is rather coarse compared with other green-culmed species. The arching culms have long branches bearing large terminal leaves. Moreover, it can easily grow too large for the smaller urban garden, although it can often be reluctant to attain

its maximum dimensions unless given good growing conditions. The beauty of the *P. bambusoides* group is found within the many colored or distorted forms, which are often surprisingly more vigorous than the species, numbering among them some of the very best garden bamboos.

All members of the *P. bambusoides* group are of easy cultivation, so long as they are not grown in too much shade, and can be used to

Phyllostachys bambusoides. The superb setting and microclimate at Penjerrick, Cornwall, allows many bamboos to attain impressive culm dimensions for such a latitude.

make imposing specimen plants with strong structural qualities. They are mostly too big to make satisfactory container plants, unless the gardener is prepared to divide and repot them frequently, and are therefore best planted in the ground. Unfortunately, as a group they are more susceptible to attack by whitefly and aphid pests than most other bamboos. This does not greatly affect the health or vigor of the plant but renders the foliage unsightly, due to the sooty molds that live on the insects' secretions. To avoid this problem as much as possible, always site these bamboos in an open position with good air circulation.

Culms Extremely tall and very thick, more than 8 m (26 feet) tall and more than 5 cm (2 inches) in diameter. Bright green at first, maturing to yellowish green. Internodes smooth and glossy. Nodes prominent. Moderately upright in habit, with older culms arching gently from about midlength. New shoots appear from midsummer onward. **Culm sheaths** Not persistent. Greenish beige to reddish buff and conspicuously spotted with dark brown. The blade is usually short and lanceolate, with bands of wine and cream, auricles and oral setae are well developed, and the ligule is moderately prominent. **Branches** In pairs. Unequal, very long, and very stout, occasionally with a weakly developed third branch between them. **Leaves** Medium-long and medium-broad, 9 to 18 cm (3½ to 7 inches) long by 1.5 to 3 cm (⅝ to 1¼ inches) wide. Terminal leaves often much larger. Bright rich green on the upper surface, matte green on the lower surface, bluntly rounded at the base and shortly tapered at the tip. **Rhizomes** Invasive (leptomorph). Forms an open grove in warm conditions and much less so in a cool-temperate or maritime climate. **Cultivation** Sun or semi-shade. Best in a very open position with good air circulation, as this reduces the likeli-

hood of attracting insect pests onto the foliage. **Hardiness** –10°C to –20°C (14°F to –4°F).

Phyllostachys bambusoides 'Albovariegata'

Very tall bamboo—invasive

Differs from the species by having white-variegated leaves and a smaller stature. A worthy garden plant and one of the few taller variegated bamboos. There seem to be at least two clones of this cultivar, varying in intensity of variegation. The clone grown in the United States is highly variegated but less robust and vigorous than the European clone.

Culms Very tall and thick, 5 to 8 m (16 to 26 feet) tall and 3 to 5 cm (1¼ to 2 inches) in diameter. **Culm sheaths** Frequently show traces of white variegations. **Leaves** Bright rich green with varying amounts and widths of only moderately conspicuous white striping on the upper surface, the white striping often slightly orange-tinted when young, colors more matte on the lower surface. All variegations become much less conspicuous by winter. **Rhizomes** Less invasive than the species. **Cultivation** The variegations are generally better in good sunlight, but leaves that are nearly all white will be prone to scorching.

Phyllostachys bambusoides 'Castillonis'

Synonym *P. castillonis*

Very tall bamboo—invasive

Differs from the species by having yellow culms with regular green striping, and a smaller stature. This is by far the best *Phyllostachys* with this coloration. The colors are much richer and more strongly contrasting, and are retained better as the culm ages. The Japanese name for this bamboo is *kimmei-chiku*, which means "golden brilliant bamboo," an

A group of attractive young
culms of *Phyllostachys
bambusoides* 'Castillonis'.

apt description. In cooler climates this cultivar often grows more vigorously than *P. bambusoides*. There is a clone in cultivation called
'Castillonis Variegata', which has a higher incidence of white striping in the leaves. Unfortunately, this is not a very good garden plant due
to its weak constitution. Always grow straight
'Castillonis' in preference.

Culms Very tall and thick, 5 to 8 m (16 to 26
feet) tall and 3 to 5 cm (1¼ to 2 inches) in diameter. Deep golden yellow, with a rich green
panel in the sulcus, the colors eventually fading and losing their contrast with age. **Leaves**
A thin creamy yellow stripe may be found on a
leaf here and there. **Rhizomes** Slightly more invasive than *P. bambusoides*.

Phyllostachys bambusoides
'Castillonis Inversa'
Very tall bamboo—invasive
Differs from the species by having green culms
with regular yellow striping, and a smaller
stature. It is by far the best *Phyllostachys* with
this particular coloration. The colors are much
more strongly contrasting and are retained
better as the culm ages. This cultivar is rather
prone to hiding its culms behind a mass of
lower branches and foliage, particularly as a
young plant. To remedy this, cleanly snap off
any unwanted growth as the culm is in its initial growth spurt. In cooler climates it often
grows more vigorously than the species.

Culms Very tall and thick, 5 to 8 m (16 to 26
feet) tall and 3 to 5 cm (1¼ to 2 inches) in diameter. Usually attains the larger end of these dimensions. Rich green with a deep golden yellow panel in the sulcus, the colors eventually

fading and losing contrast as the green parts of
the culm mature to yellowish green. **Rhizomes**
Slightly more invasive than *P. bambusoides*.

Phyllostachys bambusoides
'Castillonis Inversa Variegata'
Tall bamboo—invasive
Differs from the species by having green culms
with regular yellow striping, white-variegated
leaves, and a much smaller stature. This beautiful form was introduced into Europe and the
United States by Tony Pike from plants culti-

The deeply contrasting culm
colors of *Phyllostachys bambusoides*
'Castillonis Inversa'.

vated in New Zealand. No other bamboo in cool-temperate gardens has quite such startlingly conspicuous variegations. The colors of the culms are really just a bonus! It is not a particularly robust grower, needing care and encouragement. Few culms live to more than two years old before dying back partially or completely, while holding on to dead or partially dead leaves. It is a luxury to have any degree of movement in the rhizomes; indeed, they lack vigor in the extreme, giving a very tight clumping habit.

Culms Tall and medium-thick, 3 to 5 m (10 to 16 feet) tall and 2 to 3 cm (¾ to 1¼ inches) in diameter. Rich green with a deep golden yellow panel in the sulcus, the colors eventually losing contrast as the green parts of the culm mature

to yellowish green. **Leaves** Bright rich green with consistent and extremely conspicuous variable amounts of white striping and bands on the upper surface, the white striping often strongly orange-tinted when young, the variegations only reducing slightly in intensity as the season progresses. Colors are more matte on the lower surface. **Rhizomes** Much less invasive than the species. Practically static and tightly clump-forming unless given very lush growing conditions. **Cultivation** Benefits from an open position, although full sun can cause slight scorching of the foliage.

The glorious foliage of *Phyllostachys bambusoides* 'Castillonis Inversa Variegata'.

Phyllostachys bambusoides 'Holochrysa'

Synonym *P. bambusoides* 'Allgold'

Very tall bamboo—invasive

Differs from the species by having completely yellow culms and a smaller stature. A superb colored-culm bamboo, achieving a depth of orange-yellow unequaled elsewhere. The color of the young culms is sumptuous, bringing light and warmth to the dullest corner of the garden. However, this cultivar needs adequate room, because the culms can arch considerably with age. In cooler climates it often grows more vigorously than the species.

The young culms of *Phyllostachys bambusoides* 'Holochrysa' are a deep orange-yellow.

Culms Very tall and thick, 5 to 8 m (16 to 26 feet) tall and 3 to 5 cm (1¼ to 2 inches) in diameter. Rich orange-yellow, almost orange, the color brightest when culms are young, then deepening, and eventually fading with age. Very occasionally with a thin green stripe on an internode here and there. Slightly more lax in habit than *P. bambusoides*. **Leaves** A thin creamy yellow stripe may be found on a leaf here and there. **Rhizomes** Slightly more invasive than the species. **Cultivation** A better habit will be achieved in an open position.

Phyllostachys bambusoides 'Kawadana'

Very tall bamboo—invasive

Differs from the species by having green culms with variable yellow striping, yellow-variegated leaves, and a smaller stature. An attractive yet subtle form still rare in cultivation but well worth seeking out. Although an open, airy position favors the *P. bambusoides* group generally, this cultivar is inclined to lose the contrast of its culm striping fairly quickly where exposed to strong sunlight. It is not particularly vigorous, and patience is needed to entice it to greater culm dimensions.

Culms Very tall and thick, 5 to 8 m (16 to 26 feet) tall and 3 to 5 cm (1¼ to 2 inches) in diameter. Rich green with varying amounts of rather inconspicuous thin yellow striping that occurs at random around the circumference of the culm. The contrast is almost completely lost with age as the green parts of the culm mature to yellowish green. **Leaves** Bright rich green with consistent, rather muted, thin, yellowish green striping on the upper surface, giving a softly variegated effect. Colors are more matte below, with the striping barely penetrating through. **Rhizomes** Much less invasive than the species. **Cultivation** Partial shade will help retain the contrast of the culm striping.

Phyllostachys bambusoides 'Marliacea'

Extremely tall bamboo—invasive

Differs from the species by having distorted culms and a less robust constitution. Commonly known as the wrinkled bamboo. This cultivar is relatively rare in cultivation, mostly because it does not propagate so readily. The culms invoke comment and curiosity with their wrinkled internodes and strange distortions. Unless given warm conditions, 'Marliacea' is a difficult bamboo to cultivate, being reluctant to put up any great number of new

Phyllostachys bambusoides 'Marliacea' produces culms with wrinkled distortions.

culms each year, although it often attains culm dimensions equal to the species. Furthermore, it often sends up shoots late in the season that fail to ripen properly before the winter. 'Katashibo' is virtually identical but tends to produce culms with lesser or no wrinkling.

Culms The internodes have prominent, rounded longitudinal ridges and troughs extending around the circumference of the culm. Upper internodes are prone to zigzag and other distortions. **Rhizomes** Less invasive than typical *P. bambusoides* and slow to build up any sort of grove.

Phyllostachys bambusoides 'Slender Crookstem'

Very tall bamboo—invasive

Differs from the species by having distorted culms and a smaller stature. Widely grown in the United States but rather obscure in Europe. The culms are noticeably slender for their height, and geniculations occur in a high percentage of culms and are often extreme.

Culms Very tall and medium-thick, 5 to 8 m (16 to 26 feet) tall and 2 to 3 cm (¾ to 1¼ inches) in diameter. Frequently with pronounced sinuous or zigzag geniculations in the lower internodes.

Phyllostachys bambusoides 'Sub-Variegata'

Extremely tall bamboo—invasive

Differs from the species by having slight variegations in the leaves. This is a very choice bamboo indeed, still uncommon in cultivation and very much sought after. From a distance it closely resembles the species, although the culms are often very slightly thicker for their height. On closer inspection, the leaves have subtle bandings of dark and light green, giving a most pleasing effect. Soil type can affect the relative lightness and darkness of the striping on the leaves. It has a slightly weaker constitution than *P. bambusoides* and needs time to become properly established.

Leaves Bright rich green with muted, thin, lighter and darker green striping on the upper surface, giving a subtly variegated effect. Colors are more matte on the lower surface, with the striping barely penetrating through. **Rhizomes** Lacking vigor and slow to spread the first few years but eventually somewhat more invasive than *P. bambusoides*.

The subtly variegated foliage of *Phyllostachys bambusoides* 'Sub-Variegata'.

Phyllostachys bambusoides 'Tanakae'

Extremely tall bamboo—invasive

Differs from the species by having green culms that become brown-spotted. Something of a collector's bamboo that is perhaps more interesting than beautiful. The brown spotting takes time to develop and is more separate and defined than the irregular but arguably more attractive blotching of *P. nigra* 'Boryana', with which it can be confused. It is thought that the spotting is caused by a virus. Many, many plants in cultivation purporting to be this cultivar are just plain *P. bambusoides* and will never develop spots, or are simply mislabeled plants of 'Boryana'.

Culms Bright green at first, slowly developing dark brown spots or patches, the green parts of the culm ripening to yellowish green and the spots becoming lighter brown with age.

Phyllostachys bambusoides 'White Crookstem'

Very tall bamboo—invasive

Differs from the species by having gray-powdered young culms that are prone to distortions, and by having a smaller stature. This is another form that is more common in the United States than in Europe. The effect of the white powder is unusual and intriguing. Too much abrasion from surrounding growth can easily remove the powder, so it is essential to maintain space among the culms and with surrounding vegetation.

Culms Very tall and medium-thick, 5 to 8 m (16 to 26 feet) tall and 2 to 3 cm (¾ to 1¼ inches) in diameter. Copiously covered in white powder from sheath fall, the powder persisting often for several seasons and obscuring the green color of the culm underneath. Prone to geniculations in the lower internodes, though usually less extremely so than in 'Slender Crookstem'.

Phyllostachys bissetii

Native to China

Very tall bamboo—invasive

Commonly known as the David Bisset bamboo. A handsome species cultivated in the United States since the 1950s but more recently introduced to Europe. It may not be the tallest or thickest *Phyllostachys* bamboo, but it is extremely hardy and weather-resistant and is usually the most fresh-looking bamboo in the garden at the end of winter. Because of its easy cultivation and pleasing growth habit, this species is likely to become a mainstay of the landscaping industry. It is the wise gardener's choice for a tall screen or windbreak in exposed locations.

Culms Very tall and medium-thick, 5 to 8 m (16 to 26 feet) tall and 2 to 3 cm (¾ to 1¼ inches) in diameter. Darkish green at first, maturing to yellowish green. Internodes slightly rough to the touch when very young but becoming glossy. Nodes prominent. Fairly upright in habit, the outer culms of the grove sometimes leaning toward the light. New shoots appear in late spring. **Culm sheaths** Not persistent. Pale yellowish green, slightly tinted pinkish wine. The blade is narrowly triangular to lanceolate, auricles are moderately developed with a few oral setae, and the ligule is moderately prominent. **Branches** In pairs. Unequal and fairly long, occasionally with a weakly developed third branch between them. **Leaves** Medium-long and medium-broad, 9 to 18 cm (3½ to 7 inches) long by 1.5 to 3 cm (⅝ to 1¼ inches) wide. Dark green with a dull shine on the upper surface, matte green with a slightly lighter strip on one side on the lower surface, tapering to a slender point at the tip. **Rhizomes** Invasive (leptomorph). Fairly slow to spread

Phyllostachys bissetii is a very tough and hardy bamboo with distinctive dark green foliage.

in cooler conditions. **Cultivation** Sun or semi-shade. Best in an open position. Tolerates cold and exposed locations better than most very tall bamboos. **Hardiness** Below −20°C (−4°F).

Phyllostachys decora

Synonym *P. mannii*

Native to China

Very tall bamboo—invasive

Sometimes known as the beautiful bamboo. An attractive and very tough species bearing a superficial similarity to *P. bissetii*. It can be distinguished by the culm sheaths, which are pleasingly striped in a way that resembles variegation, and by the leaves, which tend to develop a noticeable twist. It is an excellent choice for a hedge or windbreak in an exposed or drier location.

Culms Very tall and medium-thick, 5 to 8 m (16 to 26 feet) tall and 2 to 3 cm (¾ to 1¼ inches) in diameter. Darkish deep green at first, maturing to yellowish green. Nodes prominent. Fairly upright in habit, with older culms arching gently. New shoots appear in early summer. **Culm sheaths** Pale green flushed with purple, streaked and striped with white and tinted purple at the margins. Auricles and oral setae often absent. The blade is long and strap-shaped. **Branches** In pairs. Unequal and fairly long, occasionally having a weakly developed third branch between them. **Leaves** Medium-long and medium-broad, 9 to 18 cm (3½ to 7 inches) long by 1.5 to 3 cm (⅝ to 1¼ inches) wide. Tending toward the lower end of these dimensions. Darkish deep green with a dull shine on the upper surface, matte green on the lower surface, tapering to a fine point at the tip.

Often developing a slight curl downward at the edges or a slight twist as the leaf matures. **Rhizomes** Invasive (leptomorph). Spreads slowly unless given very lush growing conditions. **Cultivation** Sun or semi-shade. Best in an open position. **Hardiness** Below −20°C (−4°F).

Phyllostachys dulcis

Native to China

Extremely tall bamboo—very invasive

Commonly known as the sweetshoot bamboo. The shoots of this impressive species are much

Phyllostachys dulcis is likely to produce the thickest green culms in a cool-temperate climate.

prized as a culinary delicacy. In cooler climates it is grown for its ability to quickly produce thick culms in an open grove. It will rapidly become too large for an urban garden with limited space. The initiated bamboo enthusiast can identify this species from a distance by its foliage, which is a distinctive luxuriant green.

Culms Extremely tall and very thick, more than 8 m (26 feet) tall and more than 5 cm (2 inches) in diameter. Thick for their height. Bright green with almost imperceptible thin yellow stripes at first, maturing to yellowish green. Internodes with faint longitudinal ridges, becoming glossy. Nodes prominent. Very upright in habit, although some lower internodes may be curved. New shoots appear in late spring. **Culm sheaths** Not persistent. Greenish cream with small brown spots, sometimes with white stripes. The blade is lanceolate and strongly crinkled, auricles and oral setae are well developed, and the ligule is prominent and convex. **Branches** In pairs. Unequal and fairly long, occasionally with a weakly developed third branch between them. **Leaves** Medium-long and medium-broad, 9 to 18 cm (3½ to 7 inches) long by 1.5 to 3 cm (⅝ to 1¼ inches) wide. Bright intense green on the upper surface, matte grayish green on the lower surface, tapering gradually to a point at the tip. **Rhizomes** Very invasive (strongly leptomorph). Spreads vigorously even in cooler conditions. **Cultivation** Sun or semi-shade. Best in an open position. **Hardiness** −10°C to −20°C (14°F to −4°F).

Phyllostachys edulis

Synonym *P. pubescens*

Native to China

Extremely tall bamboo—invasive

A bamboo of outstanding beauty and elegance, significant in Eastern culture. It is known in China as *mo chu* and in Japan as *moso chiku*, and is cultivated extensively for the production of edible shoots and paper pulp. In its native environment, where it enjoys warm, moist conditions, this species produces huge grayish green culms surmounted by plumes of tiny light green leaves. Although quite hardy, it is a most reluctant grower in cooler climates, where it seldom reaches any great size. It is more suited to the determined enthusiast who can lavish it with fertilizer and water. It can be difficult to propagate, other than as a large division, and this work is best undertaken in spring when growth is at its strongest.

Culms Extremely tall and very thick, more than 8 m (26 feet) tall and more than 5 cm (2 inches) in diameter. These dimensions are optimistic in cool conditions. Deep green at first, maturing to yellowish green, then almost orange-green. Internodes grayish in appearance in the first two or three seasons due to a copious covering of velvety hairs and powder, losing the powder quickly but retaining the hairs for several seasons and often attracting molds onto the hairs in cooler climates. Lower internodes fairly short. Nodes prominent but less so than most other *Phyllostachys* bamboos. Usually emerging from the ground off perpendicular, then straightening to become upright with a slight arch near the summit. New shoots appear in early summer. **Culm sheaths** Not persistent. Grayish green to buff, densely covered with dark brown blotches and stiff brown hairs. The blade is lanceolate to narrowly triangular and wavy, auricles are well developed with long oral setae, and the ligule is prominent. **Branches** In pairs. Unequal and fairly long, occasionally with a weakly developed third branch between them. **Leaves** Short and narrow, 5 to 9 cm (2 to 3½ inches) long by 1 to 1.5 cm (⅜ to ⅝ inch) wide. Light green on the upper surface, matte green on the lower surface, tapering from midlength to a point at the tip. **Rhizomes** Invasive (leptomorph). Freely running in warm conditions but almost static in cool-temperate climates unless grown in a lush microclimate. **Cultivation** Sun or semi-shade. Grows best in an open position with warmth and moisture; otherwise can be very difficult to establish. **Hardiness** −10°C to −20°C (14°F to −4°F).

The ghostly effect created by young culms in a mature grove of *Phyllostachys edulis* growing in the warm-temperate conditions of the Bambouseraie de Prafrance, seen in deep shade under the canopy of foliage above.

Phyllostachys edulis 'Bicolor'

Extremely tall bamboo—invasive

Differs from the species by having yellow culms with regular green striping, and a slightly smaller stature. A supremely beautiful bamboo, described by American botanist Floyd Alonzo McClure (1966) as "a bamboo of consummate elegance." This cultivar, if well grown, displays a combination of habit and color worthy of the most premier position in the garden. The colors of the culms are softly muted by the effect of the velvety hairs and complemented perfectly by the plumes of tiny leaves. It is neither too straight nor too arching but leans gently away from the center of the grove. Regrettably for gardeners living in more cool-temperate climates, it is scarce in cultivation and even more difficult to establish than the species. *Phyllostachys edulis* 'Nabeshimana' is very similar, producing a higher percentage of green striping below the branched part of the culm—if the plant can be grown big enough to see this!

Culms Slightly smaller than those of the species. Bright light yellow, with a rich green panel in the sulcus and random striping and bands below the lowest branch bearing nodes if the culm is large enough, the colors eventually becoming dull with age. **Leaves** A thin creamy yellow stripe may be found on a leaf here and there. **Cultivation** The culm colors are better in an open position.

Phyllostachys edulis 'Bicolor'.

Phyllostachys edulis 'Heterocycla'. The distortions may be lacking entirely on thinner immature culms or on plants grown in very cool conditions.

Phyllostachys flexuosa.

Phyllostachys edulis 'Heterocycla'

Synonym *P. pubescens* 'Heterocycla'

Very tall bamboo—invasive

Differs from the species by having distorted culms and a smaller stature. Commonly known as the tortoiseshell bamboo. A sought-after form scarce in cultivation in the West. When this plant is growing strongly, the culms frequently produce the conspicuous distortions, but in cooler climates most often hardly a trace of this feature exists. *Phyllostachys edulis* 'Subconvexa' is very similar, having a smoother outline to the distortions.

Culms Very tall and thick, 5 to 8 m (16 to 26 feet) tall and 3 to 5 cm (1¼ to 2 inches) in diameter. The lower parts of the culm are prone to having a regular series of inclined nodes and compressed internodes. **Cultivation** Requires warm conditions and needs to be making vigorous growth to encourage the distortions.

Phyllostachys flexuosa

Native to China

Tall bamboo—invasive

In cooler climates this bamboo is not as garden-worthy as many of the more recently introduced species, having a rather coarse habit and seldom reaching any impressive size. It was introduced into France in 1864 and became common in cultivation until it came into flower in Western gardens in the early 1990s, whereupon most plants died out. Since then many seedlings have been raised, and it is returning to cultivation.

Culms Tall and slender, 3 to 5 m (10 to 16 feet) tall and 6 mm to 2 cm (¼ to ¾ inch) in diameter. Bright green at first, maturing to yellowish green and developing distinctive blackish markings on the very uppermost internodes of older culms. Internodes becoming glossy from an early age. Nodes prominent. Obtusely zigzag throughout and soon arching from midlength. New shoots appear in late spring. **Culm sheaths** Not persistent. Greenish beige with purplish veins and small brown spots. The blade is narrowly lanceolate, auricles and oral setae are lacking, and the ligule is strongly developed. **Branches** In pairs. Unequal and fairly long, occasionally with a weakly developed third branch between them. **Leaves** Medium-long and medium-broad, 9 to 18 cm (3½ to 7 inches) long by 1.5 to 3 cm (⅝ to 1¼ inches) wide. Deep green on the upper surface, matte grayish green on the lower surface, distinctly parallel-sided until tapering from well past midlength to a slender point at the tip. **Rhizomes** Invasive (leptomorph). Fairly slow to spread in cooler conditions. **Cultivation** Sun or semi-shade. Best in an open position. **Hardiness** −10°C to −20°C (14°F to −4°F).

Phyllostachys glauca

Native to China

Very tall bamboo—invasive

A species grown for the coloration of the young culms, which are covered in white powder when young, giving a distinctive glaucous green effect. It is otherwise very similar to *P. flexuosa*, but grows more strongly.

Culms Very tall and medium-thick, 5 to 8 m (16 to 26 feet) tall and 2 to 3 cm (¾ to 1¼ inches) in diameter. Bright green and copiously covered with white powder at sheath fall, los-

ing the powder fairly quickly, maturing to yellowish green. Nodes prominent. Fairly upright in habit, with older culms arching slightly near the summit. New shoots appear in early summer. **Culm sheaths** Not persistent. Green slightly tinted with wine, occasionally with a few brown spots. The blade is lanceolate, auricles and oral setae are completely lacking, and the ligule is short. **Branches** In pairs. Unequal and fairly long, occasionally with a weakly developed third branch between them. **Leaves** Medium-long and medium-broad, 9 to 18 cm (3½ to 7 inches) long by 1.5 to 3 cm (⅝ to 1¼ inches) wide. Bright green on the upper surface, dull matte green on the lower surface, tapering gradually to a point at the tip. **Rhizomes** Invasive (leptomorph). Fairly slow to spread in cooler conditions. **Cultivation** Sun or semi-shade. Best in an open position. **Hardiness** −10°C to −20°C (14°F to −4°F).

Phyllostachys glauca 'Yunzhu'

Very tall bamboo—invasive

Differs from the species by having green culms that become brown-spotted. Of the few bamboos with this coloration on the culms, this is probably the least garden-worthy. The spotting is not conspicuous or particularly attractive and tends to appear when the culm is past its best and ready to be cut out of the grove. A bamboo for collectors.

Culms After at least one season, more often two or three, culms slowly develop irregular and inconsistent spots and patches of dark brown. Sometimes the spotting is almost absent. **Cultivation** Grow in partial shade; otherwise the culm ripens to yellowish green before the brown spots can develop, thus reducing the contrast.

Phyllostachys heteroclada

Synonym *P. purpurata*
Native to China
Tall bamboo—invasive

Commonly known as the water bamboo. A smaller species still uncommon in cultivation and suffering from much confusion as to its nomenclature. The culms are comparatively slender for the genus, with long internodes and an unusual habit. The common name refers to the possible adaptation of this species to wetter conditions in the wild, indicated by air channels in the rhizomes. It is worth seeking out as a curiosity plant.

Culms Tall and slender, 3 to 5 m (10 to 16 feet) tall and 6 mm to 2 cm (¼ to ¾ inch) in diameter. Slender for their height. Dull green, maturing to yellowish green. Internodes comparatively long, slightly curved, and twisted in opposite directions, giving a sinuous zigzag effect, each sulcus very broad, typically with three distinct deep channels. Nodes prominent, large for the diameter of the culm. Rather weak in habit and prone to excessive arching. New shoots appear in early summer. **Culm sheaths** Not persistent. Green slightly tinted with wine red. The blade is boat-shaped and narrow, auricles and oral setae are weakly developed or lacking, and the ligule is very short. **Branches** In pairs. Unequal and fairly long, occasionally with a weakly developed third branch between them. Held very horizontally or sometimes at an angle below the horizontal. **Leaves** Short and narrow, 5 to 9 cm (2 to 3½ inches) long by 1 to 1.5 cm (⅜ to ⅝ inch) wide. Darkish green on the upper surface, matte green on the lower surface, tapering fairly abruptly to a point at the tip. **Rhizomes** Invasive (leptomorph). Not particularly invasive and quite slow in cooler conditions. **Cultivation** Sun or semi-shade. Requires good growing conditions and a position that is as open as possible to encourage a more upright habit. **Hardiness** −10°C to −20°C (14°F to −4°F).

Phyllostachys heteroclada 'Solidstem'

Synonym *P. purpurata* 'Solidstem'
Very tall bamboo—invasive

Differs from the species by having partially solid culms and a larger stature. An obscure form, very uncommon in cultivation. It is more robust in constitution, with less tendency to extreme arching of the culms, and is therefore a better garden plant. This cultivar may be the true type species.

Culms Very tall and medium-thick, 5 to 8 m (16 to 26 feet) tall and 2 to 3 cm (¾ to 1¼ inches) in diameter. Internodes completely solid, extending from the base to half or more of the length of the culm, giving a stiffer and less arching habit.

Phyllostachys heteroclada 'Straightstem'

Synonym *P. purpurata* 'Straightstem'
Very tall bamboo—invasive

Differs from the species by having a much less sinuous habit and a larger stature. Another obscure form, very uncommon in cultivation. It is also more robust in constitution and can easily be confused with 'Solidstem' as a very young plant.

Culms Very tall and medium-thick, 5 to 8 m (16 to 26 feet) tall and 2 to 3 cm (¾ to 1¼ inches) in diameter. Nodes less prominent and internodes much less sinuous or twisted, giving a more upright habit.

Phyllostachys humilis

Native to China

Tall bamboo—invasive

A useful species, not common in cultivation, small in stature compared to most *Phyllostachys* bamboos. The rhizomes seem to compensate for the lack of stature with an eager invasiveness in good growing conditions.

Culms Tall and slender, 3 to 5 m (10 to 16 feet) tall and 6 mm to 2 cm (¼ to ¾ inch) in diameter. Dark purplish green at first, becoming rich green, and maturing to yellowish green. Nodes prominent. Very upright in habit, with only minimal arching of older culms. New shoots appear in early summer. **Culm sheaths** Not persistent. Creamy green, slightly rose-tinted. The blade is short and lanceolate with occasional waves, auricles are large with a few oral setae, and the ligule is fairly well developed. **Branches** In pairs. Unequal and fairly long, occasionally with a weakly developed third branch between them. **Leaves** Medium-long and narrow, 9 to 18 cm (3½ to 7 inches) long by 1 to 1.5 cm (⅜ to ⅝ inch) wide. Very variable. Deep green on the upper surface, grayish green on the lower surface, tapering gradually at the tip to a fine point. **Rhizomes** Invasive (leptomorph). Quite invasive when established. **Cultivation** Sun or semi-shade. Best in an open position. **Hardiness** −10°C to −20°C (14°F to −4°F).

Phyllostachys iridescens

Native to China

Very tall bamboo—invasive

An interesting, vigorous species still obscure in Western gardens. It appears to be closely related to *P. violascens*. The brightly glaucous coloration of the young culms draws attention, and the older culms develop an attractive striping, although this is not very conspicuous.

Culms Very tall and thick, 5 to 8 m (16 to 26 feet) tall and 3 to 5 cm (1¼ to 2 inches) in diameter. Midgreen, with a copious covering of waxy grayish powder at first, soon losing the powder, and slowly developing variable and inconsistent amounts of muted yellowish striping around the circumference of the culm. The striping becomes brownish with age and finally reddish brown, the other parts of the culm maturing to yellowish green. Nodes prominent. Occasionally geniculate near the

The young culms of *Phyllostachys iridescens* have colorful sheaths and are covered in a luminous powdery bloom, while older culms develop moderately conspicuous longitudinal striping.

base, otherwise very upright in habit with minimal arching of older culms. New shoots appear in early summer. **Culm sheaths** Not persistent. Brownish green tinted red, with a few dark brown spots or patches. The blade is broadly lanceolate, auricles and oral setae are fairly well developed, and the ligule is moderately well developed. **Branches** In pairs. Unequal, fairly long, and rather stout, occasionally with a weakly developed third branch between them. **Leaves** Medium-long and medium-broad, 9 to 18 cm (3½ to 7 inches) long by 1.5 to 3 cm (⅝ to 1¼ inches) wide. Bright green on the upper surface, matte green on the lower surface, tapering gradually to a slender point at the tip. **Rhizomes** Invasive (leptomorph). Quickly forms an open grove in warm conditions. **Cultivation** Sun or semi-shade. Best in an open position. **Hardiness** –10°C to –20°C (14°F to –4°F).

Phyllostachys makinoi

Native to China

Very tall bamboo—invasive

An attractive and distinctive species noted for the size of its culms and their conspicuous coating of powder. In more cool-temperate climates it will only attain moderately impressive culm dimensions and is grown principally for the effect of the young culms. It is hard to obtain pieces of the true *P. makinoi*, as many plants sold under this name turn out to be *P. viridis*, which is very similar as a young plant. However, the true *P. makinoi* is one of the best bamboos that can be grown for white-powdered culms, creating an almost ghostly effect against a dark background.

Culms Very tall and thick, 5 to 8 m (16 to 26 feet) tall and 3 to 5 cm (1¼ to 2 inches) in diameter. Bright green and densely covered with white powder at first, maturing to yellowish green. Internodes with minute pigskin-like dimples on their surface. Nodes prominent. Very sturdy and upright in habit. New shoots appear in early summer. **Culm sheaths** Not persistent. Pale beige with smoky brown spots. The blade is narrowly lanceolate, auricles and oral setae are lacking, and the ligule is sparsely developed and fringed with short bristles. **Branches** In pairs. Unequal and fairly long, occasionally with a weakly developed third branch between them. **Leaves** Medium-long and medium-broad, 9 to 18 cm (3½ to 7 inches) long by 1.5 to 3 cm (⅝ to 1¼ inches)

Phyllostachys makinoi has distinctive young culms.

wide. Bright green on the upper surface, matte green on the lower surface, tapering gradually at the tip. **Rhizomes** Invasive (leptomorph). Fairly slow to spread in cooler conditions. **Cultivation** Sun or semi-shade. Best in an open position. **Hardiness** −10°C to −20°C (14°F to −4°F).

Phyllostachys nidularia

Native to China

Very tall bamboo—very invasive

A very distinctive species with enlarged nodes and sometimes other distortions on larger culms, and an easily recognized culm sheath. It is uncommon in cultivation but well worth growing in a larger garden with adequate space. It needs regular feeding to keep the foliage looking healthy and is rather prone to chlorosis when grown on poor soils. Once established, it spreads with an alarming urgency that is unequaled by any other member of the genus in cultivation.

Culms Very tall and thick, 5 to 8 m (16 to 26 feet) tall and 3 to 5 cm (1¼ to 2 inches) in diameter. Midgreen at first, maturing to yellowish green. Internodes have noticeable longitudinal ridges, are prone to moderate sinuous or zigzag distortions in the mid to upper parts of the culm, and are often nearly solid. Nodes prominent, often grossly flared or swollen, and typically have a small crack or split directly behind the base of the sulcus. The habit is more or less stiffly upright overall, apart from the distortions, with a slight tendency for older culms to arch near the summit. **Culm sheaths** Not persistent. Olive green to pale green with various streaks of creamy white and wine. The blade is large, shaped like the head of a spear, and continuous on either side into the auricles, oral setae are few, and the ligule is short and covered by the blade. **Branches** In pairs. Unequal and fairly long, occasionally with a weakly de-

veloped third branch between them, sometimes emerging from very distorted nodes at unusual angles. **Leaves** Medium-long and medium-broad, 9 to 18 cm (3½ to 7 inches) long by 1.5 to 3 cm (⅝ to 1¼ inches) wide. Light midgreen on the upper surface, matte grayish green on the lower surface, tapering fairly abruptly at the tip. **Rhizomes** Very invasive (strongly leptomorph). Very far-reaching even in cooler conditions. **Cultivation** Sun or semi-shade. Best in an open position. **Hardiness** −10°C to −20°C (14°F to −4°F).

Phyllostachys nigra

Synonyms *Bambusa nigra*, *P. puberula* var. *nigra*

Native to China

Very tall bamboo—invasive

Commonly known as the black bamboo. Although native to China, it is rare in the wild. It is thought to be the first hardy bamboo introduced into Europe, arriving long before any other bamboo. Some authorities believe the date of introduction to be 1827. It is mentioned in the second edition of Loudon's *Arboretum et Fruticetum* (1854) as having been cultivated in England at the Royal Horticultural Society's gardens for some 10 or 12 years. It is now found extensively across Europe and the United States. Its high-quality wood is much favored for handicrafts and bamboo fencing. The rhizomes are used in the manufacture of walking sticks and umbrella handles.

This species is also much prized as a garden ornamental, with its polished black culms and graceful arching habit. The very best clones develop color quickly on new culms, often beginning to turn black by the end of their first season, although growing conditions will have some effect on the rate of coloration. Only the true *P. nigra* will produce culms that become an even, complete black and glossy. Many inferior clones in cultivation do not color so quickly, nor do they achieve quite the same depth of color. Such clones are often taller, more vigorous, and produce noticeably greater culm diameters. These clones should correctly be regarded as *P. nigra* 'Punctata'. Some of the better clones of *P. nigra* have been named, such as *P. nigra* 'Hale', which is purported to turn black more quickly.

Phylogenetically, *P. nigra* 'Henonis' is really the typical form of the species, and *P. nigra* is a mutated form with black pigments. However, since 'Henonis' was discovered and named after *P. nigra*, under the rules of nomenclature it must be regarded as a cultivar.

Phyllostachys nigra flowered for the first time in Europe and the United States between 1900 and 1905, and again between 1930 and 1935. A great number of seedlings were raised from these flowerings, giving rise to the many clones now in cultivation.

Culms Very tall and medium-thick, 5 to 8 m (16 to 26 feet) tall and 2 to 3 cm (¾ to 1¼ inches) in diameter. Most often seen at the smaller end of these dimensions or even slightly less. Olive green at first, quickly becoming mottled brownish black and eventually more or less solid jet-black. Nodes prominent. Soon arching gently from midlength and only more upright in very open growing conditions. New shoots appear in early summer. **Culm sheaths** Not persistent. Green flushed with pale reddish brown, sparsely covered in fine hairs. The blade is narrowly triangular and boat-shaped, wavy on the uppermost sheaths; auricles are well developed with long, curved oral setae; and the ligule is very short. **Branches** In pairs. Unequal and fairly long, occasionally with a weakly developed third branch between them. **Leaves** Short and narrow, 5 to 9 cm (2 to 3½ inches) long by 1 to 1.5 cm (⅜ to ⅝

inch) wide. Bright green and becoming glossy on the upper surface, matte grayish green on the lower surface, tapering gradually to a point at the tip. **Rhizomes** Invasive (leptomorph). Almost static in cooler conditions. **Cultivation** Sun or semi-shade. An open position in full sun with dry, relatively poor soil will hasten the blackening process, though if taken to extremes this will be to the detriment of the foliage and general appearance. **Hardiness** –10°C to –20°C (14°F to –4°F).

Phyllostachys nigra.

Phyllostachys nigra 'Boryana'

Synonyms *P. boryana*, *P. nigra* 'Bory', *P. nigra* var. *boryanus*, *P. puberula* var. *boryana*

Extremely tall bamboo—invasive

Differs from the species by having green culms that become brown-blotched, and by having a larger stature.

Culms Extremely tall and thick, more than 8 m (26 feet) tall and 3 to 5 cm (1¼ to 2 inches) in diameter. Slender for their height and usually at the smaller end of the diameters stated here. Olive green at first, becoming blotched and spotted with dark brown until this color is almost solid, the colors eventually fading with age. Inclined to arch heavily from midlength. **Rhizomes** More invasive than the species. **Cultivation** A much better habit will be achieved in a very open position, although strong sunlight hastens the ripening of the culms and thus reduces the contrast of the colors.

Phyllostachys nigra 'Boryana'.

Phyllostachys nigra 'Henonis'

Synonyms *P. henonis*, *P. nigra* 'Henon', *P. nigra* var. *henonis*, *P. puberula* var. *henonis*

Extremely tall bamboo—invasive

Differs from the species by having completely green culms and a larger stature. Phylogenetically, 'Henonis' is really the typical form of the species, but since it was discovered and named after *P. nigra*, under the rules of nomenclature it must be regarded as a cultivar. The culms grow much more strongly than those of the species and can attain almost twice the height. It is a magnificent foliage plant, with plumes of small glossy leaves carried on gently arching culms.

Culms Extremely tall and thick, more than 8 m (26 feet) tall and 3 to 5 cm (1¼ to 2 inches) in diameter. Somewhat slender for their height. Olive green at first, maturing to yellowish green. Arching gently from midlength. **Rhizomes** More invasive than *P. nigra*. **Cultivation** Grow in a very open position for an improved habit.

Phyllostachys nigra 'Megurochiku'

Extremely tall bamboo—invasive

Differs from the species by having green culms with regular black striping, and a larger stature. This superb form is still uncommon in cultivation in the West. The black coloration takes quite a long time to appear, often requir-

Phyllostachys nigra 'Henonis' in a large private garden.

ing the passage of more than two years before it is a completely solid jet-black. The height of the culms and their thickness compared with other forms of *P. nigra* combine to give a most satisfactory effect where space permits.

Culms Extremely tall and thick, more than 8 m (26 feet) tall and 3 to 5 cm (1¼ to 2 inches) in diameter. Not so slender for their height as other forms of *P. nigra*. Olive green at first, slowly developing a black panel in the sulcus, the black deepening with age while the other

A three-year-old culm of *Phyllostachys nigra* 'Megurochiku' showing the black stripe in the sulcus well developed.

parts of the culm mature to yellowish green. Culms arch less heavily than those of the species unless this bamboo is grown in an enclosed position. **Rhizomes** More invasive than the species. **Cultivation** A much better habit is achieved in an open position, and good sunlight will hasten the appearance of the black striping.

Phyllostachys nuda

Native to China

Very tall bamboo—invasive

A very robust species with a tidy habit, useful for making hedges or screens but otherwise unremarkable. The species name refers to the absence of auricles and oral setae on both the culm and leaf sheaths.

Culms Very tall and medium-thick, 5 to 8 m (16 to 26 feet) tall and 2 to 3 cm (¾ to 1¼ inches) in diameter. Dull green, often tinted purple when very young, maturing to yellowish green. The lower internodes prone to occasional geniculations. Nodes prominent. New shoots appear in early summer. **Culm sheaths** Not persistent. Grayish green tinted red. The blade is short and lanceolate, auricles and oral setae are lacking, and the ligule is prominent. **Branches** In pairs. Unequal and fairly long, occasionally with a weakly developed third branch between them. **Leaves** Medium-long and narrow, 9 to 18 cm (3½ to 7 inches) long by 1 to 1.5 cm (⅜ to ⅝ inch) wide. Bright green on the upper surface, matte green on the lower surface, tapering fairly abruptly at the tip. **Rhizomes** Invasive (leptomorph). Fairly slow to spread in cooler conditions. **Cultivation** Sun or semi-shade. Best in an open position. **Hardiness** Below −20°C (−4°F).

Phyllostachys parvifolia

Native to China

Extremely tall bamboo—invasive

A very attractive species of architectural proportions. It has been in cultivation in Western gardens since the mid-1990s but remains fairly uncommon. Introduced to Great Britain by myself in 1995. The combination of comparatively small leaves and thick culms gives it a distinctive open appearance, which is unusual among the genus. Although of easy cultivation, it does seem to need regular feeding or a very rich soil; otherwise the older leaves are inclined to become somewhat pale and yellowed, to the detriment of the overall effect.

Phyllostachys parvifolia.

Culms Extremely tall and very thick, more than 8 m (26 feet) tall and more than 5 cm (2 inches) in diameter. Deep green at first, quickly ripening to pale green and then pale yellowish green. Nodes prominent, with a conspicuous, broad farinose zone beneath that persists as the culm ages. Typically just less than upright in habit, and very sturdy, with little or no arching of older culms. New shoots appear in early summer. **Culm sheaths** Pale pinkish rose. The blade is small and narrowly lanceolate, auricles and oral setae are weakly developed, and the ligule is not prominent. **Branches** In pairs. Unequal and fairly long, occasionally with a weakly developed third branch between them. **Leaves** Short and medium-broad, 5 to 9 cm (2 to 3½ inches) long by 1.5 to 3 cm (⅝ to 1¼ inches) wide. Sparse in number. Pale green on the upper surface, matte green on the lower surface, tapering abruptly to a point at the tip. **Rhizomes** Invasive (leptomorph). Fairly slow to spread in cooler conditions, which is useful in such a thick-culmed bamboo. **Cultivation** Sun or semi-shade. Best in an open position. **Hardiness** −10°C to −20°C (14°F to −4°F).

Phyllostachys praecox

Native to China

Very tall bamboo—invasive

An obscure species rarely seen outside botanic gardens. It has a strong, robust appearance and, along with its cultivars, deserves to be more widely grown. The new shoots are favored as the chief seasonal fresh vegetable in the Shanghai and Zhejiang provinces of China.

Culms Very tall and thick, 5 to 8 m (16 to 26 feet) tall and 3 to 5 cm (1¼ to 2 inches) in diameter. Can easily attain the larger end of these dimensions. Bright green at first, with faint, thin yellow striping developing at random, particularly in the lower internodes, the striping becoming almost lost as the culm matures to yellowish green. Nodes prominent, tinted purple when young. Fairly upright, with minimal arching of older culms, and sturdy-looking. New shoots appear in late spring. **Culm sheaths** Not persistent. Greenish brown with small, darker brown spots. The blade is broadly lanceolate and crinkled, auricles and oral setae are not developed, and the ligule is prominent and convex. **Branches** In pairs. Unequal, fairly long, and very stout and sturdy in appearance, occasionally with a weakly developed third branch between them. **Leaves** Medium-long and medium-broad, 9 to 18 cm (3½ to 7 inches) long by 1.5 to 3 cm (⅝ to 1¼ inches) wide. Bright green on the upper surface, matte green on the lower surface, tapering gradually at the tip. **Rhizomes** Invasive (leptomorph). Fairly slow to spread in cooler conditions. **Cultivation** Sun or semi-shade. Best in an open position. **Hardiness** –10°C to –20°C (14°F to –4°F).

Phyllostachys praecox 'Notata'

Very tall bamboo—invasive

Differs from the species by having green culms with regular yellow striping, and a slightly smaller stature. This interesting form is worth growing but is likely to be difficult to obtain. The yellow coloration in the sulcus is rather muted and does not contrast very strongly with the rest of the culm.

    Culms Slightly smaller than those of *P. praecox*. Bright green with a softly contrasting yellow panel in the sulcus, often having thin green striping within the yellow, the contrast between the colors reducing as the culm ages to yellowish green.

Phyllostachys praecox 'Viridisulcata'

Very tall bamboo—invasive

Differs from the species by having yellow culms with regular green striping, and a slightly smaller stature. This is by far the best form of this species. I know of at least one introduction to Western cultivation, but this cultivar is likely to be very difficult to obtain for some time to come.

    Culms Slightly smaller than those of *P. praecox*. Bright light yellow with a contrasting green panel in the sulcus, and frequently with additional green stripes here and there, the colors becoming dull with age. **Leaves** A thin creamy yellow stripe may be found on a leaf here and there.

Phyllostachys propinqua

Native to China

Very tall bamboo—invasive

This species has been more widely grown in recent years, particularly in regions with colder winters, where it has proved to be very tolerant of prolonged frost and exposure. It also has the desirable characteristics of being very strong and upright. It can be identified by the culm sheaths or, upon closer inspection, by the tendency of the leaves to be perceptibly concave across their breadth, due to a slight curling up of the edges to form a shallow channel.

    Culms Very tall and thick, 5 to 8 m (16 to 26 feet) tall and 3 to 5 cm (1¼ to 2 inches) in diameter. Thick for their height. Dull green at first, maturing to yellowish green. Nodes prominent. Upright in habit with a slight arch near the summit. New shoots appear in midsummer. **Culm sheaths** Not persistent. Pale olive green with a bronzy sheen and a few small brown spots. The blade is ribbon-shaped and

Phyllostachys propinqua.

reflexed, auricles and oral setae are lacking, and the ligule is weakly developed. **Branches** In pairs. Unequal and fairly long, occasionally with a weakly developed third branch between them. **Leaves** Medium-long and medium-broad, 9 to 18 cm (3½ to 7 inches) long by 1.5 to 3 cm (⅝ to 1¼ inches) wide. Rich lime green on the upper surface, matte green on the lower surface, the edges often slightly turned up to create a concave effect, tapering to a slender point at the tip. **Rhizomes** Invasive (leptomorph). Fairly slow to spread in cooler conditions. **Cultivation** Sun or semi-shade. Best in an open position. **Hardiness** Below –20°C (–4°F).

Phyllostachys propinqua 'Bicolor'

Very tall bamboo—invasive
Differs from the species by having yellow culms with regular green striping, and a slightly smaller stature. A fine colored-culm bamboo. Unfortunately, almost all the plants brought in from China have come into flower. Hopefully some will recover; otherwise this cultivar may have to be reintroduced.

    Culms Slightly smaller than those of the species. Bright light yellow with a contrasting green panel in the sulcus, which often extends beyond each side of it, and frequently having additional green stripes here and there, the colors eventually fading with age. **Leaves** A thin creamy yellow stripe may be found on a leaf here and there.

Phyllostachys rubromarginata

Native to China
Extremely tall bamboo—invasive
An impressive species grown for the height of its culms and their very upright habit. The name *rubromarginata* refers to the red-margined culm sheaths. This species is very distinctive and unlikely to be confused with any other green-culmed *Phyllostachys*. The culms

Phyllostachys rubromarginata making attractive tall plumes of foliage.

have a very cylindrical appearance and give an effect like a series of pipes planted in the ground.

    Culms Extremely tall and thick, more than 8 m (26 feet) tall and 3 to 5 cm (1¼ to 2 inches) in diameter. Bright green at first, maturing to yellowish gray-green. Internodes comparatively long. Nodes moderately prominent and hardly breaking the contours of the culm. Very upright in habit, developing a slight arch after about three-quarters of their length. New shoots appear in midsummer. **Culm sheaths** Not persistent. Olive green to buff and bordered on the upper margins with red. The blade is narrowly triangular to ribbon-shaped, auricles and oral setae are lacking, and the ligule is dark red, short, and truncated. **Branches** In pairs. Unequal and fairly long, occasionally with a weakly developed third branch between them. **Leaves** Medium-long and medium-broad, 9 to 18 cm (3½ to 7 inches) long by 1.5 to 3 cm (⅝ to 1¼ inches) wide. Bright green on the upper surface, grayish green on the lower surface, tapering fairly abruptly to a point at the tip. **Rhizomes** Invasive (leptomorph). Fairly slow to spread in cooler conditions. **Cultivation** Sun or semi-shade. Best in an open position. **Hardiness** –10°C to –20°C (14°F to –4°F).

Phyllostachys violascens

Synonym *P. bambusoides* 'Violascens'
Native to China
Very tall bamboo—very invasive
This species has been in cultivation at least since it was introduced into Europe in 1869, but is of obscure origin in the wild. There seem to be two clones in cultivation, one of which develops its striping colorations much faster

than the other. The culms are very thin-walled and split easily when cut with secateurs. It is very vigorous and much too invasive for a small garden or restricted space. However, it is among the best bamboos to quickly create a grove effect in cooler climates. In general appearance it is very similar to *P. iridescens* but has finer foliage and develops its striping more consistently and with deeper colors.

Culms Very tall and thick, 5 to 8 m (16 to 26 feet) tall and 3 to 5 cm (1¼ to 2 inches) in diameter. Easily attaining the larger end of these dimensions. Deep purple at first when grown in

A three-year-old culm of *Phyllostachys violascens* showing the colors at their best.

sunlight, quickly becoming midgreen, and by the end of the first season developing variable amounts of muted yellowish striping around the circumference of the culm. The striping becomes reddish brown with age, then violet-purple in places, while the rest of the culm matures to yellowish green. Nodes prominent. Very upright in habit with only minimal arching of older culms. New shoots appear in early summer. **Culm sheaths** Not persistent. Deep purple when emerging from the ground, becoming greenish purple. The blade is lanceolate, auricles and oral setae are well developed, and the ligule is short and convex. **Branches** In pairs. Unequal and fairly long, occasionally with a weakly developed third branch between them. **Leaves** Medium-long and medium-broad, 9 to 18 cm (3½ to 7 inches) long by 1.5 to 3 cm (⅝ to 1¼ inches) wide. Bright green on the upper surface, matte green on the lower surface, tapering gradually to a point at the tip. **Rhizomes** Very invasive (strongly leptomorph). Rapidly spreads even in cooler conditions and quickly forms an open grove. **Cultivation** Sun or semishade. Best in an open position, although strong sunlight will ripen the culms more quickly and reduce the contrast of the striping. **Hardiness** −10°C to −20°C (14°F to −4°F).

Phyllostachys viridiglaucescens
Native to China
Very tall bamboo—invasive

This species is very common in cultivation and frequently encountered as a mature grove in older gardens. It was introduced into France in 1846 and then distributed to other parts of Europe. With practice, one can identify it from a distance by its heavy, bunched foliage and marked tendency to produce culms on a long

Phyllostachys viridiglaucescens.

curve at the edges of the grove. When grown well in warmer conditions it is impressive enough, but as a subject for cool-temperate gardens it is rather loose and coarse. Some thinner culms may fall sideways to the ground under their own weight even before developing foliage. This bamboo has been superseded by more recently introduced species.

Culms Very tall and thick, 5 to 8 m (16 to 26 feet) tall and 3 to 5 cm (1¼ to 2 inches) in diameter. Seldom seen at the larger end of these dimensions. Deep green at first, maturing to yellowish green. Internodes smooth. Nodes prominent. Moderately upright, but thinner culms inclined to be excessively lax. New shoots appear in late spring. **Culm sheaths** Not persistent. Pale buff tinted purplish green and covered in small brown spots and blotches. The blade is narrowly ribbon-shaped, reflexed, and crinkled, auricles and oral setae are usually well developed, and the ligule is prominent. **Branches** In pairs. Unequal and fairly long, occasionally with a weakly developed third branch between them. **Leaves** Medium-long and medium-broad, 9 to 18 cm (3½ to 7 inches) long by 1.5 to 3 cm (⅝ to 1¼ inches) wide. Coarse and heavy in appearance and held in bunches. Deep green on the upper surface, grayish green on the lower surface, tapering gradually to a point at the tip. **Rhizomes** Invasive (leptomorph). Quite rapid to spread once established in favorable conditions. **Cultivation** Sun or semi-shade. Best in a very open position. Can be of extremely poor habit if grown in shade. **Hardiness** Below −20°C (−4°F).

Phyllostachys viridis

Synonyms *P. mitis, P. sulphurea* 'Viridis'
Native to China
Extremely tall bamboo—invasive

A magnificent, strong species capable of growing to an immense size in warmer climates.

The thicker culms have a most architectural appearance, being almost cylindrical, with their nodes hardly breaking the outer contours of the culm, and are perfectly complemented by the small, elegant leaves. An open grove is quickly produced in which it is possible to walk between the culms. In cooler climates this species needs a little perseverance, as it can be slow to establish and very shy to produce new shoots unless growing conditions are acceptable. The whole plant is also

The culms of *Phyllostachys viridis* have a distinct farinose zone beneath the nodes when young, and the surface of the culm is minutely dimpled.

prone to wind-rock or blowing over until the rhizomes have spread out sufficiently. There is a tendency, too, for new shoots to emerge quite late in the growing season, which do not ripen sufficiently before the winter frosts. Moreover, some culms, even those of larger diameter, produce long congested branches in the lower parts of the culm. These branches often die back partially or completely in the following winter and are best quickly removed as the culm grows so as to avoid spoiling the visual effect. Once properly established, this bamboo quickly generates far-reaching rhizomes, from which emerge culms of impressive diameter, especially for cool-temperate conditions.

Culms Extremely tall and very thick, more than 8 m (26 feet) tall and more than 5 cm (2 inches) in diameter. Bright green, maturing to yellowish green. Thin-walled. Internodes minutely dimpled in a pigskin-like pattern, with a conspicuous farinose zone beneath each node. Nodes not prominent, particularly in thicker culms. Almost upright in habit, with a slight arch near the summit. New shoots appear in early summer. **Culm sheaths** Not persistent. Light rose-buff with green veins, conspicuously spotted with grayish brown. The blade is narrowly triangular to ribbon-shaped and wavy, auricles and oral setae are completely absent, and the ligule is convex. **Branches** In pairs. Unequal and fairly long, occasionally with a weakly developed third branch between them. **Leaves** Medium-long and medium-broad, 9 to 18 cm (3½ to 7 inches) long by 1.5 to 3 cm (⅝ to 1¼ inches) wide. Typically at the smaller end of these dimensions. Bright green on the upper surface, dull grayish green on the lower surface, bluntly tapering at the tip to a sharp point. **Rhizomes** Invasive (leptomorph). Takes time to establish in cool conditions but is more strongly spreading once established or if grown in warmer conditions. **Cultivation** Sun

or semi-shade. Much better in an open position with good sunlight. Far less impressive in shade. Not recommended for windy locations. **Hardiness** –10°C to –20°C (14°F to –4°F).

Phyllostachys viridis 'Houzeau'

Extremely tall bamboo—invasive

Differs from the species by having green culms with regular yellow striping, and a very slightly smaller stature. A very pleasing form that is less common in cultivation but well

Phyllostachys viridis 'Houzeau' in the Bambouseraie de Prafrance. The larger culms on the right have ripened and therefore lost the contrast of any striping.

worth seeking out. The contrast between the colors of the culm is subtle, not gaudy, and at its best when the culm is young. The stature in cool-temperate conditions is virtually as large as the species. Although this bamboo occurs in the wild, it was discovered in cultivation as a spontaneous mutation from a rhizome cutting of the green species, and named after Jean Houzeau de Lehaie, a Belgian plantsman.

Culms Very slightly smaller than those of *P. viridis*. Bright green with a softly contrasting yellow panel in the sulcus. The green parts of the culm eventually mature to yellowish green, while the yellow parts become deeper yellow with age.

Phyllostachys viridis 'Sulphurea' thriving in warm growing conditions in the Bambouseraie de Prafrance. In a cool-temperate climate the culms may not be so thick or attain such a deep color.

Phyllostachys viridis 'Sulphurea'

Synonyms *P. sulphurea*, *P. viridis* 'Robert Young'
Extremely tall bamboo—invasive

Differs from the species by having completely yellow culms and a slightly smaller stature. Commonly known as the Robert Young bamboo. A superb form that is cultivated extensively in Europe and the United States. The color of the culms is not particularly striking at sheath fall but improves with age and exposure to high light intensity. When grown in strong sunlight in warmer climates, 'Sulphurea' quickly becomes an intense, brilliant golden yellow. Even in cool-temperate conditions this is a most impressive and desirable bamboo, where its stature is almost as large as the species.

Culms Slightly smaller than those of *P. viridis*. Muted greenish yellow at first, becoming

brighter golden yellow with age. Internodes have a thin broken band of green under each node, and from this a thin green stripe will occasionally be present, particularly on lower internodes. **Leaves** A thin creamy yellow stripe may be found on a leaf here and there. **Cultivation** In cooler or more northerly (or southerly if in the southern hemisphere) climates, good light intensity is essential for proper development of culm coloration.

Phyllostachys vivax

Native to China

Extremely tall bamboo—very invasive

An impressive species, vigorous enough to reliably produce groves of reasonably thick culms, even in cooler climates. It is usefully hardier than *P. bambusoides*, with which it is most likely to be confused, and can be distinguished from

that species by its attractive, longer, drooping foliage and more upright culms with slightly ribbed internodes. In common with other large *Phyllostachys* species, *P. vivax* needs to be planted with adequate room for future growth. Although the rhizomes are not quite as diffuse as those of *P. dulcis*, they are sufficiently active to make this bamboo rather too overpowering for small urban gardens. Although the culms are fairly upright, they are comparatively thin-walled and liable to arch or lean excessively with age; it is best to remove them once they reach this stage.

Culms Extremely tall and very thick, more than 8 m (26 feet) tall and more than 5 cm (2 inches) in diameter. Deep green at first, maturing to yellowish green. Internodes with per-

Phyllostachys vivax.

ceptible longitudinal ridges. Nodes prominent. Upright in habit with a slight arch near the summit. New shoots appear in late spring. **Culm sheaths** Not persistent. Creamy buff with grayish brown to brownish black spots. The blade is narrowly triangular to ribbon-shaped, reflexed, and strongly crinkled, auricles and oral setae are lacking, and the ligule is weakly prominent. **Branches** In pairs. Unequal and fairly long, occasionally with a weakly developed third branch between them. **Leaves** Long and medium-broad, 18 to 25 cm (7 to 10 inches) long by 1.5 to 3 cm (⅝ to 1¼ inches) wide. Rich green on the upper surface, grayish green with a lighter strip on one side on the

Phyllostachys vivax 'Aureocaulis' is the best bamboo for producing thick, golden yellow culms in a cool-temperate climate.

lower surface, tapering gradually to a point at the tip. **Rhizomes** Very invasive (strongly leptomorph). Quickly forms an open grove even in cool conditions. **Cultivation** Sun or semishade. Best in an open position. **Hardiness** Below −20°C (−4°F).

Phyllostachys vivax 'Aureocaulis'

Extremely tall bamboo—very invasive Differs from the species by having completely yellow culms and a slightly smaller stature. Probably the best yellow-culmed bamboo for cooler climates. The color may not be as deep as may be found in the *P. bambusoides* group, but is a radiant butter yellow with occasional random fine green stripes that appear as if they had been painted on with extreme finesse. Taking into consideration its good foliage, habit, and hardiness, this cultivar excels all others of

similar coloration. The culms are at their best color when young, losing their attractiveness with age, whereupon they should be regularly removed.

Culms Slightly smaller than those of the species. Rich bright yellow at first, becoming deeper golden yellow, then slightly orange-yellow. Very small culms frequently have a high percentage of random green panels and stripes, while larger culms have just occasional thin green stripes here and there. **Leaves** A thin creamy yellow stripe may be found on a leaf here and there.

Phyllostachys vivax 'Haunvenzhu'.

Phyllostachys vivax 'Huanvenzhu'

Extremely tall bamboo—very invasive
Differs from the species by having green culms with regular yellow striping, and a very slightly smaller stature. This cultivar is attractive and desirable but is unfortunately rather unstable. It occurs occasionally as a mutation within groves of *P. vivax* and occurs frequently within groves of *P. vivax* 'Aureocaulis'. When such mutations are propagated, they are liable to produce new culms that are reversions to the green species or, more usually, that emerge as 'Aureocaulis'. Some may even emerge as a mixture of all three! In cool-temperate climates this cultivar is only imperceptibly smaller than the species.

Culms Very slightly smaller than those of the species. Deep green with a light golden yellow panel in the sulcus. The green parts of the culm eventually mature to yellowish green, and the yellow parts become a deeper golden yellow with age.

Phyllostachys vivax 'Huanvenzhu Inversa'

Extremely tall bamboo—very invasive
Differs from the species by having yellow culms with regular green striping, and a slightly smaller stature. An interesting and highly desirable new form that has occurred as a mutation of 'Huanvenzhu' in which the colors of the culm appear reversed. It can easily be confused with *P. bambusoides* 'Castillonis' but has the longer leaves and general habit of the *P. vivax* group. So far it is proving to be more stable than 'Huanvenzhu'.

Culms Slightly smaller than those of the species. Rich bright yellow with a strongly contrasting green panel in the sulcus and an occasional green stripe appearing on an internode here and there. The colors fade with age.

Pleioblastus

This large genus contains species very diverse in size and habit, many of which were once ascribed to *Arundinaria*. They are native to China and Japan; however, many of the early introductions to Western cultivation are of obscure provenance. While some species are attractive and useful, others are of minimal horticultural merit and are best relegated to the wilder parts of the garden. All have searching leptomorph rhizomes and a dense, thicket-forming habit.

Taller *Pleioblastus* bamboos can only be used to make specimen plants if their spread is restricted or controlled. They are really more suited to being boundary plants or a tough windbreak. With few exceptions, all species are adaptable to sun or shade and will flourish as understory plants in woodland. Among the shorter species are found some of the best groundcover bamboos, capable of quickly smothering all but the most determined of weeds. The more rampant groundcover types are very effective for stabilizing steep slopes or banks.

Identification of *Pleioblastus* species is not always straightforward. Common characteristics include the leptomorph rhizomes and the cylindrical culms with their persistent sheaths and usually multiple branches. However, many of the shorter *Pleioblastus* bamboos are sasoid in appearance, with broader leaves and sometimes solitary branches. In most cases it is easier to distinguish members of this genus by their habit and foliage.

Pleioblastus akebono

Native to Japan (known only in cultivation)
Very short bamboo—invasive

This charming dwarf species has a distinctive white coloration in the younger leaves and has a minimal rate of invasion. The name is derived from a Japanese word meaning "aurora." It is classed as a species primarily because it comes true from seed, unlike most other variegated bamboos, but some authorities believe it is merely a form of *P. humilis*. Sometimes this species can be a little difficult to establish, succeeding best in light woodland conditions. Exposure to strong sunlight can scorch the new leaves, particularly at the tips. An excellent groundcover bamboo for restricted spaces.

Culms Very short and very slender, less than 1 m (3 feet) tall and less than 6 mm (¼ inch) in diameter. Dull green, becoming yellowish green with age. Nodes not prominent. Upright in the first season, then arching over almost to the ground. New shoots appear in

Pleioblastus akebono is an unusual bamboo for a shady position at the front of a border.

midspring. **Culm sheaths** Persistent. Whitish green when first emerging from the ground and when growing strongly, becoming pale green. **Branches** Solitary. Often unbranched, otherwise solitary and long for the size of the culm. **Leaves** Medium-long and narrow, 9 to 18 cm (3½ to 7 inches) long by 1 to 1.5 cm (⅜ to ⅝ inch) wide. Almost completely white on the upper surface when growing strongly in early summer, but more usually pale green at the base progressing through greenish white to white at the tip, the colors more matte on the lower surface, tapering gradually from mid-length to a slender point at the tip. Coloration diminishes as the leaf matures, and the whole length of the leaf becomes almost completely green by winter.. **Rhizomes** Invasive (leptomorph). Spreads slowly even under good growing conditions. **Cultivation** Semi-shade or shade. Optimum leaf color is attained in partially shaded locations away from strong sunlight in summer. **Hardiness** Below −20°C (−4°F).

Pleioblastus auricomus

Synonyms *Arundinaria auricoma, A. viridistriata, P. viridistriatus*

Native to Japan

Short bamboo—invasive

This species was named *auricoma*, which means "golden-haired," by Algernon Bertram Freeman-Mitford. It is believed to have been introduced into Europe in the 1870s and has been extensively cultivated ever since. It is extensively grown throughout the United States.

Pleioblastus auricomus is widely regarded as the most satisfactory shorter variegated bamboo. The leaves are exceptionally beautiful, particularly in early summer, when leaf color is at its best. Each leaf has a widely variable amount of green striping on a brilliant golden yellow background, although this coloration is quite lost in too much shade. The upper and particularly the lower surfaces are covered in fine velvety hairs (cilia), making the foliage pleasing to the touch. As the season progresses, so the leaf color gradually loses its impact, and by the end of winter the plant can look rather leafless, a shadow of its summer glory. For this reason it is often best to cut the whole plant to the ground in early spring. The fresh new growth is then uncluttered by any dead material left from the previous season.

This is one of the few shorter bamboos that can be planted in ornamental borders without any risk of it taking over. Indeed, it can even be recommended as a taller subject for the rockery if cut to the ground each spring. The annual spread is modest, even in lush conditions, and the rhizomes usually stay close to the surface.

Although originally named as a species, this bamboo is really just a yellow-variegated mutation of some other species. Now included in *Pleioblastus*, it was named and cultivated long before any academic research had been undertaken, and its exact origin is unclear. Phylogenetically it is a sasoid bamboo, and it may be a mutation of *Sasaella ramosa*. Flowering has been a frequent occurrence for this bamboo ever since it was brought into cultivation. The flowerings are usually partial and limited to a few isolated culms, with the rest of the plant growing normally.

Culms Short and very slender, 1 to 2 m (3 to 6 feet) tall and up to 6 mm (¼ inch) in diameter. Typically seen at the lower end of this height. Dark purple-green, becoming purplish yellow-green with age. Rather thick-walled for their height. Internodes covered in fine hairs when young. Nodes not prominent. More or less upright when young, although occasionally rather zigzag in the upper parts of the culm. New shoots appear in early spring. **Culm sheaths** Persistent. Pale green. **Branches** Solitary. Sparsely branched throughout. Branches rather long in proportion to the height of the culm and occasionally in unequal pairs. **Leaves** Medium-long and medium-broad, 9 to 18 cm (3½ to 7 inches) long by 1.5 to 3 cm (⅝ to 1¼ inches) wide. Very variable. Deep, rich golden yellow on the upper surface, with variable amounts of green striping, covered in velvety hairs when young, the yellow reducing in intensity as the season progresses, colors more matte on the lower surface, tapering fairly abruptly to a point at the tip. **Rhizomes** Invasive (leptomorph). Spreads very slowly in most situations and can safely be planted in shrub borders. **Cultivation** Sun or semi-shade. In

cool-temperate climates this bamboo needs to be planted in good sunlight to get the best leaf color. In warmer localities a position in full sun may lead to a little curling and leaf scorch during very long, hot summers. **Hardiness** Below −20°C (−4°F).

Pleioblastus auricomus 'Bracken Hill'

Medium bamboo—invasive

Differs from the species by having slightly larger leaves and a larger stature. This cultivar was discovered by David McClintock in his own garden, after which it is named. Originally one of several plantings of the species, this particular grove grew to become noticeably taller than the others, with larger leaves. As a small plant, 'Bracken Hill' is indistin-

Pleioblastus auricomus in early summer when the foliage is fresh and at its best.

guishable from the species, and care should be taken to avoid mixing them up.

Culms Medium-tall and very slender, 2 to 3 m (6 to 10 feet) tall and less than 6 mm (¼ inch) in diameter. Tall for their thickness and inclined to arch unless grown in the open. **Leaves** Slightly larger than those of the species. **Cultivation** If grown in too much shade, this bamboo will become very drawn and lax, with poor leaf color.

Pleioblastus auricomus 'Chrysophyllus'

Short bamboo—invasive

Differs from the species by having completely yellow leaves. An attractive cultivar useful for

Pleioblastus auricomus 'Chrysophyllus' stands out against the contrasting foliage of other plants in a shady border at Stream Cottage.

brightening up shady corners or under large shrubs or trees. It is an excellent contrast to other plants with dark green foliage. The leaves are very sensitive to light intensity, prone to scorching in too much direct sunlight and not developing their color properly in too much shade; partial shade is ideal. This cultivar can sometimes occur spontaneously within plantings of the species.

Leaves Bright golden yellow on the upper surface, particularly when growing strongly in early summer, the yellow reducing in intensity to become greenish yellow as the season progresses. **Rhizomes** Very slightly more invasive than the species. **Cultivation** Provide shade from midday sun during summer for best leaf color and condition.

Pleioblastus chino

Synonyms *Arundinaria chino*, *A. simonii* var. *chino*

Native to Japan

Medium bamboo—very invasive

This rather dull species is of limited use and is inclined to look lackluster and scruffy in winter. The upright culms with their steepled branches resemble a scaled-down version of *P. simonii*, with which this species can sometimes be confused. Unless *P. chino* is grown in a very dry position, the rhizomes spread actively, and it can only be recommended as a screening or infill plant for the more remote parts of the garden. Despite its winter appearance, it is very hardy and sufficiently vigorous to be planted in places where other bamboos would give up. It was introduced into England in 1875. Over the years many cultivated forms of *P. chino* have appeared, with variable amounts of white or creamy yellow striping in the foliage, and the naming of these has been much confused. It is likely that some of these forms will turn out to be forms of other species. The various forms of *P. chino* are all much better garden plants than the plain green species and should be given preference in any planting scheme.

Culms Medium-tall and slender, 2 to 3 m (6 to 10 feet) tall and 6 mm to 2 cm (¼ to ¾ inch) in diameter. Dull olive green, tinted purple-green in places when young and exposed to sunlight, becoming dull yellowish green with age. Nodes moderately prominent. Stiffly upright in habit during the first season, becoming moderately arched in the upper parts with the weight of the foliage in subsequent seasons. New shoots appear in early summer. **Culm sheaths** Persistent. Pale purple when young, becoming purplish green. **Branches** Multiple. Often borne singly in the first season, with nine or more shorter branches developing thereaf-

ter. **Leaves** Long and medium-broad, 18 to 25 cm (7 to 10 inches) long by 1.5 to 3 cm (⅝ to 1¼ inches) wide. Very dark green on the upper surface, grayish green with a glossier strip of dark green on one side on the lower surface, tapering to a long, slender point at the tip. **Rhizomes** Very invasive (strongly leptomorph). Quite rampant in all but the poorest growing conditions and should be planted with care. **Cultivation** Sun or shade. Very tough and adaptable. Can be planted as a windbreak in exposed places where winter appearance is not important. **Hardiness** Below −20°C (−4°F).

Pleioblastus chino 'Aureostriata'

Short bamboo—invasive

Differs from the species by having white-variegated leaves and a smaller stature. This is

Pleioblastus chino 'Aureostriata'.

among the more attractive variegated bamboos in cultivation. It is widely cultivated and fairly easy to recognize. The striping in the leaves seems to be unaffected by light levels, making this a good variegated bamboo for shade. Although the variegation is stable, leaves are frequently produced that are completely green, giving the misleading impression that a reversion to the type has occurred.

Culms Short and very slender, 1 to 2 m (3 to 6 feet) tall and less than 6 mm (¼ inch) in diameter. Inclined to arch from midlength unless grown in a very open position. **Leaves** Midgreen with very variable amounts of white striping on the upper surface, individual leaves ranging from completely green to almost com-

pletely white, the striping quickly becoming creamy yellowish white as the season progresses, colors more matte on the lower surface, tapering more abruptly to a point at the tip. **Rhizomes** Slightly less invasive than the species.

Pleioblastus chino 'Elegantissima'

Synonym *P. chino* f. *angustifolius*

Medium bamboo—very invasive

Differs from the species by having smaller leaves with white variegations. An attractive form with a very stable and consistent variegation. The coloration of the leaves is not particularly conspicuous, even when the plant is growing strongly in early summer. Although slow to put on height, it will grow away in time to be almost as tall as the species. It can be confused with *P. simonii* 'Variegatus' but does not grow so tall, has much more consistent variegations, and as the name suggests, is also much more elegant.

Leaves Medium-long and narrow, 9 to 18 cm (3½ to 7 inches) long by 1 to 1.5 cm (⅜ to ⅝ inch) wide. Often very narrow for their length. Dark green, consistently with moderately conspicuous thin white striping on the upper surface, the white reducing slightly in brightness and intensity as the season progresses. Striping does not always penetrate through to the lower surface, where the colors are otherwise more matte. **Rhizomes** If anything, even more invasive than the species. **Cultivation** Variegations are brighter and retained better in a sunny position.

Pleioblastus chino 'Kimmei'

Short bamboo—invasive

Differs from the species by having yellow culms with variable green striping, yellow-variegated leaves, and a smaller stature. A sought-after form that is still uncommon in cultiva-

Pleioblastus chino 'Elegantissima'.

tion. Although by no means one of the principal yellow-culmed bamboos for ornamental planting, it is still an attractive shorter bamboo for planting under trees or in a shady corner, where the color of the culms can be enjoyed to best effect.

Culms Short and very slender, 1 to 2 m (3 to 6 feet) tall and less than 6 mm (¼ inch) in diameter. Sometimes slightly larger in dimension. Rather pale yellow at first, with thin green panels or stripes occurring usually above the branches, occasionally elsewhere, though sometimes absent. The yellow deepens with age to become golden yellow. **Leaves** Slightly smaller than those of the species. Dark green with very variable amounts of creamy yellow striping on the upper surface, the striping quickly becoming yellow and then deep yellow as the season progresses, colors more matte on the lower surface, tapering more abruptly to a point at the tip. **Rhizomes** Slightly less invasive than the species.

Pleioblastus chino 'Murakamianus'

Short bamboo—invasive

Differs from the species by having completely yellow culms, white-variegated leaves, and a smaller stature. This cultivar is grown primarily for the intense variegated effect of the foliage, rather than for the color of the culms, which is not particularly conspicuous. Of all the white-variegated bamboos in cultivation, this cultivar achieves the most outstanding brightness, even when grown in shade. It has been in flower since the mid-1980s, seeming to come to little harm, and frequently producing seeds with variegations on their outer surface in the same color scheme as the leaves.

Culms Short and very slender, 1 to 2 m (3 to 6 feet) tall and less than 6 mm (¼ inch) in diameter. Usually seen at the smaller end of these di-

mensions. Very pale yellow at first, occasionally with a thin green stripe on an internode here and there, the yellow deepening slightly with age. Loosely upright in habit and fairly lax when grown in shade. **Leaves** Medium-long and narrow, 9 to 18 cm (3½ to 7 inches) long by 1 to 1.5 cm (⅜ to ⅝ inch) wide. Deep green with fairly consistent, very bright creamy white striping on the upper surface, the striping becoming bright creamy yellow by winter. Leaves are seldom completely green. Colors are more matte on the lower surface. **Rhizomes** Slightly less invasive than the species.

Pleioblastus chino 'Murakamianus' is a useful shorter bamboo with brightly variegated foliage.

Pleioblastus fortunei

Synonyms *Arundinaria fortunei, P. variegatus*
Native to Japan
Short bamboo—very invasive

An excellent white-variegated semi-dwarf bamboo for general planting. The coloration seems to be little affected by light levels, and the leaves are retained through winter in fairly good condition. It is sufficiently invasive to need careful siting in ornamental borders, and is perhaps better suited to being a ground-cover. Although originally named as a species, this bamboo is really just a mutated, white-variegated form of some other species, its exact origin being obscure. It has been long cultivated

Pleioblastus fortunei.

in Japan and was introduced into Europe in 1863 by Louis Van Houtte of Ghent.

Culms Short and very slender, 1 to 2 m (3 to 6 feet) tall and less than 6 mm (¼ inch) in diameter. Pale green at first, becoming pale yellowish green with age. Nodes not prominent. Fairly upright in habit unless grown in shade, which causes the plant to grow taller and become lax. New shoots appear in late spring. **Culm sheaths** Persistent. Pale green with diffuse white striping. **Branches** Solitary. Occasionally in unequal pairs. **Leaves** Medium-long and medium-broad, 9 to 18 cm (3½ to 7 inches) long by 1.5 to 3 cm (⅝ to 1¼ inches) wide. Deep green with consistent white striping and bands on the upper surface, the colors more matte on the lower surface, tapering fairly abruptly to a point at the tip. **Rhizomes** Very invasive (strongly leptomorph). Spreads rapidly once established. Not ideal for small gardens unless restricted. **Cultivation** Sun or shade. The variegations are not much affected by light, but the habit is better in an open position. **Hardiness** Below −20°C (−4°F).

Pleioblastus gramineus

Synonym *Arundinaria graminea*
Native to Japan
Tall bamboo—very invasive

Originally thought to be a variety of *P. hindsii*, this distinctive species is a native of the Ryukyu Islands of Japan. It has the narrowest leaves in proportion to their length of any hardy bamboo in cultivation, and looks like a giant tree grass. It can only be confused with the virtually identical *P. linearis*, and can be distinguished from that species by the glabrous culm sheaths and the slight twist to the leaves. The true *P. gramineus* is rarely seen in cultivation, since nearly all plants grown under this name turn out to be *P. linearis* upon close inspection. A fine foliage bamboo for the larger garden, this species can be used for screening or as a specimen plant in a woodland setting. The rhizomes are very active and penetrating, making it unsuitable for small urban gardens.

Culms Tall and slender, 3 to 5 m (10 to 16 feet) tall and 6 mm to 2 cm (¼ to ¾ inch) in diameter. Dull olive green, becoming dull yellowish green with age. Nodes moderately prominent. Upright in habit only during the first season, becoming heavily arched with the weight of the foliage. New shoots appear in early summer. **Culm sheaths** Persistent. Midgreen, smooth and hairless on the outer surface, with small auricles and oral setae. **Branches** Multiple. Initially in pairs or threes, quickly becoming more multiple. **Leaves** Long and narrow, 18 to 25 cm (7 to 10 inches) long by 1 to 1.5 cm (⅜ to ⅝ inch) wide. Bright green on the upper surface, dull green on the lower surface, tapering to a very slender and drawn-out tip that usually has a noticeable twist. **Rhizomes** Very invasive (strongly leptomorph). Actively spreading and needs adequate space. Forms extensive thickets with ragged edges. **Cultivation** Sun or shade. Suitable for a wide range of planting positions and even reasonably tolerant of salt spray in maritime gardens. **Hardiness** −10°C to −20°C (14°F to −4°F).

Pleioblastus hindsii

Synonym *Arundinaria hindsii*

Native to China

Tall bamboo—very invasive

A tough, rampant species of limited horticultural use. When the foliage is freshly replaced in early summer it is fairly attractive and a very distinctive rich green, but by winter the plant can look rather ragged and lackluster, or even scruffy if grown in drier conditions. This species is ideal for the wilder parts of the garden and can be used as a dense screen or as an un-derstory plant in woodland. The thicker culms can be cut to make useful stakes or plant supports.

Culms Tall and slender, 3 to 5 m (10 to 16 feet) tall and 6 mm to 2 cm (¼ to ¾ inch) in diameter. Bright olive green and covered in a light waxy bloom, giving a grayish effect at first, becoming dull yellowish green with age. Thin-walled. Nodes moderately prominent. Upright in the first season, then arching quite heavily with the increasing weight of foliage. New shoots appear in late spring. **Culm sheaths** Persistent. Pale green and noticeably short, not covering the internode. **Branches** Multiple. Initially in pairs or threes, quickly becoming more multiple. Carried at an acute angle to the culm, giving an upswept brush-like appearance, particularly in the upper parts of the culm. **Leaves** Long and medium-broad, 18 to 25 cm (7 to 10 inches) long by 1.5 to 3 cm (⅝ to 1¼ inches) wide. Bright, rich green on the upper surface, grayish green on the lower surface, tapering to a drawn-out point at the tip. **Rhizomes** Very invasive (strongly leptomorph). Forms extensive thickets. Rampantly spreading even in poor growing conditions. **Cultivation** Sun or shade. Very tough and durable. Grows in a wide range of planting situations. Excellent as a windbreak in exposed localities where the condition of the foliage is not important. **Hardiness** −10°C to −20°C (14°F to −4°F).

Pleioblastus humilis

Synonyms *Arundinaria pumila, P. pumilus*

Native to Japan

Short bamboo—very invasive

This attractive and useful semi-dwarf bamboo is much planted as a tall groundcover and is invaluable for binding the soil on steep slopes or banks. The rhizomes are extremely active, rapidly colonizing large areas if unchecked. This species is one of the better tall groundcover bamboos, making lush mounds of dark green foliage that is generally retained in good condition through winter.

This species has an almost identical form regarded by many contemporary horticulturists as merely a variety: *P. humilis* var. *pumilus*. It differs only in minor morphological characteristics, the most noticeable being the almost entirely glabrous leaf blades. These two bamboos are almost indistinguishable to the naked eye and are much mixed up in cultivation. Var. *pumilus* is more widely found in European gardens; it flowered between 1964 and 1967 and again between 1998 and 2003, producing quantities of fertile seed. Both forms (under whichever name) are thought to have been introduced into England in the latter part of the 19th century.

There is a further form described in various earlier books under the name 'Gauntlettii', purporting to be smaller and less invasive. All plants that I have seen would appear to be identical to var. *pumilus*, and just as invasive if given the same growing conditions.

Culms Short and very slender, 1 to 2 m (3 to 6 feet) tall and less than 6 mm (¼ inch) in diameter. Deep green at first and often flushed with purple in sunlight, becoming dull yellowish green with age. Nodes not prominent. Moderately upright in habit unless grown in shade. New shoots appear in late spring. **Culm**

Pleioblastus humilis var. *pumilus*.

sheaths Persistent. Dull green. **Branches** Solitary. Occasionally in unequal pairs. **Leaves** Medium-long and medium-broad, 9 to 18 cm (3½ to 7 inches) long by 1.5 to 3 cm (⅝ to 1¼ inches) wide. Sometimes slightly longer than these dimensions. Deep green on the upper surface, dull matte green and slightly downy on the lower surface, with a less matte strip on one side, tapering abruptly to a point at the tip. **Rhizomes** Very invasive (strongly leptomorph). Rampant in all but the poorest growing conditions. **Cultivation** Sun or shade. The habit can become very drawn and lax in shade and is much better in an open position. **Hardiness** Below −20°C (−4°F).

Pleioblastus kongosanensis

Native to Japan

Short bamboo—very invasive

A rather drab semi-dwarf bamboo that is rare in cultivation. It is useful as a tall groundcover but otherwise has little horticultural merit. In winter it is inclined to be lackluster and scruffy.

Culms Short and very slender, 1 to 2 m (3 to 6 feet) tall and less than 6 mm (¼ inch) in diameter. Dull olive green when young and slightly purple-flushed, becoming yellowish green with age. Nodes not prominent. Fairly upright in habit, with a slight tendency to zigzag. New shoots appear in early summer. **Culm sheaths** Persistent. Dark green. **Branches** Solitary. Sparsely branched and occasionally in unequal pairs. **Leaves** Medium-long and medium-broad, 9 to 18 cm (3½ to 7 inches) long by 1.5 to 3 cm (⅝ to 1¼ inches) wide. Deep green on the upper surface, matte green on the lower surface, tapering from midlength to a fine point at the tip. **Rhizomes** Very invasive (strongly leptomorph). Fairly quick to spread. Forms dense, low patches and thickets. **Cultivation** Sun or shade. Grows almost anywhere, even in heavy shade. **Hardiness** Below −20°C (−4°F).

Pleioblastus kongosanensis 'Aureostriata'

Short bamboo—invasive

Differs from the species by having yellow-variegated leaves. An uncommon form, of interest mainly to the enthusiast or collector. The leaves are at their most attractive in early summer when the growth is fresh. By the end of winter, the striping is much less conspicuous, mainly due to the rather ragged condition of the plant at that time of year.

Leaves Deep green with variable amounts of moderately conspicuous pale yellow striping on the upper surface, the striping becoming deeper yellow as the season progresses. Colors are more matte on the lower surface.

Pleioblastus linearis

Native to Japan

Tall bamboo—very invasive

This species has narrow, grass-like leaves and is virtually identical to *P. gramineus*. It can be distinguished principally by the hairs on the outer surface of the culm sheath and by the lack of a noticeable twist in the leaves. When grown well, it is highly ornamental, though likely to be too invasive for many smaller gardens. While fairly common in cultivation, this species has been flowering sporadically since the mid-1980s or longer, and many gardeners have lost patience and dug out their specimens. Much fertile seed has been produced, giving rise to a new generation of seedlings.

Culms Tall and slender, 3 to 5 m (10 to 16 feet) tall and 6 mm to 2 cm (¼ to ¾ inch) in diameter. Dull olive green, becoming dull yellowish green with age. Nodes moderately prominent. Upright in habit only during the first season, then becoming heavily arched with the weight of the foliage. New shoots appear in early summer. **Culm sheaths** Persistent. Midgreen, with short stiff hairs on the

Pleioblastus linearis in late autumn at Stream Cottage.

outer surface when young, and with oral setae lacking or only partially developed. **Branches** Multiple. Initially in pairs or threes, quickly becoming more multiple. **Leaves** Long and narrow, 18 to 25 cm (7 to 10 inches) long by 1 to 1.5 cm (⅜ to ⅝ inch) wide. Bright green on the upper surface, dull green on the lower surface, tapering to a very slender and drawn-out point at the tip. **Rhizomes** Very invasive (strongly leptomorph). Actively spreading and needs adequate space. Forms extensive thickets with ragged edges. **Cultivation** Sun or shade. Suitable for a wide range of planting positions and even reasonably tolerant of salt spray in maritime gardens. **Hardiness** −10°C to −20°C (14°F to −4°F).

Pleioblastus pygmaeus

Synonym *Arundinaria pygmaea*

Native to Japan

Very short bamboo—very invasive

Many clones of this miniature bamboo are in cultivation. Most contemporary horticulturists now assert that the tallest clones should be regarded as *P. pygmaeus* 'Distichus' and that only the shortest clones, those less than 30 cm (1 foot) tall and possibly as short as 10 cm (4 inches), should be regarded as examples of typical *P. pygmaeus*. When well grown in an open position, good clones of this species produce a delightful lilliputian forest of slender culms topped with tiny leaves. This species is one of the very best groundcover bamboos, but it is much too invasive for general planting and should be sited with caution. Although often recommended as a rockery plant, it will rapidly invade and overrun most other plants.

Culms Very short and very slender, less than 1 m (3 feet) tall and less than 6 mm (¼ inch) in diameter. A "good" clone may attain less than a third of these dimensions. Bright green at first and sometimes faintly purple-flushed in sunlight, becoming dull yellowish green with age. Nodes not prominent. Upright in habit unless grown in shade, which causes the plant to grow taller and become lax. New shoots appear in early summer. **Culm sheaths** Persis-

tent. Olive green. **Branches** Solitary. Sparsely branched throughout and occasionally in unequal pairs. **Leaves** Very short and very narrow, less than 5 cm (2 inches) long by less than 1 cm (⅜ inch) wide. Deep green on the upper surface, dull matte green on the lower surface with a less matte strip on one side, tapering fairly abruptly to a point at the tip. Arranged tightly at the summit of the culms in two nearly opposite rows, giving a somewhat fern-like effect. Some clones have leaves that are glabrous on both surfaces. **Rhizomes** Very invasive (strongly leptomorph). Completely rampant once established and most suited for a groundcover. **Cultivation** Sun or shade. An open position will result in a much shorter, tighter, and infinitely more pleasing habit. **Hardiness** Below −20°C (−4°F).

Pleioblastus pygmaeus kept carefully under control in David Helliwell's garden in Oxford.

Pleioblastus pygmaeus 'Distichus'

Synonyms *Arundinaria disticha, P. distichus*
Short bamboo—very invasive

Differs from the species by having larger leaves and a larger stature. Commonly known as the dwarf fernleaf bamboo. This attractive low-growing bamboo is suitable for planting as a groundcover but is likely too invasive to combine with other plants in ornamental borders. The cultivar name, which means "arranged in two rows," refers to the distinctive paired arrangement of the leaves when the plant is grown in an open position. In shade the habit becomes more drawn and open, and the fern-like effect of the leaves is lost. This cultivar was introduced into Europe in the late 1860s. Many contemporary horticulturists regard it as identical to *P. pygmaeus*, to the extent that 'Distichus' is merely a taller clone of the species, and vice versa.

Culms Short and very slender, 1 to 2 m (3 to 6 feet) tall and less than 6 mm (¼ inch) in diameter. Seldom seen at much above 1 m (3 feet) and a "good" clone will be slightly shorter than that. Fairly upright in habit when grown in the open but very drawn and lax in shade. **Leaves** Short and medium-broad, 5 to 9 cm (2 to 3½ inches) long by 1.5 to 3 cm (⅝ to 1¼ inches) wide. Arranged in two almost opposite rows, giving a distinctly fern-like effect when the plant is grown in an open position.

Pleioblastus shibuyanus 'Tsuboi'

Synonym *P. argenteostriatus* 'Glaber Tsuboi'
Native to Japan
Short bamboo—invasive

This is by far the best of the smaller white-variegated bamboos in cultivation. It is not at all gaudy but gives a subtle and highly pleasing effect that is at its brightest when the plant is grown in partial shade. Although capable of reaching the dimensions stated here, it is very slow to put on height and is best regarded as a semi-dwarf bamboo for garden purposes. It was introduced into Europe and the United States in the early 1980s. The plain species is unknown in cultivation in Western gardens.

Culms Short and very slender, 1 to 2 m (3 to 6 feet) tall and less than 6 mm (¼ inch) in diameter. Taller culms may have diameters slightly exceeding these dimensions. Pale midgreen when young, becoming pale yellowish green with age. Nodes moderately prominent. Very upright in the first two seasons, then arching quite heavily with increasing weight of foliage. New shoots appear in late spring. **Culm**

The attractive fern-like effect produced by a mass planting of *Pleioblastus pygmaeus* 'Distichus'.

Pleioblastus shibuyanus 'Tsuboi'.

sheaths Persistent. Pale green. **Branches** Multiple. Initially in twos or threes, later becoming surrounded by three or more smaller branches to give a more multiple effect. Usually quite short and closely upswept in a fairly acute angle to the culm. **Leaves** Medium-long and narrow, 9 to 18 cm (3½ to 7 inches) long by 1 to 1.5 cm (⅜ to ⅝ inch) wide. Very variable. Deep green with softly defined creamy white stripes and bands on the upper surface, the variegations becoming almost creamy yellow as the season progresses. Colors are slightly more matte on the lower surface. **Rhizomes** Invasive (leptomorph). Spread is fairly modest and very controllable, making this cultivar suitable for growing in mixed borders. **Cultivation** Sun or shade. More satisfactory in partially shaded situations. **Hardiness** –10°C to –20°C (14°F to –4°F).

Pleioblastus simonii

Synonym *Ar*undinaria simonii
Native to China, Japan
Very tall bamboo—very invasive

A strong-growing, rampant species with a distinctly upright habit, and more useful than ornamental. While satisfactory as a tough, tall screen or windbreak, it is better suited to the wilder or more remote parts of the garden. Although this is a very hardy bamboo, the fo-

Pleioblastus simonii growing
in a suburban garden.

liage is inclined to look excessively brown-
edged and scruffy by the end of winter unless
the plant is grown in a very wind-free environment. The culms are somewhat thin-walled,
but nonetheless this is one of the best species
for the production of garden canes and plant
supports. Now widely cultivated, it was introduced into France in 1862 by an M. Simon and
named after him by an M. Carriere. This species has flowered on several occasions, producing large quantities of fertile seed.

Culms Very tall and medium-thick, 5 to 8 m
(16 to 26 feet) tall and 2 to 3 cm (¾ to 1¼ inches)
in diameter. Deep olive green and lightly
dusted with white powder at first, becoming
dull yellowish green with age. Thin-walled.
Nodes not prominent. Very upright in habit,
only arching slightly with age. New shoots appear in early summer. **Culm sheaths** Persistent. Very persistent on the culm branches.
Midgreen with margins tinted purple.
Branches Multiple. Solitary or in pairs at first,
quickly becoming more multiple, arranged in
a distinct steeple-like formation. **Leaves** Long
and medium-broad, 18 to 25 cm (7 to 10 inches)
long by 1.5 to 3 cm (⅝ to 1¼ inches) wide. Deep
green and developing a dull shine on the upper
surface, matte grayish green on the lower surface, with a less matte strip on one side, tapering to a slender, drawn-out point at the tip.
Rhizomes Very invasive (strongly leptomorph). Completely rampant once established,
and rather deep compared with most bamboos.
Cultivation Sun or shade. Grows almost anywhere but can attract whitefly and aphids onto
the foliage in airless, very shady situations.
Hardiness Below −20°C (−4°F).

Pleioblastus simonii 'Variegatus'

Synonyms *Arundinaria simonii* 'Variegatus',
P. simonii var. *heterophyllus*
Very tall bamboo—very invasive

Differs from the species by having leaves that
vary in shape and that may have white variegations. This cultivar is common in cultivation
and is often mistaken for the species, since the
variegations are minimal and inconsistent. It
is not a very garden-worthy bamboo and does
not merit planting in preference to the species.

Leaves Appearing normal on culms in their
first year. In subsequent years, clusters of
leaves are produced that are often much narrower for their length, sometimes with moderately conspicuous thin white striping on the

Pleioblastus simonii 'Variegatus' growing at my first nursery in Essex. This extremely invasive bamboo quickly became a nuisance and eventually had to be dug up and confined within a big pot.

upper surface, the striping partially penetrating through to the lower surface.

Pseudosasa

This is a small genus of mostly taller bamboos having an upright, boldly architectural appearance, with the foliage arranged in palmate effect at the summit of the culms. They can be distinguished in cultivation mainly by their persistent culm sheaths, their strong and usu-ally solitary branches, and their comparatively large leaves, with the exception of *P. owatarii*. All species and forms of this genus make attractive garden plants of many uses. Their leptomorph rhizomes are seldom so invasive as to cause problems.

Pseudosasa amabilis

Synonym *Arundinaria amabilis*
Native to China
Tall bamboo—invasive

Commonly known as the Tonkin cane. This upright, strong-growing species is distinctive for its longer leaves. The culms are thick-walled but pliable and only develop branches in their uppermost parts, making this species particularly well-suited for cutting for garden canes. In China it is grown commercially on a large scale for this purpose. Although capable of making an impressive specimen plant in any garden, this bamboo is rather difficult to grow unless given warm conditions, and it is still rare in cultivation in most of Europe and the United States. It is hardy enough to be grown outside in most cool-temperate climates, sometimes tolerating temperatures below −10°C (14°F). However, unless the growing conditions are very favorable, this species can be slow to establish and can look rather dilapidated and tatty in winter.

Culms Tall and slender, 3 to 5 m (10 to 16 feet) tall and 6 mm to 2 cm (¼ to ¾ inch) in diameter. Sometimes attaining a slightly larger diameter than this. Olive green at first, becoming dull yellowish green with age, then brownish black in places. Very thick-walled and strong. The internodes are covered in fine hairs during the first season. Nodes not prominent. Very upright in habit, developing a slight arch in later seasons. New shoots appear in early summer. **Culm sheaths** Persistent. Midgreen, with a distinctive dense tuft of brown

tion Sun or shade. Best in a warm and open but very sheltered situation, and in good soil. **Hardiness** −5°C to −10°C (23°F to 14°F).

Pseudosasa japonica

Synonyms *Arundinaria japonica, Bambusa metake*
Native to China, Japan, Korea
Tall bamboo—invasive

This species, commonly known as the arrow bamboo, was one of the first bamboos to be cultivated in European gardens, having been introduced into France in 1850 by Van Siebold, and brought to England shortly after. In the United States it has been cultivated since the beginning of the 20th century. Since its introduction, *P. japonica* has undoubtedly been the most widely cultivated bamboo in cool-temperate gardens, and still enjoys considerable popularity despite the greatly increased range of bamboos available. In some regions it has escaped from cultivation to become partially naturalized. As a garden plant it is without equal, being very tough and hardy, and well able to withstand exposed growing conditions. Very cold winters can cause some damage to the foliage, but this is quickly replaced in spring. When well grown, it has a most architectural appearance and is eminently suitable for making imposing screens or for use as a specimen plant, and also makes a fine container plant for the terrace or patio.

Culms Tall and slender, 3 to 5 m (10 to 16 feet) tall and 6 mm to 2 cm (¼ to ¾ inch) in diameter. May sometimes attain slightly larger dimensions. Olive green at first, becoming yellowish green with age. Thin-walled. Nodes not prominent. Very upright in habit during the first season, gradually developing an arch as the weight of foliage increases in later years. New shoots appear in late spring. **Culm sheaths** Persistent. Very persistent on the culm branches. Dull green and coarse. Covered in

Pseudosasa amabilis can be identified by the prominent long tuft of coarse hairs on the outer surface of the culm sheath.

hairs usually extending along the middle of the sheath from the base to halfway up or more. Upper sheaths may exhibit this feature much less conspicuously. **Branches** Solitary. Sometimes in pairs or threes in upper parts of the culm. **Leaves** Very long and medium-broad, more than 25 cm (10 inches) long by 1.5 to 3 cm (⅝ to 1¼ inches) wide. Deep green on the upper surface, matte grayish green on the lower surface, tapering to a drawn-out point at the tip. **Rhizomes** Invasive (leptomorph). Almost static unless given very warm conditions. **Cultiva-**

A fine stand of *Pseudosasa japonica* at Carwinion.

fine hairs when young. **Branches** Solitary. Occasionally in twos or threes, particularly in the upper parts of the culm. **Leaves** Long and medium-broad, 18 to 25 cm (7 to 10 inches) long by 1.5 to 3 cm (⅝ to 1¼ inches) wide. Deep green and with a dull shine on the upper surface, matte silvery green on the lower surface, tapering gradually to a drawn-out point at the tip. **Rhizomes** Invasive (leptomorph). Spread is fairly moderate and thus can be managed in smaller gardens. **Cultivation** Sun or shade. Happy in a wide range of growing situations but liable to attract whitefly and aphids in airless conditions with too much shade. **Hardiness** −10°C to −20°C (14°F to −4°F).

Pseudosasa japonica 'Akebono'

Tall bamboo—invasive

Differs from the species by having completely white leaves and a slightly smaller stature. This attractive form is fairly consistent, with only an occasional culm or branch bearing completely green leaves. It often occurs spontaneously from 'Akebonosuji'.

Culms Almost as large as those of the species. **Leaves** Most leaves are conspicuously almost completely white on the upper surface when growing strongly in early summer, thereafter white at the tip, shading gradually to green at the base. Some leaves have a thin green stripe. The white coloration rapidly becomes pale yellowish white as the season progresses and is much less conspicuous by winter. Coloration is more matte on the lower surface. **Cultivation** Inclined to scorch in full sun, so best planted in at least some shade.

The leaves of *Pseudosasa japonica* 'Akebono' can be almost completely white.

Pseudosasa japonica 'Akebonosuji'

Tall bamboo—invasive

Differs from the species by having white-variegated leaves and a slightly smaller stature. An attractive form that is inclined to revert, so frequent cutting out of completely green-leaved culms is required to maintain the effect. Culms often emerge that have some branches bearing variegated leaves and other branches bearing completely green leaves. 'Akebono' frequently occurs spontaneously within the clump and can be removed if desired; otherwise it is inclined to take over.

Pseudosasa japonica 'Akebonosuji'

Culms Almost as large as those of the species. **Leaves** Most leaves have very variable and moderately conspicuous amounts of creamy whitish striping on the upper surface, but some leaves are completely whitish and others are completely green. The whitish parts of the leaves quickly become yellowish white as the season progresses. Colors are more matte on the lower surface.

Pseudosasa japonica 'Tsutsumiana'

Medium bamboo—invasive

Differs from the species by having distorted culms and a smaller stature. This is an interesting form, well worth cultivating. It can take time for the plant to mature sufficiently to produce culms with noticeable distortions. Unfortunately, the culms hide their distortions behind the very persistent culm sheaths, only revealing them fully after two or more seasons. The rhizomes have similar distortions, though this is seldom seen unless they come to the surface of their own accord or are dug up. As a small plant this cultivar is easily confused with the plain species.

Culms Medium-tall and slender, 2 to 3 m (6 to 10 feet) tall and 6 mm to 2 cm (¼ to ¾ inch) in diameter. May attain slightly greater dimensions than stated here, and generally thick for their height. Thicker culms consistently have

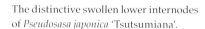
The distinctive swollen lower internodes of *Pseudosasa japonica* 'Tsutsumiana'.

Pseudosasa owatarii. This plant is only 46 cm (18 inches) high.

a series of swollen, bottle-like internodes in the lower parts of the culm. **Leaves** Are often stiffer and slightly narrower for their length than those of the species. **Rhizomes** Slightly more invasive than the species.

Pseudosasa owatarii

Native to Japan

Very short bamboo—very invasive

A delightful, if somewhat invasive, miniature bamboo that resembles the shorter clones of *Pleioblastus pygmaeus*. It is found growing on Yaku Island, Japan, where there seems to be two distinct forms growing spontaneously.

The description here refers to the shorter form, which seems to be the one found in cultivation.

Culms Very short and very slender, less than 1 m (3 feet) tall and less than 6 mm (¼ inch) in diameter. Typically only half these dimensions. Dull green at first, maturing quickly to dull yellowish green. Nodes not prominent. Very upright in habit, becoming slightly less so in subsequent years. New shoots appear in late spring. **Culm sheaths** Persistent. Pale green, purple-flushed at the base. **Branches** Solitary. Older culms can develop one or two shorter branches alongside. **Leaves** Very short and very narrow, less than 5 cm (2 inches) long by less than 1 cm (⅜ inch) wide. Glossy, dark green on the upper surface, silvery matte green on the lower surface, tapering gradually to a drawn-out point at the tip. Prone to developing tip withering in winter. **Rhizomes** Very invasive (strongly leptomorph). When established, this bamboo makes up for its lack of height with its eager spread. Quickly colonizes to make a groundcover. **Cultivation** Sun or shade. The habit is only slightly extended by growing this plant in shade, but it is usually seen at its best in an open position. **Hardiness** –10°C to –20°C (14°F to –4°F).

Pseudosasa pleioblastoides

Native to China, Japan

Tall bamboo—invasive

This species closely resembles and so is easily confused with *P. japonica*, but it is more robust in appearance and grows more strongly. The main distinguishing characteristic is the usually more multiple effect of the culm branches. The leaves are also darker and sometimes narrower for their length. This species is not very common in cultivation but is worth seeking out, particularly for use as a windbreak in exposed locations.

Culms Tall and slender, 3 to 5 m (10 to 16 feet) tall and 6 mm to 2 cm (¼ to ¾ inch) in diameter. Can easily attain the larger end of these dimensions or slightly more. Olive green when young, sometimes slightly purple-flushed, becoming yellowish green with age. Somewhat thin-walled. Nodes not prominent. Upright in habit and sturdy, becoming slightly arched with the weight of foliage in later years. **Culm sheaths** Persistent. Very persistent on the culm branches. Dull green and coarse. **Branches** Solitary. Usually a number of smaller branches develop later from the base of the first one, giving the effect of more multiple branching. **Leaves** Long and medium-broad, 18 to 25 cm (7 to 10

inches) long by 1.5 to 3 cm (⅝ to 1¼ inches) wide. Dark deep green on the upper surface, matte silvery green on the lower surface, tapering gradually to a drawn-out tip. **Rhizomes** Invasive (leptomorph). Spreads moderately in average growing conditions. **Cultivation** Sun or shade. Can sometimes draw whitefly and aphids onto the foliage in airless conditions with too much shade. **Hardiness** –10°C to –20°C (14°F to –4°F).

Sasa

This is a very large genus comprising numerous closely related species, often differing only in very minor morphological characteristics. The greatest number of species are found in Japan and surrounding islands, but *Sasa* bamboos are also found in Korea and China. In their native environment, they cover large tracts of upland hillside and forest floor, almost completely suppressing other vegetation.

The gardener can recognize most species of *Sasa* by their comparatively large leaves, which are usually broad for their length and which often develop pronounced marginal and tip withering in winter. When viewed from a distance, the withering can resemble variegation. Established plants have a dense, jungle-like canopy of leaves supported by curved, slender culms bearing solitary branches. All species have very vigorous leptomorph rhizomes and so are excellent subjects for groundcover but unsuitable for planting in shrub borders.

Sasa kurilensis

Native to Japan, Kuril Islands, Sakhalin (Russia)

Medium bamboo—very invasive

An extremely vigorous species that has the distinction of being the world's most northerly growing bamboo in the wild, being found naturally in the Kuril Islands and on the island of Sakhalin. All the main structural parts of this bamboo, the nodes and internodes and sheathing organs, are glabrous. There are two clearly recognizable clones in cultivation, differing mainly in stature and garden worthiness. The larger clone described here is not a particularly good garden plant. It is rampant and looks scruffy for much of the year, perhaps attaining some level of attractiveness in midsummer, when the new culms and new leaves are at their best.

Culms Medium-tall and slender, 2 to 3 m (6 to 10 feet) tall and 6 mm to 2 cm (¼ to ¾ inch) in diameter. Very light green when young, quickly ripening to a rich, glossy light green, the color slowly changing to light yellowish green with age. Nodes not prominent. Strongly curved at the base and arching near the summit with the weight of the large leaves. New shoots appear in late spring. **Culm sheaths** Semi-persistent. Almost translucent pale green. **Branches** Solitary. Some older culms may develop three or four smaller branches alongside, particularly near the summit. **Leaves** Long and broad, 18 to 25 cm (7 to 10 inches) long by 3 to 6 cm (1¼ to 2½ inches) wide. Midgreen and glossy on the upper surface, matte green on the lower surface, very bluntly rounded at the base, tapering abruptly to a point at the tip. Depending on growing conditions, there will be some degree of withering at the tips and along the

Sasa kurilensis growing under deciduous trees in the Sir Harold Hillier Gardens (formerly Hillier Arboretum), Hampshire.

margins in winter, which is not particularly attractive. **Rhizomes** Very invasive (strongly leptomorph). Too invasive for all but the largest gardens or estates. Can be used for colonizing areas of wasteland. **Cultivation** Sun or shade. This bamboo thrives almost anywhere and makes a good understory plant for deciduous woodland. **Hardiness** Below −20°C (−4°F).

Sasa kurilensis dwarf form

Short bamboo—very invasive

Differs from the species by having slightly darker leaves and a smaller stature. A much

better bamboo for general planting. The name used here is not properly recognized botanically but serves to identify the plant in horticulture. While still too invasive for very small gardens, this attractive form can be used to make a dense groundcover under deciduous trees, or as a leafy small specimen if kept rigorously under control. The foliage will usually be retained more freshly through winter than the typical form, especially if the plant is grown in a lush, sheltered position free from excessive summer and autumn drought.

Culms Short and very slender, 1 to 2 m (3 to 6 feet) tall and less than 6 mm (¼ inch) in diameter. **Leaves** Slightly darker green than the typical form and slightly broader for their length.

This specimen clearly demonstrates the greater attractiveness of the dwarf form of *Sasa kurilensis*, compared with the typical form.

Sasa kurilensis 'Shimofuri'

Medium bamboo—very invasive

Differs from the species by having white-variegated leaves. There are many forms of *S. kurilensis* in cultivation with varying amounts of white striping in the leaves, too numerous to list here. However, 'Shimofuri' is by far the most stable, in terms of being very constant with the degree of striping in each leaf, and by retaining the white color through winter. It is an excellent and very pleasing garden plant, though it needs to be kept well under control in smaller gardens.

The beautiful foliage of *Sasa kurilensis* 'Shimofuri'. This is an excellent variegated bamboo for shade.

Culms New shoots and young culms are an even paler, more translucent green than those of the species. **Leaves** Dark green on the upper surface, with consistent, moderately conspicuous, very thin white striping, the coloration not changing much through the season. Very grayish matte on the lower surface, with the striping slightly penetrating through. Some degree of tip and marginal withering may occur in winter. **Cultivation** This bamboo can almost tolerate full sun without scorching, but leaf colors are kept more freshly if shade is given for at least part of the day through the middle months of summer.

Sasa megalophylla f. *nobilis*

Synonym *S. senanensis* f. *aureovariegata*

Native to Japan

Short bamboo—very invasive

This wonderful form is one of the better variegated *Sasa* bamboos, with thick bands of luscious butter yellow in the leaves. It was introduced into Western gardens in the mid-1980s, but unfortunately, all plants came into flower shortly afterward and promptly died. I was given a piece by the late Gerald Bol around this time, but my plant only lived for about a year before flowering. This bamboo is listed here in the hope that it has survived somewhere or will be reintroduced from Japan. The plain green species is currently not in general cultivation in Western gardens.

Culms Short and very slender, 1 to 2 m (3 to 6 feet) tall and up to 6 mm (¼ inch) in diameter. Deep green at first, slightly flushed with purple, ripening to yellowish green. Nodes not prominent. Strongly curved at the base and soon leaning or arching under the weight of the large leaves. New shoots appear in late spring. **Culm sheaths** Persistent. Rich green slightly flushed with purple. **Branches** Solitary. Older culms may develop one or two secondary branches in the upper parts of the culm. **Leaves** Long and very broad, 18 to 25 cm (7 to 10 inches) long by more than 6 cm (2½ inches) wide. Glossy, rich green on the upper surface, with variable amounts of highly conspicuous rich yellow bands or striping, the yellow color deepening as the season progresses, the colors more matte on the lower surface. Fairly consistent, with few reversions. Bluntly rounded at the base, tapering abruptly to a fine point at the tip. Slight marginal and tip with-

Sasa megalophylla f. *nobilis* growing at my first nursery in Essex. This rare and sought-after bamboo became effectively extinct in cultivation in Western gardens due to flowering a few years after this picture was taken.

ering may occur in winter. **Rhizomes** Very invasive (strongly leptomorph). Will quickly colonize surrounding areas. **Cultivation** Sun or shade. The variegations are still produced in shade, but an open position gives a better habit. Shelter from strong winds is advisable to keep the leaves in good condition. **Hardiness** Below −20°C (−4°F).

Sasa nipponica

Native to Japan

Very short bamboo—very invasive

A delightful smaller species, recalling *Sasaella ramosa*. Ideal as a groundcover in woodland. Its dark glossy leaves are distinctively narrow for the genus.

Culms Very short and very slender, less than 1 m (3 feet) tall and less than 6 mm (¼ inch) in diameter. Dull midgreen and slightly purple-flushed when young, ripening slowly to dull yellowish green. Nodes moderately prominent for the thickness of the culm. Usually curved at the base but fairly upright thereafter. New shoots appear in early summer. **Culm sheaths** Persistent. Midgreen, slightly purple-flushed at the edges. **Branches** Solitary. Older culms sometimes develop three or more smaller branches in the upper parts of the culm. **Leaves** Medium-long and medium-broad, 9 to 18 cm (3½ to 7 inches) long by 1.5 to 3 cm (⅝ to 1¼ inches) wide. Very dark green and glossy on the upper surface, dull matte green on the lower surface, tapering to an abrupt point at the tip. The lower surface is covered with fine, short hairs. There is considerable withering in winter of leaf tips and margins, which looks quite attractive in mass effect. **Rhizomes** Very invasive (strongly leptomorph). Ideal as a groundcover but too invasive for most other uses. **Cultivation** Sun or shade. Tolerant of a wide range of growing situations. **Hardiness** −10°C to −20°C (14°F to −4°F).

Sasa nipponica 'Aureostriata'

Very short bamboo—very invasive
Differs from the species by having yellow-variegated leaves. An obscure form that is of moderate garden worthiness. The variegations are pleasing but highly unstable, with frequent reversions that should be removed assiduously.

Leaves Dark green with variable amounts of broad dull yellow striping on the upper surface that is not particularly conspicuous, colors more matte on the lower surface. Many culms are produced that altogether lack striping in the leaves. **Cultivation** The variegations are not particularly affected by light levels, though heavy shade is not recommended.

Sasa nipponica.

Sasa palmata 'Nebulosa'

Synonym *S. cernua* 'Nebulosa'
Native to Japan
Medium bamboo—very invasive
A magnificent large-leaved bamboo for the larger garden. The name *palmata* refers to the palm or hand-like arrangement of the leaves at the apex of the culms, while the name 'Nebulosa' refers to the cloud-like brown markings to be found on older culms. It is one of the longest-cultivated bamboos in Western gardens, introduced into Britain in 1889 and into the United States in 1925. There is some confusion as to whether the typical species, which lacks the brown blotches, is actually in cultivation, and certainly all the plants I have ever seen are the bamboo described here.

Sasa palmata 'Nebulosa'.

As a garden plant, *S. palmata* 'Nebulosa' has contributed in part to the negative perception that some people have regarding bamboos. This is largely due to misguided plantings made many years ago in which this bamboo's very invasive nature was not properly appreciated. Indeed, in many parts of Europe and the United States it has taken over neglected gardens and has become to some extent naturalized in places. Nonetheless, this bamboo imparts a tropical air to any planting, with its fine, glossy, large leaves reflecting the sun like flickering mirrors. It is an excellent bamboo and well worth the effort needed to keep it under control in smaller gardens.

Culms Medium-tall and slender, 2 to 3 m (6 to 10 feet) tall and 6 mm to 2 cm (¼ to ¾ inch) in diameter. Slender for their height. Rich midgreen when young, ripening to dull yellowish green with irregular brown blotching, particularly in the lower parts of the culm. The brown blotching merges together over time to more or less completely cover the culm internodes. Nodes not prominent. Strongly curved at the base and arching increasingly with time under the weight of the large leaves. New shoots appear in midspring. **Culm sheaths** Persistent. Purple-green at first, quickly becoming pale green. **Branches** Solitary. Older culms may develop one or two secondary branches in the upper parts of the culm. **Leaves** Long and very broad, 18 to 25 cm (7 to 10 inches) long by more than 6 cm (2½ inches) wide. Glossy, rich green on the upper surface, light matte green on the lower surface, bluntly rounded at the base, abruptly tapering to a fine point at the tip. Some marginal and tip withering may occur through the winter months in drier locations; otherwise the foliage may survive the winter more or less intact. **Rhizomes** Very invasive (strongly leptomorph). Needs adequate space. Searching rhizomes quickly colonize considerable areas. **Cultivation** Sun or shade. Very adaptable to being grown out in the open or under deciduous woodland. Not the best bamboo for very windy locations, as the foliage is easily shredded. Wind also increases the chance of winter withering. **Hardiness** Below −20°C (−4°F).

Sasa palmata 'Warley Place'

Medium bamboo—very invasive

Differs from the species by having yellow-variegated leaves. This interesting form was discovered by David McClintock while we were visiting Ellen Willmott's old garden at Warley Place in Essex. It existed as a few culms bearing variegated leaves, amid a vast area completely colonized by 'Nebulosa' over the decades since the garden was last properly cultivated. I returned to the garden a few weeks later and managed to dig up enough variegated material to bring this new form into cultivation. A bamboo truly for the dedicated collector! The variegations, when present, are all that could be desired. The large lustrous leaves are boldly streaked with deep golden yellow in different tones amid the plain green. However, culms bearing variegated leaves are tantalizingly scarce, since reversions are so frequent. It is best to cultivate this bamboo in the ground rather than a container, so that the green-leaved culms and connecting rhizomes can more easily be differentiated and removed.

Leaves Glossy, rich green on the upper surface, with highly variable amounts of moderately conspicuous yellow striping and bands in tones from deep yellow to very pale yellow and almost green, some leaves completely yellow. Color intensity does not change much as the season progresses. Colors are more matte on the lower surface. Not consistent and very prone to reversion. **Cultivation** Semi-shade. Any pale yellow and green or completely yellow leaves are liable to scorch in midsummer sun.

Sasa quelpartensis

Synonym *S. veitchii* 'Nana'
Native to Japan
Very short bamboo—very invasive

This charming bamboo resembles *S. veitchii* at approximately half the height. It can most easily be distinguished from that species by its leaves, which are less broad for their length, and by the lesser degree of marginal and tip withering in winter unless grown in very dry locations. It is a delightful subject for ground-cover work, quickly making low leafy mounds and carpets, even in quite inhospitable places. It is much too invasive for ornamental borders.

Culms Very short and very slender, less than 1 m (3 feet) tall and less than 6 mm (¼ inch) in diameter. Dull olive green and slightly purple-flushed when young, particularly on the side exposed to more light, ripening to dull purplish yellow-green. Nodes moderately prominent for the size of the culm. Rather lax in habit, but this is not obvious due to the very short stature. New shoots appear in late spring. **Culm sheaths** Persistent. Light green. **Branches** Solitary. Older culms very occasionally develop one or two secondary branches in the upper parts of the culm. **Leaves** Medium-long and broad, 9 to 18 cm (3½ to 7 inches) long by 3 to 6 cm (1¼ to 2½ inches) wide. Dark green and lustrous on the upper surface, matte green on the lower surface, bluntly rounded

Sasa quelpartensis.

Sasa tsuboiana.

at the base, tapering fairly abruptly to a point at the tip. Moderate marginal and tip withering occurs in winter. **Rhizomes** Very invasive (strongly leptomorph). Only suitable as a groundcover or as an extensive colonizing plant in large gardens. **Cultivation** Sun or shade. Thrives almost anywhere. **Hardiness** −10°C to −20°C (14°F to −4°F).

Sasa tsuboiana

Native to Japan
Short bamboo—very invasive

Although less well known than other *Sasa* bamboos in cultivation, this species is worth seeking out for its more upright habit and at-tractive leaves, which have very little marginal withering in winter and are rather long for their width. A possible subject for use as a specimen plant if kept rigorously under control.

Culms Short and slender, 1 to 2 m (3 to 6 feet) tall and 6 mm to 2 cm (¼ to ¾ inch) in diameter. Midgreen at first and slightly glossy, ripening to yellowish green. Nodes not prominent. Of fairly upright habit despite the weight of the large leaves. New shoots appear in mid to late spring. **Culm sheaths** Persistent. Midgreen, slightly purple-flushed. **Branches** Solitary. One or two additional branches occasionally develop near the summit of older culms.

A recently established plant of *Sasa veitchii*, seen in early spring with last year's leaves still looking attractive.

Leaves Long and broad, 18 to 25 cm (7 to 10 inches) long by 3 to 6 cm (1¼ to 2½ inches) wide. Rich midgreen and glossy on the upper surface, light matte green on the lower surface, bluntly rounded at the base, tapering more gradually than usual for a *Sasa* to a fine point at the tip. **Rhizomes** Very invasive (strongly leptomorph). Very slightly less invasive than other species of this genus. **Cultivation** Sun or shade. This plant is capable of growing almost anywhere, but best results are obtained in lush, wind-free environments. **Hardiness** –10°C to –20°C (14°F to –4°F).

Sasa veitchii

Native to Japan

Short bamboo—very invasive

A long-cultivated bamboo important in landscaping and amenity horticulture. Introduced into the United Kingdom in 1880. This species is somewhat inconspicuous in summer but easily recognized in winter, with its distinctive withered leaf margins, which look from a distance so like variegation. It is very attractive en masse and ideal for a large groundcover planting, the invasive rhizomes quickly colonizing to form dense tracts of vegetation. It is equally suited to open areas or as vegetation of the woodland floor.

Culms Short and very slender, 1 to 2 m (3 to 6 feet) tall and less than 6 mm (¼ inch) in diameter. Deep purple-green and covered by a grayish bloom at first, ripening quickly to yellowish midgreen. Nodes not prominent. Usually curved at the base and having a rather lax habit. New shoots appear in late spring. **Culm sheaths** Semi-persistent. Purple-tinted at first, becoming light green. **Branches** Solitary. Older culms frequently have one or two secondary branches develop around the base of the main branch, especially near the summit of the culm. **Leaves** Long and broad, 18 to 25 cm (7 to 10 inches) long by 3 to 6 cm (1¼ to 2½ inches) wide. Very dark green and glossy on the upper surface, dull grayish green on the lower surface, very bluntly rounded at the base, tapering abruptly to a point at the tip. Marginal and tip withering is pronounced, occurring as soon as the weather cools in late autumn or early winter. **Rhizomes** Very invasive (strongly leptomorph). Slow to establish in some soils but soon spreading rampantly. An ideal taller groundcover bamboo. **Cultivation** Sun or shade. Very tough, tolerant, and adaptable, thriving in a wide range of situations. **Hardiness** Below −20°C (−4°F).

Sasaella

Originally a large genus, *Sasaella* now includes only a few valid species, with many having been transferred to the very closely related *Sasa*. The principal distinguishing characteristics are the generally smaller leaves, which are less broad for their length than those of true *Sasa*, and the shorter stature. They are highly suitable subjects for groundcover plantings and can be used very effectively to bind the soil on steep banks or unstable ground.

Sasaella bitchuensis

Native to Japan

Short bamboo—very invasive

Although this bamboo has crept into cultivation in Western gardens, it has little merit ornamentally and is best left to the bamboo collector. By the end of most winters it looks ragged and dismal, and even its summer appearance is nothing special. It is, however, very tough and rampant, and could be utilized to colonize the wilder parts of large gardens or to make game coverts.

Culms Short and very slender, 1 to 2 m (3 to 6 feet) tall and less than 6 mm (¼ inch) in diameter. Dull olive green and slightly purple-flushed when young, maturing to dull yellowish green. Nodes moderately prominent. Generally lax and leaning in habit. New shoots appear in late spring or early summer. **Culm sheaths** Persistent. Purple-green at first, quickly becoming light green, and covered in dense hairs. **Branches** Solitary. Most older culms develop one or two secondary branches alongside the first. **Leaves** Medium-long and broad, 9 to 18 cm (3½ to 7 inches) long by 3 to 6 cm (1¼ to 2½ inches) wide. Dark green with a dull shine on the upper surface, grayish matte green on the lower surface, moderately rounded at the base, tapering gradually to a blunt point at the tip. Some marginal and tip withering occurs in winter, though this may become pronounced when the plant is grown in dry or exposed situations. **Rhizomes** Very invasive (strongly leptomorph). Too invasive for all but the largest gardens. **Cultivation** Sun or shade. Very durable and adaptable but inclined to extreme scruffiness in poor growing conditions. **Hardiness** −10°C to −20°C (14°F to −4°F).

Sasaella masamuneana

Synonym *S. glabra*

Native to Japan

Very short bamboo—very invasive

This species exists in cultivation mostly as reverted plants from the more popular variegated forms. It is a good, though unexciting, groundcover bamboo and creates a dense, leafy canopy carried on short, sturdy culms.

Culms Very short and very slender, less than 1 m (3 feet) tall and less than 6 mm (¼ inch) in diameter. May be taller in heavy shade. Mid-green and flushed reddish purple at first, quickly ripening to yellowish green. Nodes not prominent. Fairly upright in habit for a sasoid bamboo, even when grown in shade.

New shoots appear in midspring. **Culm sheaths** Persistent. Light green, slightly purple-flushed. **Branches** Solitary. One or two secondary branches occasionally develop on older culms. **Leaves** Long and broad, 18 to 25 cm (7 to 10 inches) long by 3 to 6 cm (1¼ to 2½ inches) wide. Rich deep green with a dull shine on the upper surface, light matte green on the lower surface, moderately rounded at the base, tapering fairly abruptly to a point at the tip. Slight marginal and tip withering may occur in winter. **Rhizomes** Very invasive (strongly leptomorph). Too invasive for ornamental borders but

Sasaella masamuneana is used to make a dense groundcover bordering a path.

ideal for making a shortish leafy groundcover. **Cultivation** Sun or shade. Very tough and tolerant and will grow almost anywhere. **Hardiness** −10°C to −20°C (14°F to −4°F).

Sasaella masamuneana 'Albostriata'

Synonym *S. glabra* 'Albostriata'

Very short bamboo—very invasive

Differs from the species by having white-variegated leaves and a slightly smaller stature. An excellent variegated groundcover bamboo for general planting that is slightly less invasive than the species. The cultivar name is somewhat misleading since the variegations are never very white, even when young, and quickly become yellowish. The leaves are at their most striking in early summer with the new growth, and the variegations are almost faded away on many leaves by the onset of winter. This cultivar has a compact habit and seldom needs the periodic trimming to ground level that is so beneficial to other dwarf bamboos.

Culms Slightly shorter than those of the species. Completely reverted culms may occasionally be produced, bearing no variegated leaves. These are best removed. **Culm sheaths** Frequently with creamy white variegations. **Leaves** Rich deep green on the upper surface, with variable amounts of creamy white striping that is often slightly pink-tinted when young. Some leaves are completely green or almost green with minimal striping. Most variegations quickly become creamy yellow, turning almost yellow by the onset of winter, becoming much less conspicuous, with many leaves having nearly lost their striping. Colors are more matte on the lower surface.

Sasaella masamuneana 'Albostriata'.

Sasaella masamuneana 'Aureostriata'

Synonym *S. glabra* 'Aureostriata'

Very short bamboo—very invasive

Differs from the species by having yellow-variegated leaves. A very dull variegated bamboo only for the collector. The variegations are unspectacular and only attractive for a brief period from very late summer into winter.

Leaves Dull, indistinct, thick, dark yellow stripes occasionally develop on the upper surface of some leaves as the season progresses. The striping is usually absent in young leaves and appears quite suddenly after midsummer, though it is seldom conspicuous. By early winter the striping becomes more dull yellow and tired-looking. The lower surface is matte green, with any striping hardly penetrating through.

Cultivation Plant in a more open position to encourage the development and deepening of the variegations, although they will still appear in shade.

Sasaella ramosa

Synonyms *Arundinaria vagans*, *Sasa vagans*

Native to Japan

Very short bamboo—very invasive

A very useful and attractive dwarf bamboo that has been cultivated since the 19th century in Western gardens. It was introduced into the United Kingdom in 1892 as *Arundinaria vagans*. The original specific name, *vagans*, means "roving" or "wandering" and is very apt for one of the most invasive bamboos in cultivation. It is highly unsuitable for ornamental borders or containers, where its searching rhizomes

The foliage of *Sasaella masamuneana* 'Aureostriata' at the peak of its attractiveness in late summer.

will be a nuisance. However, as a groundcover bamboo it has no equal. The best example of this bamboo I have ever seen was at David Mc-Clintock's garden in Kent, where *S. ramosa* covered a considerable area under light woodland, marching inexorably over hummock and dip in an apple green swathe. The foliage does become quite withered by the end of winter, but in mass effect this is not to any detriment of its appearance. Many plants of this species flowered on and off in the 1980s, though coming to little harm and barely checking in growth. It is most likely to be confused with *Pleioblastus humilis* and its variety *pumilus*, from which it can be distinguished by the noticeably hairy undersides to the leaves.

Culms Very short and very slender, less than 1 m (3 feet) tall and less than 6 mm (¼ inch) in diameter. May be taller in heavy shade. Bright light green at first, ripening to light yellowish green. Nodes not prominent. Although the habit is rather lax, there is such a density of culms and branches that the appearance is held stiffly compact. New shoots appear in late spring. **Culm sheaths** Persistent. Pale green. **Branches** Solitary. Occasionally a second branch develops alongside the first. **Leaves** Medium-long and medium-broad, 9 to 18 cm (3½ to 7 inches) long by 1.5 to 3 cm (⅝ to 1¼ inches) wide. Light green and slightly matte on the upper surface due to the presence of very fine hairs, becoming darker green and losing the fine hairs as the season progresses,

Sasaella ramosa makes an attractive groundcover on either side of a path.

matte green and distinctly covered in dense fine hairs on the lower surface, fairly bluntly rounded at the base, tapering quickly to a point at the tip. Considerable withering may occur along the margins and at the tip in autumn and winter. **Rhizomes** Very invasive (strongly leptomorph). Very quickly spreading once established in anything but poor growing conditions. The perfect groundcover bamboo. **Cultivation** Sun or shade. Extremely tough, tolerant, and adaptable, but resents very dry locations. **Hardiness** Below −20°C (−4°F).

Sasamorpha

A small genus that is very closely related to *Sasa* and that some botanists do not recognize as being sufficiently distinct. The bamboos in this genus differ mostly by having a more upright habit and less prominent nodes. *Sasamorpha borealis* is the only species likely to be found in cultivation.

Sasamorpha borealis

Synonym *Sasa borealis*
Native to Japan
Short bamboo—very invasive

A rather dull and dismal bamboo of little horticultural merit. The new leaves in early summer can look attractive if the plant has been well maintained. But sadly, this bamboo spends most of the year looking ragged and scruffy and can only be recommended for tall groundcover or game coverts in the more remote parts of the garden.

Culms Short and very slender, 1 to 2 m (3 to 6 feet) tall and less than 6 mm (¼ inch) in diameter. Dull olive green flushed with purple, ripening to dull light green. Nodes not prominent. More or less upright in habit when young, the older culms becoming steadily more lax. New shoots appear in late spring. **Culm sheaths** Persistent. Purple-green at first, becoming light green. **Branches** Solitary. Older culms may develop one or more secondary branches near the summit. **Leaves** Long and broad, 18 to 25 cm (7 to 10 inches) long by 3 to 6 cm (1¼ to 2½ inches) wide. Dark green on the upper surface, dull matte green on the lower surface, bluntly rounded at the base, tapering fairly abruptly to a point at the tip. Considerable marginal and tip withering occurs in winter. **Rhizomes** Very invasive (strongly leptomorph). Too invasive and untidy for anything but the wildest parts of a larger garden. **Cultivation** Sun or shade. Grows almost anywhere. **Hardiness** Below −20°C (−4°F).

Semiarundinaria

An attractive genus of mostly architectural bamboos distinguished by their upright stature and cylindrical culms, which often have a partially developed shallow sulcus in the upper internodes. Considered by some botanists to be a hybrid genus crossing *Phyllostachys* with *Pleioblastus*.

This genus includes some of the most garden-worthy bamboos. The species with stouter culms are remarkably wind-tolerant, often able to withstand maritime exposure with little damage to the foliage. All *Semiarundinaria* species are useful for upright tall hedges and screens, with the exception of *S. yamadorii*, which is inclined to be looser in habit.

Semiarundinaria fastuosa

Synonyms *Arundinaria fastuosa, Bambusa fastuosa*
Native to Japan
Extremely tall bamboo—invasive

This species is native to Honshū, Shikoku, and Kyūshū. It is known in Japan as *narihiradake*, after Ariwara no Narihira, a hero of mythical romantic literature in the 11th century. It was named *Arundinaria fastuosa* and introduced into France by Bory Latour Marliac in 1892, and came to England in 1895. It has long been culti-vated in the United States.

The specific name *fastuosa* means "stately," and that is exactly the right name for this bam-boo. It can be easily distinguished from a dis-tance by its ramrod-straight culms, which pro-duce a stiffly upright habit. It is among the tall-est bamboos that can be grown in cool-tem-perate climates and will impart a distinct architectural quality to any planting scheme. It is important to stress, however, that unless given reasonable growing conditions, this spe-cies will not attain anything like its possible maximum height. It is an ideal subject for a tall hedge or screen in restricted spaces, because the very short branches give a plume-like effect of foliage at the tops of the culms. In this re-spect it can sometimes be confused with *Pleio-blastus simonii*. However, *S. fastuosa* is more refined and usually produces much thicker culms as a mature specimen. The culms are comparatively short-lived, so frequent cutting out of dead material is necessary to maintain a good appearance. This is one of the most wind-tolerant bamboos, along with *S. fastuosa* var. *viridis*, and is therefore suitable for planting as a windbreak in quite exposed localities. It is also an excellent subject for making a tall up-right screen in a narrow border where it is re-stricted at the edges.

In Western gardens this species flowered sporadically from the late 1950s until the early 1980s, though very few clumps came to any great harm, and most regained their former stature.

Culms Extremely tall and thick, more than 8 m (26 feet) tall and 3 to 5 cm (1¼ to 2 inches) in diameter. Rich deep green and glossy when young, becoming a distinctive purple-green on most lower internodes where exposed to sun-light, and maturing to yellowish green where not directly exposed to sunlight. Thin-walled

and prone to splitting when cut, even with the sharpest secateurs. Nodes not prominent. Very upright and straight and remaining so, with an occasional trace of zigzag sometimes in the lower parts of the culm. New shoots ap-pear in late spring. **Culm sheaths** Not per-sistent. Green tinted faint purple on the out-side, deep reddish purple on the inside, the lat-ter color lasting for some while after the sheath has become desiccated and faded, which is a useful guide to identification. Covered in fine hairs. Often remaining partially attached to

Newer and older culms of
Semiarundinaria fastuosa.

the culm in the early part of the first season, giving a distinctive effect. **Branches** In pairs or threes. Higher up the culm, particularly on older culms, the branches are frequently more multiple. Very short and upwardly inclined. **Leaves** Long and medium-broad, 18 to 25 cm (7 to 10 inches) long by 1.5 to 3 cm (⅝ to 1¼ inches) wide. Deep green and with a dull shine on the upper surface, matte green and with a less matte strip on one side on the lower surface, tapering gradually to a slender, drawn-out point at the tip. **Rhizomes** Invasive (leptomorph). Fairly slow to spread in cooler conditions. Remains in a tight clump initially, putting out occasional long runners when established in favorable conditions. **Cultivation** Sun or semishade. Best in an open, sunny position but will tolerate being grown under deciduous trees. Able to withstand strong winds and maritime exposure. **Hardiness** −10°C to −20°C (14°F to −4°F).

Semiarundinaria fastuosa var. viridis

Synonym *Arundinaria fastuosa* var. *viridis*

Extremely tall bamboo—very invasive

Differs from the species by having more richly green leaves and culms and by being more invasive. A superb bamboo well worth seeking out. It is an asset to any garden, keeping itself attractive and fresh-looking throughout the year. One of the finest bamboos for a tall hedge and happy as an underplanting to deciduous trees. It is perhaps too invasive to be recommended for the very small garden unless kept under tight control.

Culms Slightly lighter, richer green than the species, not developing the distinctive purple colorations, and slowly ripening to yellowish green. Generally less thick for their height than those of the species and often thicker just above a node than below. **Leaves** Slightly smaller and a pleasing, distinctly richer green.

The effect is more obvious on larger plants. **Rhizomes** More invasive than the species in most situations.

Semiarundinaria kagamiana

Native to Japan

Very tall bamboo—very invasive

A very vigorous and useful bamboo of upright habit. It can be planted as an alternative to *S. fastuosa* where less height and more density are needed. In common with that species, *S. kagamiana* makes a first-class windbreak, being able

Semiarundinaria fastuosa var. *viridis*.

to withstand very exposed conditions, including maritime exposure. It can be distinguished from the *S. fastuosa* types by its culms, which are thinner for their height, and by the more reddish coloration on its sunny side.

There is some confusion in Western gardens between this species and a bamboo introduced under the name *S. makinoi*. Some authorities state that although very similar in appearance, they should be regarded as separate species. In my experience, all the plants grown in Europe and the United States seem to be *S. kagamiana*; therefore, the true *S. makinoi* is probably not yet in general cultivation outside of Japan.

Semiarundinaria kagamiana.

Culms Very tall and medium-thick, 5 to 8 m (16 to 26 feet) tall and 2 to 3 cm (¾ to 1¼ inches) in diameter. Light midgreen at first, quickly ripening to dull yellowish green and distinctly tinted purplish red where exposed to good sunlight. Shortening of the internodal distance occurs here and there on thicker culms. Nodes moderately prominent, with some thicker culms having a distinct swelling under most nodes in the mid to lower parts of the culm. Stiffly upright in habit. New shoots appear in early summer. **Culm sheaths** Not persistent. Pale green slightly flushed with wine red. More or less glabrous and lacking auricles or oral setae. **Branches** In threes. Older culms usually develop more multiple branches. Very short and upwardly inclined. **Leaves** Medium-long and medium-broad, 9 to 18 cm (3½ to 7 inches) long by 1.5 to 3 cm (⅝ to 1¼ inches) wide. Midgreen with a dull shine on the upper surface, very light matte green on the lower surface, tapering quickly to a sharp point at the tip. **Rhizomes** Very invasive (strongly leptomorph). Far-reaching and penetrating once properly established. **Cultivation** Sun or shade. Very adaptable to a wide range of growing situations. Tolerant of strong winds and maritime exposure. **Hardiness** −10°C to −20°C (14°F to −4°F).

Semiarundinaria lubrica

Synonym Oligostachyum lubricum
Native to Japan
Very tall bamboo—very invasive

This handsome, uncommonly cultivated species recalls a more strong-looking ×*Hibanobambusa tranquillans*. The glossy, dark green culms carry largish, firm-textured, dark green leaves, giving an air of health and robust vigor. Although not as tall as other species in the genus, this bamboo is a fine addition to any garden and is worthy of wider appreciation. It seems happy in most planting situations, including in close proximity to deciduous trees. The rhizomes are very active, making this bamboo too invasive for the smaller garden.

Culms Very tall and medium-thick, 5 to 8 m (16 to 26 feet) tall and 2 to 3 cm (¾ to 1¼ inches) in diameter. Dark olive green and very glossy when young, ripening to yellowish green. Nodes moderately prominent. Sometimes slightly zigzag in the lower parts of the culm, otherwise very upright and staying upright in habit. New shoots appear in late spring. **Culm sheaths** Not persistent. Dark green and slightly purple-flushed when young. **Branches** In threes. Older culms gradually develop more multiple branches. **Leaves** Medium-long and medium-broad, 9 to 18 cm (3½ to 7 inches) long by 1.5 to 3 cm (⅝ to 1¼ inches) wide. Terminal leaves at the summit of the culm and at the ends of branches are noticeably broader for their length. Very dark green and lustrous on the upper surface, light matte green with a trace of a less matte strip on one side on the lower surface, tapering to a slender, drawn-out point at the tip. **Rhizomes** Very invasive (strongly leptomorph). Slow to spread until established, then very far-reaching and penetrating. **Cultivation** Sun or shade. Perhaps the most adaptable *Semiarundinaria* bamboo for less than ideal conditions. **Hardiness** Below −20°C (−4°F).

Semiarundinaria okuboi

Synonym *S. villosa*
Native to Japan
Tall bamboo—very invasive

This species is most easily distinguished from other *Semiarundinaria* bamboos by its comparatively slender culms and larger leaves. While quite imposing as a mature specimen, it is inclined to look uninspiring as a small plant, with its thin culms and somewhat untidy habit.

The larger leaves are a little less tough than those of species with thicker culms, and are prone to some winter damage. However, this species provides gardeners with an upright specimen that can reach a height greater than most other large-leaved bamboos in cultivation. Beware of the eager rhizomes, which will rapidly colonize surrounding areas.

Culms Tall and slender, 3 to 5 m (10 to 16 feet) tall and 6 mm to 2 cm (¼ to ¾ inch) in diameter. Can be slightly taller in good growing conditions. Deep green quickly ripening to yellowish green. Nodes not prominent. Fairly upright in habit, with older and very small culms arching slightly. New shoots appear in late spring. **Culm sheaths** Not persistent. Midgreen. **Branches** In threes. Older culms develop one or more shorter secondary branches, giving a more multiple effect. **Leaves** Medium-long and broad, 9 to 18 cm (3½ to 7 inches) long by 3 to 6 cm (1¼ to 2½ inches) wide. Dark green with a dull shine on the upper surface, matte green with a slightly less matte strip on one side on the lower surface, tapering fairly abruptly to a point at the tip. Terminal leaves at the summit of the culm and at the end of some branches are often larger. **Rhizomes** Very invasive (strongly leptomorph). Vigorous and far-reaching in all but the poorest growing conditions. **Cultivation** Sun or shade. Very adaptable to a wide range of growing situations, but not quite so tolerant of strong winds and exposure as other members of the genus. **Hardiness** −10°C to −20°C (14°F to −4°F).

Semiarundinaria yamadorii

Synonyms *Arundinaria yamadorii*, *S.* ‘Angers’
Native to Japan
Tall bamboo—invasive

A less robust species obscure in Eastern writings but fairly common in Western gardens. It is distinguished from other species in the

Semiarundinaria yamadorii.

genus by its larger terminal leaves and much less upright habit. While still a good garden plant, it has a weaker constitution than most *Semiarundinaria* bamboos and is not recommended for exposed positions, where the foliage will be rendered brown-edged and scruffy by the end of winter.

Culms Tall and slender, 3 to 5 m (10 to 16 feet) tall and 6 mm to 2 cm (¼ to ¾ inch) in diameter. Light green at first, ripening quickly to yellowish green and easily abraded, giving rise to marks and discolorations in older culms. Nodes moderately prominent. Prone to weak geniculations in the lower internodes and generally somewhat zigzag throughout the length of the culm. Much less upright than other *Semiarundinaria* bamboos, with older culms arching considerably under the weight of the large terminal leaves. New shoots appear in early summer. **Culm sheaths** Not persistent. Pale green. **Branches** In threes. Most older culms develop more multiple branches. **Leaves** Medium-long and medium-broad, 9 to 18 cm (3½ to 7 inches) long by 1.5 to 3 cm (⅝ to 1¼ inches) wide. Rich, rather light green on the upper surface, light matte green on the lower surface, tapering fairly abruptly to a sharp point at the tip. Terminal leaves at the summit of the culm and at the end of some branches are often considerably larger. **Rhizomes** Invasive (leptomorph). Can be considerably more invasive when given lush growing conditions. **Cultivation** Sun or semi-shade. Tolerant of most situations but dislikes any sort of exposure. **Hardiness** –10°C to –20°C (14°F to –4°F).

Semiarundinaria yamadorii **'Brimscombe'**

Tall bamboo—invasive

Differs from the species by having yellow variegations in the younger leaves. I discovered this cultivar growing in the middle (always in the middle, never at the edge!) of a clump of the species in the Oxford garden of John Vlitos. With some difficulty we managed to extract some propagating material, and the resulting plant was named after his garden. To get the best from this cultivar, always plant it in as sunny a position as possible. It is a curious and pleasing form, though unspectacular, and is likely to remain a collector's plant.

Leaves In early summer the younger leaves are very light yellow on the upper surface, some with variable amounts of thin green striping in the style of *Pleioblastus auricomus*, others completely yellow. The coloration requires strong light to develop properly and will appear more or less plain green if the plant is grown in shade. The yellow color is short-lived, quickly changing to green as the season progresses. The yellow coloration is hardly noticeable on the lower surface, which is effectively matte light green. **Cultivation** Sun. If this bamboo is planted in any position away from direct sunlight, its coloration is guaranteed to be insubstantial, if present at all.

Semiarundinaria yashadake

Synonym *Arundinaria yashadake*
Native to Japan
Extremely tall bamboo—invasive

A superb species, generally less common than *S. fastuosa* var. *viridis*, with which it is superficially similar. It can be distinguished from that form by its culms, which are generally thinner for their height; by its culm sheaths, which lack the reddish coloration on the inner surface; and by its leaves, which are usually less rich green and thinner for their length. To the keen bamboo gardener this species represents an excellent subject for an imposing upright specimen plant or for a very tall screening bamboo that will give a wall-like effect. Useful as an unusual alternative to taller *Phyllostachys* bamboos where the planting position is less open.

Culms Extremely tall and medium-thick, more than 8 m (26 feet) tall and 2 to 3 cm (¾ to 1¼ inches) in diameter. Rich midgreen and glossy when young, ripening to dull yellowish green. Nodes not prominent. Very upright in habit and only developing a slight arch when grown in shade, which causes the habit to become slightly lax. New shoots appear in late spring. **Culm sheaths** Not persistent. Midgreen and covered in brownish hairs. **Branches** In threes. Higher up the culm, particularly in older culms, the branches often become more multiple. Very short and upwardly inclined. **Leaves** Medium-long and medium-broad, 9 to 18 cm (3½ to 7 inches) long by 1.5 to 3 cm (⅝ to 1¼ inches) wide. Deep green with a dull shine on the upper surface, light matte green with a slightly less matte strip on one side on the lower surface, more or less parallel-sided for most of their length, tapering gradually to a slender, drawn-out point at the tip. **Rhizomes** Invasive (leptomorph). As with *S. fastuosa* there is usually little spread in the early years after planting, but then occasional long runners are produced. **Cultivation** Sun or shade. Very adaptable to a wide range of planting situations and tolerant of strong wind and maritime exposure. **Hardiness** −10°C to −20°C (14°F to −4°F).

Semiarundinaria yashadake 'Kimmei'

Tall bamboo—invasive

Differs from the species by having yellow culms with variable green striping, and a much smaller stature. A useful and very attractive bamboo, ideal as a shorter and more compact shade-tolerant alternative to the principal yellow *Phyllostachys* bamboos. The bright golden yellow color is very pleasing, with the complimentary green stripes appearing here and there, and all displayed with minimal interference due to the sparse foliage. In basic morphological characteristics, this bamboo would seem to be more closely related to *S. yamadorii* or something similar, rather than being a cultivar of *S. yashadake*. It is much less sturdy and structural in appearance than the species to which it is attributed, having much thinner culms and larger, less robust leaves. There is also a bamboo in cultivation that seems to be the inverse of this form—that is, the culms are green with a yellow stripe above the branches. It is called *S. yashadake* 'Gimmei'.

Culms Tall and slender, 3 to 5 m (10 to 16 feet) tall and 6 mm to 2 cm (¼ to ¾ inch) in diameter. Very bright, light golden yellow at first, with thin green stripes appearing at random. Sometimes the green coloring appears as a panel in the partially developed sulcus above the branches, and sometimes the culms are completely yellow throughout. The yellow parts of the culm that are exposed to sunlight when young usually develop a pinkish red coloration temporarily in the first season. With

maturity the yellow becomes a deep golden yellow and the green striping becomes lighter and less vivid. **Culm sheaths** Frequently with creamy white variegations. **Branches** Sparsely branched throughout. **Leaves** Coarser than those of *S. yashadake*. Darker green on the upper surface, occasionally with thin cream stripes that become a deeper yellow with age, colors muted and grayish matte on the lower surface. **Cultivation** Less robust than the species and less tolerant of strong winds.

Semiarundinaria yashadake 'Kimmei' is an excellent yellow-culmed bamboo for smaller gardens.

Shibataea

An attractive small genus of low-growing bamboos with a distinctive appearance. They are quickly recognized by their short culms, which are triangular in cross section due to a flat sulcus above the very short culm branches, and by their unusual small leaves, which are broad for their length. Each culm has three to seven branches that seldom additionally ramify. Each branch has only one or two internodes terminating abruptly with one leaf, though occasionally two may be found. The new shoots are colorfully tinted in a shade from red to purple and are curiously flattened.

Shibataea species are very useful in the garden. They produce pleasantly innocuous mounds of leafy vegetation and can be used as smaller specimen plants or tallish groundcover. They are happy in sun or a certain amount of shade, though too much shade causes a loss of the attractive tidy habit. These bamboos do not make good subjects for dry places, where their main fault will quickly reveal itself. Most species are very reluctant to shed their scruffy older leaves, even with the impetus of new growth in early summer. Some older culms will hang on to last year's leaves almost indefinitely. The solution is to maintain vigor by feeding the plant, providing copious water during dry periods, and ruthlessly pruning out the older culms. This genus has a dislike of very alkaline soils, which tend to cause chlorosis. Wherever possible, plant in neutral to acid soils.

Shibataea bamboos are native to eastern China, and in the case of the most commonly cultivated species, *S. kumasasa*, also southern Japan.

Shibataea chiangshanensis

Native to China

Very short bamboo—invasive

A delightful miniature bamboo still rare in cultivation but likely to become very popular. The very short culms, which are rarely taller than half a meter (1½ feet), carry distinctly ovate leaves held in neat formation. This bamboo has great potential for the garden, where it can be used as an edging plant along large borders or as a slow-spreading groundcover.

Culms Very short and very slender, less than 1 m (3 feet) tall and up to 6 mm (¼ inch) in diameter. Seldom attaining more than half these dimensions. Light midgreen at first, slowly ripening to dull yellowish green. Internodes almost semicircular in cross section. Nodes moderately prominent for the size of the culm. Upright in habit, although slightly zigzag in the upper parts of the culm, some culms having a slight lean toward the strongest light. New shoots appear in early summer. **Culm sheaths** Not persistent. Reddish purple at first, becoming reddish green. **Branches** In threes. Extremely short, with each branch usually not ramifying further in subsequent years. **Leaves** Short and medium-broad, 5 to 9 cm (2 to 3½ inches) long by 1.5 to 3 cm (⅝ to 1¼ inches) wide. Rich green with a dull shine on the upper surface, matte green on the lower surface, bluntly rounded at the base, broad for their length, distinctly broadest near the base, tapering fairly abruptly to a sharp point at the tip. **Rhizomes** Invasive (leptomorph). Spreads slowly under most gardening conditions and can safely be planted in shrub borders. **Cultivation** Sun or semi-shade. Adaptable to most situations but needs adequate moisture and dislikes very alkaline soils. **Hardiness** −10°C to −20°C (14°F to −4°F).

Shibataea chinensis

Native to China

Short bamboo—invasive

This charming bamboo is easily confused with *S. kumasasa*, but its culms and leaves are smaller and neater in appearance. It can be distinguished from *S. chiangshanensis* by its greater height and slightly longer leaves. It has a tidy vertical habit, giving the effect of a miniature bamboo forest. In its native China it is often used to make low hedges, an application for which it is well suited. This species is most likely to be found in the gardens of bamboo collectors, but it is gradually becoming more widely available.

Culms Very short and very slender, less than 1 m (3 feet) tall and up to 6 mm (¼ inch) in diameter. Light midgreen at first, slowly ripening to dull yellowish green. Internodes somewhat triangular in cross section higher up the culm, and more circular near the base. Nodes moderately prominent. Upright in habit, with a slight tendency to zigzag in the upper parts of the culm, and tidy-looking. New shoots appear in early summer. **Culm sheaths** Not persistent. Light green, slightly purple-flushed. **Branches** In threes. Very short, with each branch usually not ramifying further in subsequent years. **Leaves** Short and medium-broad, 5 to 9 cm (2 to 3½ inches) long by 1.5 to 3 cm (⅝ to 1¼ inches) wide. Rich green with a dull shine on the upper surface, matte green on the lower surface, bluntly rounded at the base, broad for their length, broadest near the base, tapering abruptly to a point at the tip. **Rhizomes** Invasive (leptomorph). The rate of spread is very modest, making this species suitable for smaller gardens. **Cultivation** Sun or semishade. Adaptable to most situations but needs adequate moisture and dislikes very alkaline soils. **Hardiness** –10°C to –20°C (14°F to –4°F).

The pleasing foliage of *Shibataea chinensis*.

Shibataea kumasasa

Synonym *Phyllostachys ruscifolia*

Native to China, Japan

Short bamboo—invasive

A good smaller bamboo for general planting. It is capable of growing higher than most other species in the genus but is usually seen as a plant about 1 m (3 feet) tall. This species is extensively used in Japan to make large areas of groundcover and is sometimes clipped regularly to make rounded balls or undulating hummocks. It is ideal for making low hedges.

Shibataea kumasasa is an excellent smaller
bamboo for the front of an ornamental border.

In common with other species of the genus, it
prefers acid rather than alkaline soils and requires adequate moisture during the growing season to avoid looking scruffy and dreary.
This species is among the longest-cultivated
bamboos in Western gardens and is usually
represented in even the smallest bamboo collection. Introduced into the United Kingdom in
1861 and into the United States in 1902.

Culms Short and very slender, 1 to 2 m (3 to
6 feet) tall and up to 6 mm (¼ inch) in diameter.
Seldom reaches more than 1 m tall. Light midgreen at first, slowly ripening to dull yellowish
green. Internodes very triangular in cross section. Nodes moderately prominent. Fairly upright in habit with a slight zigzag in the upper
parts of the culm, some older culms developing a slight lean due to their slenderness and
the weight of the foliage. New shoots appear in
early summer. **Culm sheaths** Not persistent.
Purplish green with a slight yellow hue, particularly at the margins. **Branches** In threes. Very
short, with little further ramification in subsequent years. **Leaves** Short and medium-broad,

5 to 9 cm (2 to 3½ inches) long by 1.5 to 3 cm (⅝ to 1¼ inches) wide. Rich deep green with a dull shine on the upper surface, light matte green on the lower surface, bluntly rounded at the base, broad for their length, broadest near the base, tapering fairly abruptly to a point at the tip. **Rhizomes** Invasive (leptomorph). The rate of spread is very modest, making this species suitable for small gardens. **Cultivation** Sun or semi-shade. Adaptable to most situations but needs adequate moisture and dislikes very alkaline soils. **Hardiness** –10°C to –20°C (14°F to –4°F).

Shibataea kumasasa 'Albostriata'

Short bamboo—invasive

Differs from the species by having white-variegated leaves. This, the white-variegated form, is very similar to the yellow-variegated form, 'Aureostriata', with which it is easily mistaken. Plants correctly identified as the white-variegated form should have originated from plant material collected in the forest in Sakashita-cho, Aichi Prefecture, Japan, in 1967. At its best, this cultivar is singularly beautiful and a joy to behold. The ideal planting position is in light shade, as the white parts of the leaves are liable to scorching in strong midsummer sun. Unfortunately, like 'Aureostriata', it is very unstable, producing many culms that are completely green-leaved. These reverted culms will quickly dominate and suppress the variegated-leaved culms and so should be rigorously removed. It is a good idea to periodically dig up the whole clump and wash the soil from the rhizomes to find and remove the reverted culms. This bamboo is a labor of love for the dedicated collector.

Culm sheaths Frequently with creamy white variegations. **Leaves** Rich deep green with highly variable amounts of creamy white striping on the upper surface at first, some leaves completely white and others completely green, colors more matte on the lower surface. As the season progresses, the white parts of most leaves become more creamy white, turning creamy yellow by winter. Not consistent, with frequent reversions. **Cultivation** A position in semi-shade is needed for best results.

Shibataea kumasasa 'Aureostriata'

Short bamboo—invasive

Differs from the species by having yellow-variegated leaves. This, the yellow-variegated

A young plant of *Shibataea kumasasa* 'Aureostriata'. Unfortunately, this bamboo and the form 'Albostriata' are very prone to reversions, in which culms are produced with completely green foliage.

form, is very similar to the white-variegated form, 'Albostriata', with which it is easily mistaken. Plants correctly identified as the yellow-variegated form should have originated from material introduced into Germany from Japan around 1865. At its best, this cultivar is almost as beautiful as the white-variegated form. It is a little more tolerant of strong sunlight but still benefits from planting in light shade. It is just as unstable and should be treated in the same way by periodically digging up the whole clump and removing the reverted culms.

Culm sheaths Frequently with light yellow variegations. **Leaves** Most leaves are rich deep green with highly variable amounts of light yellow striping on the upper surface at first, while some leaves are completely light yellow and others are completely green, colors more matte on the lower surface. As the season progresses, the yellow parts of most leaves become deeper yellow. Not consistent, with frequent reversions. **Cultivation** A position in semishade is recommended for best results.

Shibataea lancifolia

Native to China

Short bamboo—invasive

Undoubtedly the best species of *Shibataea* for ornamental plantings. This species has distinctively longer leaves that are drawn out almost endlessly at the tip to a very fine point. It makes an attractive mass of light green, rather grayish foliage that can be used in front of taller colored-culm bamboos. In common with other species of the genus, this plant's spread is very slow, unless it is grown in warmer conditions, and it is therefore suitable for even the smallest garden. I acquired this species in the late 1980s as part of an exchange with Jim Waddick of the American Bamboo Society. Shortly afterward I had propagated enough material to introduce it into cultivation in the United King-

dom. It quickly proved to be an excellent garden plant, but did seem even more prone than other species of the genus to becoming chlorotic on alkaline soils. This can be overcome to some extent with occasional copious top-dressings of peat or flowers of sulfur or sequestered iron, which will help to keep the foliage green.

Culms Short and very slender, 1 to 2 m (3 to 6 feet) tall and up to 6 mm (¼ inch) in diameter. Light midgreen at first, slowly ripening to dull yellowish green. Internodes almost semicircular in cross section, more circular near the base of the culm. Nodes moderately prominent. Fairly upright in habit, with a slight tendency

Shibataea lancifolia.

to zigzag in the upper parts of the culm. New shoots appear in early summer. **Culm sheaths** Not persistent. Light green with a slight purple tint when young, glabrous throughout. **Branches** In threes. Very short, with little or no further ramification in subsequent years. **Leaves** Medium-long and medium-broad, 9 to 18 cm (3½ to 7 inches) long by 1.5 to 3 cm (⅝ to 1¼ inches) wide. Light green and slightly matte at first on the upper surface, becoming midgreen with a very dull shine, matte midgreen on the lower surface, acutely rounded at the base, long for their breadth, tapering to a long, drawn-out point at the tip. **Rhizomes** Invasive (leptomorph). Slightly more invasive than some species in the genus but still slow to spread. **Cultivation** Sun or semi-shade. Adaptable to most situations but needs adequate moisture and dislikes very alkaline soils. **Hardiness** −10°C to −20°C (14°F to −4°F).

Sinobambusa

A genus of subtropical bamboos that are native to southern and southeastern China and naturalized in some parts of Japan. They are hardier than might be expected from their provenance, and can be grown outside in cool-temperate gardens with reasonable success. They have a generally upright appearance rather recalling *Semiarundinaria* and can be distinguished by their main branches, which are more or less equal in length, and by the culm sheaths, which abscise almost immediately to leave a curiously prominent corky sheath scar.

Sinobambusa bamboos make statuesque garden plants, thriving in milder areas. Their only obvious fault is a tendency for the culms to be quickly marked and abraded by contact with each other. Care should be taken when choosing a location, since the rhizomes are very penetrating once established.

All members of this genus, especially *Sino-*

bambusa tootsik, are poor choices for container growing. Their active rhizomes quickly circle round inside a pot and sooner or later explode right through its sides. Furthermore, upon becoming starved of nutrients in a container, these bamboos are prone to looking extremely tired and lackluster, and are even apt to die suddenly. If you live in a cold district and container growing is your only option, be sure to keep *Sinobambusa* species well fed and healthy, with regular dividing and repotting into fresh compost.

Sinobambusa intermedia

Native to China

Tall bamboo—very invasive

This elegant species is cultivated widely in the United States but is much less common in Britain and continental Europe. From a distance it can be quickly recognized by the white powdery coating on the young culms. This white appearance persists well into midseason and contrasts nicely with the older culms. The foliage is carried in pleasing plume-like tufts on the relatively short branches. A most garden-worthy bamboo indeed.

Culms Tall and medium-thick, 3 to 5 m (10 to 16 feet) tall and 2 to 3 cm (¾ to 1¼ inches) in diameter. Light rich green at first, with a very white coating of fine powder adhering to fine bristly hairs on the surface of the internodes, which are somewhat rough to touch; the coating and the hairs are lost as the culm ripens to deeper green, then yellowish green, then brown. From an early age the internodal surface usually acquires various marks and abrasions that are lighter in color. The powdery coating is retained under the culm nodes as a farinose zone. Nodes moderately prominent, with a distinctive corky sheath scar, and spaced apart with a long internodal distance, often as much as 50 to 60 cm (1⅝ to 2 feet). Very upright in habit, with only moderate arching near the summit of older culms. New shoots appear mostly in early summer but can appear at other times of year when the weather is mild. **Culm sheaths** Not persistent. Midgreen and distinctly hairy on the outer surface, particularly around the base of the sheath. **Branches** In threes. Usually more or less equal in length. Sometimes reduced to one or two on lower nodes. **Leaves** Medium-long and medium-broad, 9 to 18 cm (3½ to 7 inches) long by 1.5 to 3 cm (⅝ to 1¼ inches) wide. Deep green, glossy, and glabrous on the upper surface, matte green and glabrous or nearly so on the lower surface and very firm-textured, tapering to a gradual point at the tip. **Rhizomes** Very invasive (strongly leptomorph). Can spread rapidly in favorable conditions and very mild climates. **Cultivation** Sun or shade. The habit will be more upright in an open position. Dislikes cold dry winds in winter. **Hardiness** –5°C to –10°C (23°F to 14°F).

Sinobambusa tootsik

Native to China

Tall bamboo—very invasive

Commonly known as the Chinese temple bamboo, a reference to its traditional use for planting around temples and religious institutions. This noble bamboo has been cultivated since ancient times. In Japan, where it is widely naturalized, it has been used as an ornamental plant for more than a thousand years. It is often seen there with its already short branches further trimmed back to create a pompom-like effect. This, the most commonly grown representative of the genus *Sinobambusa*, is a good subject for Western gardens. It is hardy enough to be ventured outdoors in locations free from severe frost, and seems to impart a restful quality to any planting. Unfortunately, perhaps even more than other members of the genus,

Sinobambusa tootsik can be identified by the prominent ring of purple-brown hairs at the base of the culm sheath.

the young culms become marked and discolored very quickly, so frequent pruning out of older material is recommended.

Culms Tall and medium-thick, 3 to 5 m (10 to 16 feet) tall and 2 to 3 cm (¾ to 1¼ inches) in diameter. Light midgreen at first, with a slight whitish powdery coating adhering to fine hairs on the internodal surface (not as distinctive as in *S. intermedia*), quickly becoming deep rich green, then gradually ripening to yellowish green and then brown. From an early age the internodal surface usually acquires an abundance of marks and abrasions that are lighter in color. Nodes moderately prominent, with a distinctive corky sheath scar and a slight farinose zone below each node that persists beyond the first season. Very upright in habit, with only a slight arch developing on older culms. New shoots appear in early summer but can appear at other times of year when the weather is mild. **Culm sheaths** Not persistent. Light green tinted reddish brown, more purple-red at the base, hairy on the outer surface and with a distinctive tuft of purple-brown hairs around the base of the sheath. **Branches** In threes. The middle branch is usually longer than those on each side. Sometimes reduced to two or one on lower nodes. **Leaves** Medium-long and medium-broad, 9 to 18 cm (3½ to 7 inches) long by 1.5 to 3 cm (⅝ to 1¼ inches) wide. Very variable in size throughout the plant. Dark green, with a dull shine, and healthy-looking on the upper surface, light matte green on the lower surface, tapering fairly abruptly at the tip. **Rhizomes** Very invasive (strongly leptomorph). Can spread rapidly in favorable conditions and very mild climates. **Cultivation** Sun or shade. An open position is preferable if this bamboo is to be seen at its best. Dislikes cold dry winds in winter. **Hardiness** −5°C to −10°C (23°F to 14°F).

Sinobambusa tootsik 'Variegata'

Synonym *S. tootsik* f. *albostriata*

Tall bamboo—very invasive

Differs from the species by having white-variegated leaves and a slightly smaller stature. This is an absolutely wonderful variegated bamboo, all the more special for being one of the few really good, taller, variegated forms in cultivation. While the white stripes in the leaves are probably at their brightest in early summer, the loss of intensity by winter is only slight, lit-

tle more than a deepening of color. This superb bamboo should always be planted against a dark background for best effect.

Culms Slightly smaller than those of the species. **Leaves** Deep green, with conspicuous white striping that becomes more creamy white as the season progresses. The striping is fairly consistent from leaf to leaf, with only a few leaves tending to be nearly all white or all green. Colors are more matte on the lower surface, with only some of the white striping penetrating through. **Cultivation** Sun or semi-

Sinobambusa tootsik 'Variegata' growing in a big pot by the greenhouse at Stream Cottage.

shade. When this plant is grown in shade, variegations are retained but are less striking.

Thamnocalamus

A fine genus of clump-forming species, containing some of the most elegant and garden-worthy bamboos in cultivation. With the exception of the robust *Thamnocalamus tessellatus*, which is native to South Africa, all species are indigenous to the more high-altitude forest and forest fringes of the Himalaya. The taxonomy of the high-altitude bamboos is still very confused, particularly the distinctions between *Borinda*, *Drepanostachyum*, *Fargesia*, *Himalayacalamus*, and *Thamnocalamus*, and there is likely to be further changes to the classification of these bamboos by botanists over the coming years.

The Himalayan species of *Thamnocalamus* are characterized by their generally delicate and elegant appearance, and can be distinguished from other high-altitude genera by their many fewer branches and by their leaves, which have distinct and noticeable tessellation. All species of *Thamnocalamus* tend to have their culm sheath blades held upright rather than bent outward.

Thamnocalamus bamboos are of easy cultivation. The Himalayan species are well suited to shade but seem to thrive best in partially shaded positions where there is some sunlight but also shelter from cold winds. In strong sunlight these bamboos tend to suffer from leaf curl, but this does no harm to the plants and is hardly noticeable on the forms with smaller leaves. Contrarily, I have found that *T. tessellatus* seems to resent shelter or shade and is usually seen at its best when grown right out in the open.

Thamnocalamus crassinodus

Synonym *T. spathiflorus* var. *crassinodus*
Native to Nepal, Tibet
Tall bamboo—clump-forming

This highly desirable species manages to be elegant as well as imposing. The habit is pleasingly upright, and the waxy gray young culms have clearly noticeable swellings at each node. This is complemented by just the right amount of smallish delicate-looking leaves, which are carried on branches bending outward from the culm to a uniform 45 degrees. It is a fine subject for partial shade in association with deciduous trees, perhaps needing this location more than the other species and forms of *Thamnocalamus* described here. This species is easy to identify as a mature clump, but thinner culms on immature plants will lack the nodal swellings. It is most likely to be confused with *T. spathiflorus*, from which it can be separated by the slightly smaller leaves and distinctive culms. Many of the examples of *T. crassinodus* found in Western gardens originate from seedlings collected by Merlyn Edwards during a trip to Nepal in 1973. They were found at altitudes of about 3200 m (10,500 feet) above sea level. The small-leaved forms 'Kew Beauty', 'Langtang', and 'Merlyn' were collected in the Langtang Valley during a trip to Nepal in 1971, along with various other *T. crassinodus* seedlings that, as yet, are not widely cultivated.

Culms Tall and slender, 3 to 5 m (10 to 16 feet) tall and 6 mm to 2 cm (¼ to ¾ inch) in diameter. Midgreen at first with a waxy gray-blue powdery coating that persists throughout the first season, ripening to light yellowish green, the upper parts of the culm and most of the branches quickly becoming tinted deep wine red, particularly where exposed to sunlight. Nodes moderately prominent, with a noticeable swelling on thicker culms that extends some 1 cm (⅜ inch) on either side of the node. Fairly upright in habit when young, with some older culms developing a moderate lean, or an arch from midculm upward. New shoots appear in late spring. **Culm sheaths** Semi-persistent. Light green, slightly purple-tinted at first, and covered in fine hairs, although some wild plants have glabrous culm sheaths. **Branches** In threes. The middle branch is thicker and longer and usually has greater secondary ramification than those on either side. Often reduced to just one or two branches on lower nodes. **Leaves** Medium-long and narrow, 9 to 18 cm (3½ to 7 inches) long by 1 to 1.5 cm (⅜ to ⅝ inch) wide. Dullish, slightly matte midgreen on the upper surface, grayish matte green on the lower surface, tapering very abruptly to a point at the tip. **Rhizomes** Clump-forming (pachymorph). Makes a fairly dense clump that does not become much more open in maturity. **Cultivation** Sun or shade. By far the best position for this bamboo is partial or dappled shade under light tree cover. It is very susceptible to leaf curl when planted in strong sunlight. Provide shelter from cold winds in winter. **Hardiness** −5°C to −10°C (23°F to 14°F).

Thamnocalamus crassinodus 'Gosainkund'

Synonym *T. crassinodus* 'Glauca'

Tall bamboo—clump-forming

Differs from the species by having a slightly more distinct gray-blue powdery coating on the young culms, and by being slightly less hardy. One of the many *T. crassinodus* seedlings collected by Merlyn Edwards was given to Nathan Mutch at Pitt White in Devon. After growing there for some years, it was eventually recognized as a particularly good clone. The habit was supremely elegant, and the young culms had a particularly well-developed grayish color. Although by this time propagating ma-

Thamnocalamus crassinodus 'Gosainkund' has striking young culms that are covered in a gray-blue powdery deposit.

terial had filtered into the nursery trade under the unofficial cultivar name 'Glauca', it has since been called 'Gosainkund' to commemorate the sacred lake nearby to where it was collected. Unfortunately, this cultivar is not so hardy as the other forms in cultivation, being liable to lose much of the foliage or even being cut down completely at temperatures much below −5°C (23°F).

Culms Young culms have a slightly whiter and more persistent powdery coating. **Hardiness** Slightly less hardy than the species.

Thamnocalamus crassinodus 'Kew Beauty'

Tall bamboo—clump-forming

Differs from the species by having a more extended reddish coloration on the culms and culm branches and by having smaller leaves. This is by far the easiest of the Langtang seedlings to identify. All plants of this cultivar originate from a seedling that was given to the Royal Botanic Gardens, Kew, and later named 'Kew Beauty' by David McClintock. This particular form is regarded by many (myself included) as the finest clump-forming bamboo in cultivation. If I found myself restricted to growing only one taller bamboo in my garden, it would have to be 'Kew Beauty'.

Culms Very slightly deeper green under the powdery coating when young, as compared with the species, and developing a much more pronounced reddish coloration that can extend almost to the base of the culm where exposed to sunlight. The coloration persists often into the third or even fourth season, the most reddish culms sometimes ripening to blackish brown-red without passing through the yellowish green phase. **Branches** Much more noticeably reddish where exposed to sunlight, but often having this coloration in shade. **Leaves** Short and very narrow, 5 to 9 cm (2 to 3½ inches) long by less than 1 cm (⅜ inch) wide. An open position produces leaves slightly darker green on the upper surface than those of the species. **Cultivation** A position in good sunlight maximizes the reddish effect.

Page 280: *Thamnocalamus crassinodus* 'Kew Beauty' growing in my garden.

Thamnocalamus crassinodus 'Langtang'

Tall bamboo—clump-forming

Differs from the species by lacking the reddish coloration in the upper parts of the culm and by having smaller leaves. In average growing conditions the leaves are only slightly smaller than those of 'Merlyn', a cultivar with which it is very easy to confuse. Nonetheless, it has the smallest leaves of the taller temperate bamboos in cultivation.

Culms Ripening to light yellowish green with age and almost completely lacking any reddish coloration in the upper parts of the culm and on the branches. **Leaves** Very short and very narrow, less than 5 cm (2 inches) long by less than 1 cm (⅜ inch) wide. Sometimes smaller than two-thirds of these dimensions. The upper surface of the leaves is a slightly lighter green than those of the species when the plant is grown in an open position.

Thamnocalamus crassinodus 'Merlyn'

Tall bamboo—clump-forming

Differs from the species by lacking the reddish coloration in the upper parts of the culm and by having slightly smaller leaves. A completely superb clump-forming bamboo of virtually equal merit to 'Kew Beauty', differing mainly in the lighter color of the older culms. This would be the logical choice where one of the two has to be planted in a shady location. It is very easy to confuse with 'Langtang', the only obvious difference being the size of the leaves.

Culms Almost completely lacking any signs of reddish coloration in the upper parts of the

Page 281: An impressive foliage effect created by *Thamnocalamus crassinodus* 'Merlyn'.

culm and on the branches. **Leaves** Short and very narrow, 5 to 9 cm (2 to 3½ inches) long by less than 1 cm (⅜ inch) wide. Slightly lighter green on the upper surface than those of the species when the plant is grown in an open position.

Thamnocalamus spathiflorus

Synonyms *Arundinaria spathiflora*, *T. aristatus*
Native to Nepal, Bhutan, India, Sikkim
Tall bamboo—clump-forming
An extremely elegant species occurring at altitudes of 2100 to 3300 m (7000 to 11,000 feet)

in the Himalaya. In the wild it is very variable, with forms and subspecies associated with different altitudes and regions. In northwestern India this bamboo once provided most of the material used for home artifacts such as sticks, poles, handles, weaving, and furniture.

A bamboo from the same region named *T. aristatus* now appears to be identical with *T. spathiflorus*. Since the name *T. spathiflorus* was published some 30 years earlier, under the rules of taxonomy this name must prevail. Plants grown in the United States as *T. aristatus* are most likely *T. spathiflorus* or possibly misidentified plants of *T. crassinodus*. Unlike *T. crassinodus* and its cultivated forms, *T. spathiflorus* is less upright and looser in habit, has

Thamnocalamus spathiflorus produces gently arching culms topped by elegant foliage.

slightly larger, lighter green leaves, and has little if any obvious nodal swelling.

Thamnocalamus spathiflorus is recorded by Émile-Gustave Camus (1913) as having flowered extensively in India in 1821, 1881–1882, and 1893. This species was introduced into England in 1886, and some plants flowered here with little permanent effect in the early 1990s.

This bamboo makes a fine garden plant and imparts a Himalayan flavor to any planting. The foliage is most attractive, and the plant is only marginally let down by the somewhat ungainly culms, which are seldom straight. It is compact enough to be used in a small urban garden and is not out of place in a traditional cottage garden. In common with other delicate Himalayan bamboos, a lot of dead culms are produced each year and will need to be removed. By far the most satisfactory planting position is where there is partial or dappled shade and shelter from strong cold winds.

Culms Tall and slender, 3 to 5 m (10 to 16 feet) tall and 6 mm to 2 cm (¼ to ¾ inch) in diameter. Bright light green at first with a faint dusting of whitish gray powder, quickly ripening to pale yellowish green, tinted pinkish purple where exposed to sunlight, particularly in the upper parts of the culm and on the branches. Thin-walled and easily split. Nodes not prominent. Only moderately upright and somewhat loose in habit, often slightly zigzag in the lower parts of many culms, with most older culms developing an arch or lean with the weight of increasing foliage. New shoots appear in late spring and early summer. **Culm sheaths** Semi-persistent. Pale green, tinted and spotted purple, with fine hairs on the outer surface. **Branches** In threes. Older culms usually develop further branches alongside, while on lower nodes there may be only one or two.

Leaves Medium-long and narrow, 9 to 18 cm (3½ to 7 inches) long by 1 to 1.5 cm (⅜ to ⅝ inch) wide. Light, dullish, slightly matte green on the upper surface, light grayish matte green on the lower surface, tapering gradually to a fine point at the tip. **Rhizomes** Clump-forming (pachymorph). Makes a rather open clump from an early age but is still compact enough for the smaller garden. **Cultivation** Sun or shade. Succeeds best where there is at least some shade in the middle part of the day. Provide shelter from harsh winds. **Hardiness** –5°C to –10°C (23°F to 14°F).

Thamnocalamus spathiflorus subsp. *nepalensis*

Synonym *Fargesia nepalensis*
Native to Nepal
Tall bamboo—clump-forming

Differs from the species by having a sparse, more upright habit and larger leaves. Most plants in cultivation in Western gardens originate from a specimen collected by Tony Schilling and planted at Wakehurst Place in West Sussex, United Kingdom. It is a good garden plant but not so elegant or graceful as the species. Liable to lose foliage quickly in cold winters.

Culms Slightly more slender than those of the species and ripening more uniformly to yellowish green with much less obvious pinkish purple tinting where exposed to sunlight. Noticeably more upright in habit, with only minimal arching of older culms. **Culm sheaths** Glabrous. **Branches** Often shorter than those of *T. spathiflorus* and developed more sparsely. **Leaves** Medium-long and medium-broad, 9 to 18 cm (3½ to 7 inches) long by 1.5 to 3 cm (⅝ to 1¼ inches) wide. Slightly lighter green on the upper surface than those of the species in most growing situations, very sparse in number, ta-

Thamnocalamus spathiflorus subsp. *nepalensis* grows by the vegetable garden at Carwinion. Note the line of CDs used to scare away birds!

pering less gradually to a fine point at the tip.
Cultivation Very prone to chlorosis of the foliage when grown in poor soils or in containers.
Hardiness Slightly less hardy than the species.

Thamnocalamus tessellatus

Synonym *Arundinaria tessellata*
Native to South Africa
Tall bamboo—clump-forming

This, the only bamboo native to South Africa, is closely allied botanically to *T. spathiflorus* but is of much tougher constitution. Accord-

ing to the theory of continental drift, the land-masses of Asia and Africa were once joined, and it is believed that as they drifted apart, this species was separated and isolated from other *Thamnocalamus* species. It occurs over a large area, sometimes sparsely and sometimes in vast tracts, from the Table Mountain northward, mostly at high altitudes of 1500 to 2500 m (5000 to 8000 feet). In more open, drier places it is sometimes found dwarfed and stunted, little more than 1 m (3 feet) tall, but it may reach more than five times that height in wetter, more sheltered places. It is known in its native country by the Afrikaans name *bergbamboes* and is the namesake of the mountain Bamboesberg, where this bamboo grows so prolifically.

The culms of this species are thick-walled and strong, particularly in their lower halves. At one time Zulu warriors used these culms in the structure of their hide-covered shields, and other tribes used the culms as shafts for arrows and spears.

As a garden plant this bamboo can just as easily look dull, uninspiring, and scruffy as it can look thriving and attractive. The difference is caused by the planting position and maintenance regime. This species needs an open, airy, almost windy position to look its best. Any sort of shelter, and particularly shade, causes the culms to become drawn and lax, with dull foliage. The culms often live to a great age and can become very untidy, with little remaining good foliage and a tendency to hold on to desiccated bits and pieces, so regular cutting out of older culms is essential.

Given the right planting position and regular maintenance, *T. tessellatus* makes a really useful and worthwhile garden plant. It is tough and hardy, tolerating conditions that would defeat other bamboos. Moreover, it is much more drought-tolerant than many other bamboos. In exposed localities it is ideal as a windbreak or hedge. This species can be quickly identified by the noticeable gray cast in the foliage, which is uncommon in bamboos, and by the dazzlingly white sheaths of the culms in their first season. In general appearance it bears a passing resemblance to *Chusquea culeou* but is much less impressive.

Culms Tall and slender, 3 to 5 m (10 to 16 feet) tall and 6 mm to 2 cm (¼ to ¾ inch) in diameter. Often stout in appearance for their height. Pale green at first with a light dusting of grayish white powder, becoming dull midgreen with traces of the powdery deposit retained after the first season, slowly ripening to dull yellowish green. The upper parts of the culm and exposed branches may develop a purplish tint where facing sunlight. Nodes not prominent. Almost upright in habit in open positions, with outer culms emerging and staying at a slight angle from the ground, older culms arching over near the summit and much more so in shade. New shoots appear in early summer. **Culm sheaths** Semi-persistent. Pale creamy green sometimes flushed with pinkish mauve at first, becoming intensely white before fading. Covered in fine hairs when young. **Branches** In threes. Slow to develop or developing partially in the first season, quickly becoming more multiple in the second season with smaller branches developing from the

Thamnocalamus tessellatus can be recognized by the conspicuously white culm sheaths.

base of the main branches. Short and tufted in a bottlebrush effect, with many twigs. **Leaves** Medium-long and narrow, 9 to 18 cm (3½ to 7 inches) long by 1 to 1.5 cm (⅜ to ⅝ inch) wide. Slightly grayish pale green at first, becoming a dark dull olive green with a slight dark grayish cast and a dull shine on the upper surface, grayish matte green on the lower surface, tapering gradually to a fine point at the tip. Many older leaves develop a desiccated tip in winter. **Rhizomes** Clump-forming (pachymorph). Makes quite a dense, sturdy-looking clump unless grown in heavy shade. **Cultivation** Sun or semi-shade. Best in a very open position. One of the few clump-forming bamboos that grows poorly in shade. **Hardiness** –10°C to –20°C (14°F to –4°F).

Yushania

An attractive genus of high-altitude bamboos occurring naturally at 1800 to 3600 m (6000 to 12,000 feet) in the Himalaya. In their native environment they form large, thicket-like tracts sometimes stunted in height due to grazing by wild or domestic animals. The spreading, rather weed-like growth habit can inhibit or suppress other vegetation after clear-felling of the forest by native peoples.

Most species of *Yushania* have at some time been attributed to other genera, and their nomenclature is still uncertain. Only a few species are currently grown in Western gardens, and of these, only *Y. anceps* is common in cultivation. Although superficially similar to the main clump-forming genera, *Drepanostachyum*, *Fargesia*, and *Thamnocalamus*, *Yushania* species are distinguished principally by their rhizomes. These bamboos have pachymorph rhizomes with elongated necks. The elongated necks can be solid or hollow, lack any dividing walls, and are rootless. At the end of each neck the growth turns upward to become a culm,

and at this point, nodes are produced that bear roots and buds. From these buds, new necks emerge. This gives an open clump habit, with culms in scattered groups, and a more rapid rate of invasion.

All species described here have attractive foliage, and the mature culms can be harvested for use as plant supports. *Yushania* bamboos will tolerate considerable shade and can be grown in close association with deciduous and some evergreen trees. Some species make useful and highly ornamental hedges and screens, in places where their moderately invasive habit is acceptable. Care needs to be taken in confined planting situations with limited access to the application of a spade, because the outward march of the rather deep rhizomes may be moderate, but there are a lot of them and they are inexorable and relentless! For this reason, *Yushania* bamboos are not the best choice for long-term container growing. Much rhizome will accumulate at the bottom of the container, eventually pushing the whole bamboo up and out, or the container will simply split.

Yushania anceps

Synonyms *Arundinaria anceps*, *A. jaunsarensis*
Native to India

Tall bamboo—moderately invasive
Yushania anceps occurs in the northwestern Himalaya at altitudes of 3000 to 3300 m (10,000 to 11,00 feet), where it has traditional uses as fodder for grazing animals and for weaving into household utilities such as baskets and mats. This is one of the longest-cultivated bamboos in Western gardens, having been introduced into England in 1865 by a Colonel E. Smyth and first grown at Elkington Hall in Lincolnshire. At the time of its introduction there was uncertainty as to its true provenance, and it was named *anceps*, or the "doubtful" bamboo, by Algernon Bertram Freeman-Mitford in *The*

Older clumps of *Yushania anceps* can produce this remarkable habit, particularly if grown in an open position.

Bamboo Garden (1896). The specific name *anceps* has taxonomic precedence over *jaunsarensis*, the name given to wild plants of this species in India later the same year. More recently the generic name was changed from *Arundinaria* to produce the combination *Yushania anceps*.

This species is on record as having flowered several times in cultivation, notably in 1911, 1935, 1955, and the early 1980s. In the gardens where this bamboo flowered most recently, in Britain, across continental Europe, and in the United States, the clumps more or less died out. But after a year or two, fresh growth emerged here and there from whatever life remained in the roots and rhizomes of the plants not grubbed out by their owners. Within a few years, these clumps completely regained their former stature.

As a garden plant *Y. anceps* is widely distributed in cultivation. Specimens can be found in most older botanic gardens, and it is quite usual to see it growing in private gardens large and small. This species is one of the best taller bamboos for planting in shade or under trees so long as there is adequate moisture. In very dry locations it quickly becomes stunted and lackluster. Otherwise it is almost too easy to grow and is often seen taking over far beyond its allotted growing space. In full sun the delicate leaves are very susceptible to leaf curl, and so, for best visual effect, plant this bamboo in a position where it will receive at least some shade for the middle part of the day. It is reasonably hardy, sometimes tolerating lower temperatures than those stated below, with just some loss of foliage.

Culms Tall and slender, 3 to 5 m (10 to 16 feet) tall and 6 mm to 2 cm (¼ to ¾ inch) in diameter. Deep rich green at first, with a light coating of white powder, particularly at the nodes, the internodes quickly losing the powder, becoming glossy olive green, maturing to yellowish green. Nodes not prominent, with a longish distance between nodes, often more than 30 cm (1 foot). Upright in habit in the first season but quickly cascading from near the summit thereafter with the increasing weight of foliage. New shoots appear in early summer. **Culm sheaths** Semi-persistent. Light green, sometimes flushed with faint purple at the edges. **Branches** Multiple. One to three branches of unequal length at first, quickly developing two or three shorter branches alongside, then becoming more multiple. **Leaves** Short and narrow, 5 to 9 cm (2 to 3½ inches) long by 1 to 1.5 cm (⅜ to ⅝ inch) wide. Sometimes slightly longer than these dimensions. Rich bright green on the upper surface with a dull shine, matte grayish green on the lower surface, tapering fairly abruptly to a fine point at the tip. **Rhizomes** Moderately invasive (pachymorph with extended neck). Rather too invasive for very small gardens. **Cultivation** Sun or shade. Quite happy in a range of planting situations but at its best in at least partial shade. Susceptible to leaf curl when planted in full sun. **Hardiness** −5°C to −10°C (23°F to 14°F).

Yushania anceps 'Pitt White'

Synonym *Arundinaria niitakayamensis*
Extremely tall bamboo—moderately invasive
Differs from the species by having slightly smaller leaves and a much larger stature. Named after Nathan Mutch's famous garden at Pitt White in Devon, this remarkable, sought-after bamboo was originally misidentified as *Arundinaria niitakayamensis* (Pitt White clone). It originates from plant material obtained by Mutch at Perry's Hardy Plant Farm in Enfield, Middlesex, in 1940. All stock at the nursery was destroyed during ground clearing for food crops at the outset of the Second World War, and it is thought that the plant grown by Mutch at Pitt White was the only survivor.

When still a small plant, 'Pitt White' is virtually indistinguishable from the species. However, when the culms of a mature plant are seen upright at the end of their first season, before the weight of the foliage causes the culms to arch, it is easy to recognize how incredibly tall this form is, compared with other cool-temperate, high-altitude bamboos. The effect is accentuated by the relative slenderness of the culms.

The plant at Pitt White flowered along with the typical *Y. anceps* in the early 1980s. This invites speculation that it may have originally occurred as a culm sport or mutation from the species, rather than as a separate seedling clone. When I visited the garden shortly after the death of Nathan Mutch, the clumps had almost died out from the flowering. But on a return visit a few years later I was pleasantly surprised to see healthy new culms some 2 m (6 feet) high. By 2004 this plant had regained most of its former glory. There are a great many seedlings in cultivation purporting to be from the flowering of this bamboo, and some do attain quite impressive mature heights. However, all the seedlings I have seen, including one growing in my own garden, seem to have the larger leaf dimensions of the species and lack the purple coloration of the older culms. It is worth seeking out propagations of the regenerated original plant at Pitt White in order to have this bamboo in its best form.

Culms Extremely tall and medium-thick, more than 8 m (26 feet) tall and 2 to 3 cm (¾ to 1¼ inches) in diameter. Older culms often develop a purple-brown coloration. Mature culms are thin-walled for their dimensions and can cascade very heavily, almost to the ground, in their second and third seasons. **Leaves** Slightly but distinctly smaller than those of the species.

Yushania maculata

Native to China

Tall bamboo—moderately invasive

A superb species that is proving to be the toughest and hardiest representative of the genus in cultivation. *Yushania maculata* is a native mostly of Sichuan and Yunnan provinces and is found at heights of 1700 to 3300 m (5500 to 11,000 feet). It occurs as an understory plant in mountain forest and also in vast open tracts that are often kept reduced to stunted proportions by grazing animals. It is thought to have been first introduced to Western gardens as an unidentified wild-collected bamboo in the mid-1970s.

This species is quickly recognized by its striking blue-gray young culms with their colorful sheaths. The habit is pleasingly upright and tidy without being too formal, giving a "curtain of bamboo" effect where grown as a linear shaped clump. Perhaps most attrac-

tive of all is the wonderful foliage, which is firm, longish and finely tapering, and a deep shining green. The overall effect is sturdy and healthy-looking. *Yushania maculata* can be used in a wide variety of garden situations, being very happy in the open or under trees. It is one of the best bamboos for making a hedge or screen where some spread can be tolerated. As a windbreak it is nearly indestructible.

Culms Tall and slender, 3 to 5 m (10 to 16 feet) tall and 6 mm to 2 cm (¼ to ¾ inch) in diameter. Deep midgreen at first and covered with waxy grayish powder that often persists into the second season, maturing to yellow-

Yushania maculata.

ish olive green and sometimes tinted orange-brown. Internodes swollen just above the node, the swellings tapering off quickly at first, then more gradually, so that the most slender point of the internode is in the approaches to the next node. Upright in habit, sometimes with a slight zigzag in the lower internodes, and tending to stay fairly upright with only minimal arching of older culms. New shoots appear in early summer. **Culm sheaths** Persistent. Reddish brown with darker brown spots and patches. Covered in stiff short hairs and fringed at the base with a tuft of brownish hairs. **Branches** Multiple. Usually three to six branches of unequal length at first, with other shorter branches developing alongside. **Leaves** Medium-long and narrow, 9 to 18 cm (3½ to 7 inches) long by 1 to 1.5 cm (⅜ to ⅝ inch) wide. Deep, dark, rich green and with a lustrous shine on the upper surface, matte green on the lower surface, tapering gradually to a fine point at the tip. **Rhizomes** Moderately invasive (pachymorph with extended neck). Rhizomes can be quite deep under the soil surface, often 30 cm (1 foot), making this bamboo difficult to control in restricted spaces. **Cultivation** Sun or shade. Well suited to a wide range of positions and can be grown in full sun without suffering from leaf curl. **Hardiness** –10°C to –20°C (14°F to –4°F).

Yushania maling

Synonyms *Arundinaria maling*, *A. racemosa*
Native to India, Nepal, Bhutan, Sikkim
Tall bamboo—moderately invasive
An uncommon species originally misidentified in cultivation as *Arundinaria racemosa*. It is easily distinguished from other species of this genus by the rough culms and comparatively large leaves. It is the most common spreading bamboo in eastern Nepal, where it occurs at altitudes of 1500 to 2700 m (5000 to 9000 feet).

Although an impressive foliage bamboo, *Y. maling* is not particularly hardy due to the late emergence of the culms, which often fall susceptible to the first frosts of winter due to insufficient ripening. Surviving older culms are fairly hardy, but a typical plant grown anywhere other than in the mildest gardens will be an unattractive mixture of brownish older culms and dead or partially cut-down newer culms. In mild localities this species, once established, can become something of a weed. The active rhizomes can be deep and the an-

The new culms of *Yushania maling* are rough to touch due to the presence of stiff short hairs on the culm surface.

nual spread rather far-reaching for the genus. Perhaps a bamboo more suited to the enthusiast than to the average gardener.

Culms Tall and slender, 3 to 5 m (10 to 16 feet) tall and 6 mm to 2 cm (¼ to ¾ inch) in diameter. Light green at first with a copious covering of waxy gray powder, maturing very quickly to yellowish green and often by the end of the second season turning brownish green, this color persisting for many seasons thereafter. Internodes covered in coarse, stiff hairs that make the newer culms rough to touch. Nodes not prominent. Upright at first, then arching near the summit with the weight of foliage in later seasons. New shoots appear in mid to late summer. **Culm sheaths** Persistent. Pale green and coarsely striated. Covered with fine hairs. **Branches** Multiple. Usually three to five branches of unequal length at first, with other shorter branches developing alongside. The first and longest branch (and occasionally the second longest) becomes much longer than all the others, arching down with age and development of secondary branching. **Leaves** Medium-long and medium-broad, 9 to 18 cm (3½ to 7 inches) long by 1.5 to 3 cm (⅝ to 1¼ inches) wide. Deep rich green with a very slight shine on the upper surface, matte green on the lower surface, tapering to a fine point at the tip. **Rhizomes** Moderately invasive (pachymorph with extended neck). The rhizomes are not only quite deep under the soil surface, often 30 cm (1 foot), but also tend to reach further than other species of this genus. **Cultivation** Sun or shade. Prefers partial shade or even deep shade. Susceptible to leaf curl when planted in full sun. **Hardiness** −5°C to −10°C (23°F to 14°F).

Lists of Bamboos for Specific Purposes

Bamboos for Groundcover
Indocalamus longiauritus
Indocalamus tessellatus
Pleioblastus akebono
Pleioblastus auricomus
Pleioblastus auricomus 'Chryso-
   phyllus'
Pleioblastus chino 'Murakamianus'
Pleioblastus fortunei
Pleioblastus humilis
Pleioblastus humilis var. *pumilus*
Pleioblastus kongosanensis 'Aureo-
   striata'
Pleioblastus pygmaeus
Pleioblastus pygmaeus 'Distichus'
Pseudosasa owatarii
Sasa kurilensis dwarf form
Sasa nipponica
Sasa quelpartensis
Sasa veitchii
Sasaella masamuneana 'Albos-
   triata'
Sasaella ramosa
Shibataea (all species)

Bamboos for Small to Medium Hedges and Screens
Fargesia dracocephala
Fargesia murielae 'Simba'
Fargesia rufa
Shibataea (all species)

A mature clump of
Fargesia nitida.

Bamboos for Medium to Tall Hedges and Screens
Chusquea culeou
Fargesia denudata
Fargesia murielae
Fargesia nitida
Fargesia robusta
Pseudosasa japonica
Pseudosasa pleioblastoides
Thamnocalamus (all species)
Yushania (all species)

Bamboos for Very Tall to Extremely Tall Hedges and Screens
Phyllostachys aurea (and forms)
Phyllostachys aureosulcata (and
   forms)
Phyllostachys bissetii
Phyllostachys decora
Phyllostachys nigra (and forms)
Phyllostachys parvifolia
Phyllostachys rubromarginata
Phyllostachys viridiglaucescens
Pleioblastus simonii
Semiarundinaria (all species)

Bamboos for Producing Cut Canes
Chimonobambusa quadrangularis
Chusquea culeou
Chusquea gigantea
Fargesia murielae
Fargesia nitida
Fargesia robusta
Phyllostachys aurea (and forms)
Phyllostachys nigra (and forms)

Phyllostachys rubromarginata
Pleioblastus simonii
Pseudosasa japonica
Pseudosasa pleioblastoides
Semiarundinaria fastuosa
Semiarundinaria fastuosa var.
   viridis
Semiarundinaria kagamiana
Semiarundinaria yashadake
Sinobambusa tootsik
Thamnocalamus tessellatus
Yushania (all species)

Bamboos for Cold Gardens
Chusquea culeou
Fargesia (all species)
×*Hibanobambusa tranquillans*
×*Hibanobambusa tranquillans* 'Shi-
   roshima'
Indocalamus (all species)
Phyllostachys arcana
Phyllostachys arcana 'Luteosul-
   cata'
Phyllostachys aureosulcata (and
   forms)
Phyllostachys bissetii
Phyllostachys decora
Phyllostachys nuda
Phyllostachys propinqua
Phyllostachys propinqua 'Bicolor'
Phyllostachys rubromarginata
Phyllostachys vivax (and forms)
Pleioblastus chino
Pleioblastus chino 'Elegantissima'
Pleioblastus fortunei
Pleioblastus kongosanensis 'Aureo-
   striata'

Pleioblastus pygmaeus
Pleioblastus simonii
Sasa kurilensis (and forms)
Sasa palmata 'Nebulosa'
Semiarundinaria fastuosa
Semiarundinaria fastuosa var.
  viridis
Shibataea kumasasa

Bamboos for Windy or Exposed Gardens

Chusquea culeou
Fargesia denudata
Fargesia robusta
Phyllostachys arcana
Phyllostachys arcana 'Luteosulcata'
Phyllostachys aurea (and forms)
Phyllostachys aureosulcata (and
  forms)
Phyllostachys bissetii
Phyllostachys decora
Phyllostachys glauca
Phyllostachys nuda
Phyllostachys parvifolia
Phyllostachys propinqua
Phyllostachys propinqua 'Bicolor'
Pleioblastus chino (and forms)
Pleioblastus fortunei
Pleioblastus gramineus
Pleioblastus humilis
Pleioblastus humilis var. *pumilus*
Pleioblastus linearis
Pleioblastus pygmaeus
Pleioblastus shibuyanus 'Tsuboi'
Pleioblastus simonii
Pseudosasa japonica
Pseudosasa japonica 'Tsutsumiana'
Pseudosasa pleioblastoides
Sasaella masamuneana 'Albos-
  triata'
Sasaella ramosa
Semiarundinaria fastuosa
Semiarundinaria fastuosa var.
  viridis

Semiarundinaria kagamiana
Semiarundinaria yashadake
Thamnocalamus tessellatus
Yushania maculata

Bamboos for Smaller Containers

Fargesia murielae 'Simba'
Fargesia rufa
Pleioblastus auricomus
Pleioblastus auricomus 'Chryso-
  phyllus'
Pleioblastus chino 'Murakamia-
  nus'
Pleioblastus shibuyanus 'Tsuboi'
Shibataea (all species)

Bamboos for Larger Containers

Borinda (all species)
Chusquea culeou
Drepanostachyum (all species)
Fargesia denudata
Fargesia dracocephala
Fargesia murielae
Fargesia nitida
Fargesia robusta
Fargesia utilis
×*Hibanobambusa tranquillans*
×*Hibanobambusa tranquillans* 'Shi-
  roshima'
Himalayacalamus (all species)
Phyllostachys aurea (and forms)
Phyllostachys aureosulcata (and
  forms)
Phyllostachys bambusoides (col-
  ored forms)
Phyllostachys bissetii
Phyllostachys decora
Phyllostachys edulis (and forms)
Phyllostachys heteroclada
Phyllostachys nigra (and forms)
Phyllostachys nuda
Pseudosasa japonica
Thamnocalamus (all species)

Bamboos for Growing Permanently Indoors

Bambusa multiplex 'Alphonse
  Karr'
Bambusa multiplex 'Fernleaf'
Bambusa ventricosa
Chusquea coronalis
Chusquea cumingii
Drepanostachyum falcatum
Otatea acuminata subsp. *aztecorum*

Bamboos for Heavy Shade

Borinda (most species)
Chimonobambusa (all species)
Chusquea culeou
Fargesia murielae (and forms)
Fargesia nitida
Fargesia utilis
Indocalamus (all species)
Pleioblastus akebono
Pleioblastus chino
Pleioblastus gramineus
Pleioblastus linearis
Sasa (all species)
Sasaella (all species)
Yushania (all species)

Bamboos for Periodically Drier Locations

Chusquea culeou
Chusquea cumingii
Chusquea gigantea
×*Hibanobambusa tranquillans*
×*Hibanobambusa tranquillans* 'Shi-
  roshima'
Pleioblastus gramineus
Pleioblastus linearis
Pseudosasa japonica
Pseudosasa japonica 'Tsutsumiana'
Pseudosasa pleioblastoides
Sasaella (all species)
Thamnocalamus tessellatus
Yushania maculata

Bamboos for Periodically Wetter Locations

Arundinaria gigantea subsp. *tecta*
Chusquea uliginosa
Phyllostachys atrovaginata
Phyllostachys heteroclada
Phyllostachys nidularia
Sasa palmata 'Nebulosa'

Bamboos for Maritime Exposure

Chusquea culeou
Pleioblastus gramineus
Pleioblastus hindsii
Pleioblastus linearis
Pleioblastus simonii
Pseudosasa japonica
Pseudosasa japonica 'Tsutsumiana'
Pseudosasa pleioblastoides
Semiarundinaria fastuosa
Semiarundinaria fastuosa var. *viridis*
Semiarundinaria kagamiana
Semiarundinaria yashadake

Bamboos with Variegated Foliage

Chimonobambusa marmorea 'Variegata'
×*Hibanobambusa tranquillans* 'Shiroshima'
Phyllostachys aurea 'Albovariegata'
Phyllostachys bambusoides 'Castillonis Inversa Variegata'
Phyllostachys bambusoides 'Castillonis Variegata'
Pleioblastus akebono
Pleioblastus auricomus (and forms)
Pleioblastus chino 'Aureostriata'
Pleioblastus chino 'Elegantissima'
Pleioblastus chino 'Murakamianus'
Pleioblastus fortunei

Pleioblastus kongosanensis 'Aureostriata'
Pleioblastus shibuyanus 'Tsuboi'
Pseudosasa japonica 'Akebono'
Pseudosasa japonica 'Akebonosuji'
Sasa kurilensis 'Shimofuri'
Sasa nipponica 'Aureostriata'
Sasa palmata 'Warley Place'
Sasaella masamuneana 'Albostriata'
Sasaella masamuneana 'Aureostriata'
Semiarundinaria yamadorii 'Brimscombe'
Shibataea kumasasa 'Albostriata'
Shibataea kumasasa 'Aureostriata'
Sinobambusa tootsik 'Variegata'

Bamboos with Colored Culms

Bambusa multiplex 'Alphonse Karr'
Chimonobambusa marmorea 'Variegata'
Chimonobambusa quadrangularis 'Nagamineus'
Chimonobambusa quadrangularis 'Suow'
Himalayacalamus falconeri 'Damarapa'
Phyllostachys arcana 'Luteosulcata'
Phyllostachys aurea 'Flavescens Inversa'
Phyllostachys aurea 'Holochrysa'
Phyllostachys aurea 'Koi'
Phyllostachys aureosulcata
Phyllostachys aureosulcata 'Aureocaulis'
Phyllostachys aureosulcata 'Spectabilis'
Phyllostachys bambusoides 'Castillonis'
Phyllostachys bambusoides 'Castillonis Inversa'

Phyllostachys bambusoides 'Castillonis Inversa Variegata'
Phyllostachys bambusoides 'Castillonis Variegata'
Phyllostachys bambusoides 'Holochrysa'
Phyllostachys bambusoides 'Kawadana'
Phyllostachys bambusoides 'Tanakae'
Phyllostachys edulis 'Bicolor'
Phyllostachys edulis 'Nabeshimana'
Phyllostachys glauca 'Yunzhu'
Phyllostachys iridescens
Phyllostachys nigra
Phyllostachys nigra 'Boryana'
Phyllostachys nigra 'Megurochiku'
Phyllostachys nigra 'Punctata'
Phyllostachys propinqua 'Bicolor'
Phyllostachys violascens
Phyllostachys viridis 'Houzeau'
Phyllostachys viridis 'Sulphurea'
Phyllostachys vivax 'Aureocaulis'
Phyllostachys vivax 'Huanvenzhu'
Pleioblastus chino 'Murakamianus'
Semiarundinaria yashadake 'Gimmei'

Bamboos with Small or Narrow Leaves

Bambusa multiplex (and forms)
Borinda (most species)
Chimonobambusa marmorea
Chimonobambusa tumidissinoda
Chusquea culeou (some forms)
Chusquea cumingii
Chusquea gigantea
Drepanostachyum (all species)
Fargesia (most species)
Himalayacalamus (all species)

Pleioblastus akebono
Pleioblastus chino 'Elegantissima'
Pleioblastus gramineus
Pleioblastus linearis
Pleioblastus pygmaeus
Pseudosasa owatarii
Thamnocalamus crassinodus (and forms)
Yushania anceps
Yushania anceps 'Pitt White'

Bamboos with Large Leaves
×*Hibanobambusa tranquillans*
×*Hibanobambusa tranquillans* 'Shiroshima'
Indocalamus (all species)
Phyllostachys vivax (and forms)
Pseudosasa japonica
Pseudosasa pleioblastoides
Sasa (most species)
Sasaella bitchuensis
Semiarundinaria okuboi

Bamboos for Forming Open Groves
Chusquea gigantea
Phyllostachys bambusoides (and forms)
Phyllostachys dulcis
Phyllostachys edulis (and forms)
Phyllostachys iridescens
Phyllostachys violascens
Phyllostachys vivax (and forms)

Glossary

ABSCISSION. the process of cutting off, releasing

ACUTE. sharply or narrowly angled

ADPRESSED. pressed on, pressed against

ADVENTITIOUS. occurring at an unusual or unexpected position

AERIAL. above soil level

ANGIOSPERM. a highly developed flowering plant, not simple

APEX. the uppermost part

AURICLE. an ear-like appendage, a small prominence flanking the ligule

AXIS, AXES. a branch or section(s) of growth, a main stem from which other plant parts are arrayed

BAMBUSOID. bamboo-like, resembling a bamboo

BLADE. a flattened, leaf-like projection from the top of a sheath

BLOOM. on a culm, a grayish or whitish, waxy, powdery deposit

BRANCH COMPLEMENT. a branch grouping at a node

BRANCH SHEATH. a protective foliar organ enclosing a section of stem that is part of the branch complement

BUD. a dormant growth point

CAESPITOSE. growing closely together, in close proximity

CARYOPSIS. a one-seeded fruit with the pericarp fused to the seed, the characteristic seed of grasses

CHLOROSIS. yellowing of the foliage caused by mineral deficiencies or imbalance

CILIA. small, fine hairs at the margin of a structure

CLONE. a group of plants produced by vegetative propagation from one original seedling or stock

CLUMP-FORMING. having a growth habit in which the culms are close together, rhizomes spreading slowly

CULM SHEATH. a protective foliar organ enclosing a complete node and internode of a culm at the time of its first development

CULM. the jointed aerial stem of a grass, also known as a *cane*

CULTIVAR. a variety maintained only in cultivation where there may not be any significant wild populations

DECIDUOUS. shedding or falling away at a specific time of year or season

DESICCATED. devoid of all moisture, dried up

DICOTYLEDON. a plant bearing two cotyledons (seed leaves)

DIFFUSE. open, spread out, arising singly rather than in groups

ENTIRE. complete, not serrated, toothed, or indented

FARINOSE. covered in waxy gray or white powder, flour-like

FIMBRIAE. stiff or bristly hairs usually emerging from an auricle, also known as *oral setae*

FORM (F.). a taxonomic rank below that of subspecies or variety

GENICULATION. bending from side to side, not straight

GLABROUS. smooth and lacking hairs

GLAUCOUS. dull bluish green

GREGARIOUS FLOWERING. occurs when plants flower simultaneously

HARDY. the ability to withstand cold winters

HERBACEOUS. not woody, having no persistent aerial growing parts

HORTICULTURE. the cultivation of plants

INTERNODE. the part of a culm that is between two nodes

INVASIVE. having a growth habit in which the culms are widely spaced, rhizomes spreading rapidly

LANCEOLATE. long and narrow and tapering at both ends, shaped like the head of a lance

LEAF. the primary photosynthetic organ of a plant, usually green and flattened

LEPTOMORPH. a type of rhizome that is long and thin and does not always turn upward to become a culm

LIGNIFIED, LIGNIFICATION. woody, the process of becoming woody

LIGULE. the rim-like projection at the apex of a sheath on the inner side at the junction with the blade

LIMBUS. the flattened blade-like projection from the top of a sheath

LINEAR. long and narrow with parallel sides

MERISTEM. the growing point of a stem or root, a group of actively dividing undifferentiated cells where growth takes place

MICROCLIMATE. a highly localized set of climatic conditions

MICROPROPAGATION. the growing or culturing of cells from various parts of a plant in order to produce new plants

MIDRIB. a hardened structure running along the middle of the leaf, the continuation of the leaf stalk into the leaf

MONOCARPIC. dying after flowering

MONOCOTYLEDON. a plant bearing only one cotyledon (seed leaf)

MONOPODIAL. a branching pattern in which a dominant branch or stem gives rise to secondary branches or stems

MORPHOLOGY. the study of the forms of plants and animals

NECK. the constricted basal portion of a stem or main axis

NODE. the joint of a bamboo stem, the point where all further branches or growth originates

OBTUSE. bluntly or broadly angled

ORAL SETAE. stiff hairs or bristles emerging from an auricle or the place where an auricle would normally be present, also known as *fimbriae*

OVARY. the organ of the female reproductive system containing an ovule

PACHYMORPH. a type of rhizome that is short and thick and turns upward to become a culm

PALMATE. palm or hand-like

PERSISTENT. remaining attached after dying

PETIOLE. a stalk or connecting stem

PHLOEM. the part of the plant that transports nutrients from the leaves to the rest of the plant

PHOTOSYNTHESIS. the conversion of carbon dioxide into carbohydrates in parts of plants that contain chlorophyll, under the influence of light

PHYLLOSTACHOID. having characteristics of the genus *Phyllostachys*, notably thick culms bearing a sulcus on the internode

PSEUDOPETIOLE. a short, stem-like connection between a leaf blade of a bamboo and the leaf sheath

RAMIFICATION. branching into many divisions

RHIZOME. an underground stem

ROOT. the usually underground part of a plant that absorbs water and nutrients from the soil and helps to anchor the plant

ROOT PRIMORDIA. partially developed roots, root buds

SASOID. having characteristics of the genus *Sasa*, notably a short stature and large leaves carried on solitary main branches

SCALE. a rudimentary or degenerate foliar organ

SCANDENT. leaning, scrambling, or loosely climbing

SESSILE. attached directly by the base without a stalk

SHEATH. a protective foliar organ that encloses a section of stem at the time of its first development

SHOOTING SEASON. the time of year when most bamboos produce their new shoots

SINUOUS. waving or bending smoothly, without sharp corners

SPIKELET. the fundamental unit of a grass flower cluster

STOMATA. minute orifices in the epidermis of plants, mouth-like organs

STRIATION. thin lines or stripes

SUBSPECIES (SUBSP.). a taxonomic rank below that

of species, used sometimes instead of variety and often signifying a geographic difference

SULCUS. a flattened or groove-like structure running along an internode

SUPRANODAL RIDGE. the uppermost part of a node that may vary in prominence

SYMPODIAL. a branching habit in which each succeeding branch becomes dominant

TAXONOMY. the study of the relationships between groups of plants, including their definition and naming

TESSELLATION. divided into small squares or oblongs, leaf veins having a pattern of small squares

TILLER. putting up further stems from the base of a stem

TRANSPIRATION. the evaporation of water from the surface of a leaf or stem

VARIEGATED, VARIEGATION. having more than one color

VARIETY (VAR.). a taxonomic rank below that of species, used sometimes instead of subspecies

WOODY. hardened and strong, having persistent aerial parts, not herbaceous

Further Reading

Bell, Michael. 2000. *A Gardener's Guide to Growing Temperate Bamboos*. Newton Abbot, Devon: David and Charles.

But, Paul Pui-Hay, Liang-chi Chia, Hok-lam Fung, and Shiu-Ying Hu. 1985. *Hong Kong Bamboos*. Hong Kong: The Urban Council, Hong Kong.

Camus, Émile-Gustave. 1913. *Les bambusées*. Paris: Paul Lechevalier.

Chao, C. S. 1989. *A Guide to Bamboos Grown in Britain*. Kew, Surrey: Royal Botanic Gardens, Kew.

Farrelly, David. 1984. *The Book of Bamboo*. San Francisco: Sierra Club Books.

Freeman-Mitford, Algernon Bertram. 1896. *The Bamboo Garden*. London: Macmillan.

Grounds, Roger. 1989. *Ornamental Grasses*. London: Christopher Helm.

Hakluyt, Richard. 1589. *Principall Navigations, Voyages, and Discoveries of the English Nation*. London: George Bishop and Ralph Newberie.

Judziewicz, Emmet J. (ed.), Lynn G. Clark, Ximena Londono, and Margaret J. Stern. 1999. *American Bamboos*. Washington, D.C.: Smithsonian Institution Press.

Lawson, Alexander High. 1968. *Bamboos: A Gardener's Guide to Their Cultivation in Temperate Climates*. New York: Taplinger.

Linschoten, Jan Huygen van. 1598. *Discours of Voyages into ye East & West Indies*. English translation. London: Wolfe.

Loudon, John Claudius. 1854. *Arboretum et Fruticetum*. 2nd ed.

McClure, Floyd Alonzo. 1957. *Bamboos of the Genus* Phyllostachys *Under Cultivation in the United States*. Agricultural Handbook 114. Washington, D.C.: U.S. Department of Agriculture, Agricultural Research Service.

McClure, Floyd Alonzo. 1966. *The Bamboos: A Fresh Perspective*. Cambridge, Massachusetts: Harvard University Press.

Meredith, Ted Jordan. 2001. *Bamboo for Gardens*. Portland, Oregon: Timber Press.

Munro, William. 1868. *A Monograph of the Bambusaceae*. Transactions of the Linnean Society of London 26: 1.

Ohrnburger, Dieter, and Josef Goerrings. 1983, 1984. *Bamboos of the World*. A series of illustrated booklets. Odenthal, Germany: Ohrnburger and Goerrings.

Okamura, Hata, and Yukio Tanaka. 1986 *The Horticultural Bamboo Species in Japan*. Kobe: Haato.

Orta, Garcia de. 1563. *Colloquios dos simples e drogas e cousas medicinaes da India*.

Recht, Christine, and Max F. Wetterwald. 1992. *Bamboos*. English translation edited by David Crampton. London: Batsford.

Ruprecht, F. J. 1839. *Bambuseas Monographice Exponit*. Saint Petersburg: Mem. Acad.

Stapleton, Chris. 1994. *Bamboos of Bhutan: An Illustrated Guide*. Kew, Surrey: Royal Botanic Gardens, Kew.

Stapleton, Chris. 1994. *Bamboos of Nepal: An Illustrated Guide*. Kew, Surrey: Royal Botanic Gardens, Kew.

Suzuki, Sadao. 1978. *Index to Japanese Bambusaceae*. Tokyo: Gakken.

Wang, Dajun, and Shen Shao-Jin. 1987. *Bamboos of China*. Portland, Oregon: Timber Press.

Whittaker, Paul. 2005. *Hardy Bamboos: Taming the Dragon*. Portland, Oregon: Timber Press.

Yule, Henry, and Arthur Coke Burnell. 1886. *Hobson-Jobson: Being a Glossary of Anglo-Indian Colloquial Words and Phrases*. London: John Murray.

Shilin, Zhu (ed.), Ma Naixun, and Fu Maoyi. 1994. *A Compendium of Chinese Bamboo*. Peking: China Forestry Publishing House.

Index of Plant Names